THE PEACEMAKERS

EDITED BY
GHAZALA WAHAB

ALEPH

ALEPH

ALEPH BOOK COMPANY
An independent publishing firm
promoted by ***Rupa Publications India***

First published in India in 2023
by Aleph Book Company
7/16 Ansari Road, Daryaganj
New Delhi 110 002

ISBN: 978-93-95853-26-2

1 3 5 7 9 10 8 6 4 2

Printed in India.

To each one of us who believe that a nation is not just a piece of land, but the people who inhabit it.

CONTENTS

INTRODUCTION

Ghazala Wahab

Though peace and conflict are often regarded as opposite ends of the same spectrum, absence of the latter does not automatically lead to the former. Peace is as much a physical reality as it is a state of mind. A multi-dimensional phenomenon, peace can neither be assumed nor taken for granted. Along with the absence of violence, it includes justice; security of life, livelihood, and honour; optimism; and a comfortable familiarity with the environment—a sense of being home. This is the reason it takes refugees years to find peace, even when they no longer face violence.

Not surprising then that a country as diverse as India, whose emergence as an independent nation state was preceded and succeeded by prolonged cycles of unprecedented violence inflicted by civilians on other civilians in the name of religion, would experience frequent periods of peacelessness. People rendered homeless by physical violence live with mental and emotional violence for years before they can feel at home in a new place. And at peace.

As violence begets violence, people without peace often find relief in denying it to those they consider the cause of their suffering. The Partition refugees who came to India had not only suffered brutalization at the hands of those they regarded as their neighbours or acquaintances, but had probably witnessed much worse, without the ability or willingness to help. Some might even have participated in the brutalization of others. Broken by trauma and terrible secrets, people usually take a long time to rediscover the natural human instincts of empathy and kindness. They are also most susceptible to the other human instincts—blame and need for revenge.

While the history of independent India's struggle with peace and conflict can be traced to the violent sundering of 1947, it would be unfair to heap all the blame of the subsequent violence on the people who were fighting their own mental and emotional demons. Opportunist politics played on anger-driven religious prejudice to create emotional borders within the nation. Citizens were cast as opponents to one another—while one group had a natural claim to the nation, others were deemed usurpers. Since both sought a share in the scarce national resources, a state of permanent conflict developed over who had the first right to those resources, leading to frequent spurts of violence.

In her book *The Violence in Our Bones* (2021), Neera Chandhoke writes, 'The vast size of India, a highly differentiated population, uneven economic development, linguistic differentiation, regional imbalances, class and caste hierarchies, politicization of religious identities, appropriation of tribal lands, agrarian distress, joblessness, poverty, and deep inequality breed frustration. We see frustration at the subhuman quality of life led by a majority of our people, and anger at the non-performance of various governments.'[1]

Communal violence has been one of the major internal destabilizers in India, which in the last seventy-five years has created not only a huge chunk of internally displaced people but has also led to community-specific ghettos within cities, forcing people to live subhuman and alienated lives.[2] There is a lot of literature chronicling post-independence communal violence in India. These books and research papers point out how stray incidents have been used as triggers for well-planned and pre-meditated violence against the target community, in most cases, Muslim.[3]

Two common threads run through most incidents of communal violence. One is the systemic fanning of insecurity among the majority community, using tropes which affect them the most. For instance, they are told that unchecked growth of Muslim population might turn them into a majority. This will make them a dominant community and they will take away the privileges and the 'first right' that Hindus enjoy in a 'Hindu' India; or that virile Muslim men are seducing Hindu women, both to humiliate the Hindu community as well as to add numbers to their ranks, depleting Hindu numbers in turn! Or Muslims are untrustworthy because they are always conspiring to wage a jihad against India, and so on. Since Independence, such tropes have been used to not only push the Muslims to the margins, but also to mobilize Hindus, turning them into one homogenous group, overcoming intra-religious, geographical, and cultural differences.[4]

The second thread has been the broad complicity of law-enforcement agencies who, afflicted by 'few hours syndrome', have, in most violent situations, allowed the rioting mob a free run, either to get even with the 'other' or to vent their rage for a few hours before they and the local administration finally swing into action.

At a joint press conference called by health and civil society groups in March 2020 after the February 2020 violence in Delhi, former bureaucrat and activist Harsh Mander told the media, 'Even the biggest riot cannot go on if the state does not want it. There are standard protocols to control such situations. Even a very big riot can be controlled within about six hours.'[5]

A somewhat similar comment was made by the Uttar

Pradesh cadre police officer, Vibhuti N. Rai in 1995. An Indian Police Service officer, Rai wrote two books on police complicity in communal violence—*Shahar Mein Curfew* (2014) based on his personal experience during the 1980 riots in Allahabad (the book was publicly burnt by the general secretary of Vishva Hindu Parishad Ashok Singhal for being anti-Hindu[6]), and *Hashimpura 22 May: The Forgotten Story of India's Biggest Custodial Killing* (2016). In a 1995 interview to *Communalism Combat*, which was later uploaded to the *Sabrang* website, he said, 'Communal prejudice and bias is so deep and widespread that I feel some drastic steps need to be taken and fast. Especially by the senior leadership within the Indian police.... It is heart-warming to come across instances of decent, non-partisan police officers. But, and I say this with deep regret, such examples are more the exception than the rule. It is useless to constantly put blame only on politicians. We in the police force have to accept that our house is not in order.... In almost every riot in UP over the past twenty years the PAC (Provincial Armed Constabulary) has been indicted.'[7]

While the loss of life and dislocation of victims during a communal conflagration draw maximum attention (and rightly so), the invisible, but equally long-term impact is financial, which is a consequence of both direct violence and curfew, as well as a decline in trust and business sentiment in violence-affected areas. In his book *Communal Riots After Independence* (2004), Engineer considers the financial loss after each incident. For instance, after the 1969 Gujarat riots, while the official loss of life was 512, of which 430 were Muslims, the total loss of property aggregated to ₹42,324,069.54. Similarly, in the 1992–93 Bombay riots, the financial loss was estimated to be up to ₹4,000 crore.[8]

Hence, even if quantitatively the weaker side loses more, in terms of value, the stronger side incurs greater loss. Perhaps it is in this small detail that the truth about declining large-scale communal violence lies. One of the motives of any communal incident in India has been to degrade the economic and social standing of the target community. However, when the cost of this became higher than the benefits accrued then large-scale riots became tactics with diminishing returns. Once a low-cost mechanism of economic and social deprivation was found through legal injunctions against certain business activities, such as meat and leather, public violence by mob as well as select economic boycott of small-scale vendors, riots were no longer required.

As I wrote in *Born a Muslim*, 'The government frequently claims that since 2014, there hasn't been any major communal conflagration in India. The truth is there have been multiple minor communal incidents at such frequency that they have created an atmosphere of perpetual tension and fear. By Government of India's own statistics, there has been a 41 per cent increase in communal incidents across India.[9] And victims have mostly been Muslims, followed by Christians.

Multiple Mutinies

Absence of peace has not been the only reality of independent India. Another has been the presence of conflict, in many cases, vicious armed conflict, and not just at the periphery. So, while insurgencies in the Northeast and Kashmir have been the prolonged hangover of Independence, left-wing extremism, colloquially referred to as Naxalism because of the Naxalbari village in West Bengal, was the consequence of ill-conceived, and unjustly executed post-independence government policies.

In the autumn of 2005, when the current national security advisor Ajit Doval was a few months into his retirement as the director of the Intelligence Bureau (IB), I met him for an informal chat on the state of India's internal health. Through his career, Doval was known for his ears to the ground approach, which gave him exceptional insights into various separatist movements in India's border states.

According to Doval, there was a tendency at the lowest level of governance to deny the existence of a problem and continue to overlook it for as long as it was possible to do so. Once it was no longer possible to deny it, the lowest administrative level usually unleashed unimaginable brutality to quieten it. This second response inadvertently worsened the problem by further alienating the people. At this stage, the administration, unable to keep the issue under wraps, usually tried to buy silence either by pumping in money in the name of development or by cultivating local leaders to keep the flock in check. Unfortunately, even as money repeatedly failed to buy peace, it created vested interests over a period of time, who benefitted as long as the problem remained on a boil. Hence, the problem lingered, sapping resources, both in terms of manpower and money, which otherwise could be used elsewhere for growth.[10]

If one were to take a broad sweep across India, from the north to northeast through the central plateau, lying amidst the iron pillars of a promising future, such as smooth roads, industries, and highspeed railways, are the remains of consistent policy failure. One after another, each more avoidable than the other. Take Kashmir first. Enough has been written on the origins of the conflict that pins the blame on Pakistan and the invasion by the Pakistan Army in the garb of a tribal attack.

It has also been pointed out by many scholars that the roots of the conflict were sown much earlier and that the Pakistani invasion was simply the consequence of those roots. Had the principle that was applied to other princely states, such as

Junagadh and Hyderabad, been applied to Kashmir as well, the situation would have been different. Both Junagadh and Hyderabad were ruled by Muslim rulers, but the population was largely Hindu. Hence, the will of the people took precedence over the ruler. In Kashmir, the situation was the opposite, so first there was an attempt to force a demographic change by pushing the Muslims of Jammu into Pakistan, leading to terrible bloodshed.[11] There was also an uprising in the Poonch district of the Jammu region in 1947 against the maharaja by Muslims who wanted to join Pakistan. That was also brutally quelled.[12] Later, of course, Pakistan invaded Kashmir and that became the popular discourse. All of this is now frozen in the past, and no amount of hand-wringling can undo it.

Despite the tumultuous beginnings and a latent separatist sentiment which gradually dissipated into wishful thinking, the part of Kashmir Valley that remained in Indian control after 1949 made peace with the status quo. Of course, the feeling of separateness remained, as the people of the Valley identified as Kashmiris and not Indians, but there was no active desire to break away from the larger nation state. They were reconciled to coexisting under the garb of autonomy, howsoever shrunken. There could have been no greater example of this than the 1965 India–Pakistan War, in which Pakistan tried to orchestrate a revolt in the Valley by having soldiers infiltrate the populace. However, Kashmiris caught the infiltrators and handed them over to Indian security forces.[13]

Former chief of naval staff and a Kashmiri, Admiral Arun Prakash dwelled on this duality in the article he wrote for *FORCE*. ‘Growing up in the Valley in the 1950s and 1960s, my neighbours and playmates were all Kashmiris; of Muslim, Hindu, and Sikh faith. Our parents were friends, we ate in each others’ homes, and celebrated all festivals together. But even as children, we clearly understood that Kashmir was not India, and that the average Kashmiri's attitude towards India was at best ambivalent, while he definitely had an empathy for Pakistan.'[14]

But ambivalence was not hostility. This distance was covered slowly over a few decades, mostly because of the Indian government's lethal mix of short-sightedness and high-handedness. In his book *Nehru and the Spirit of India* (2022), Manash Firaq Bhattacharjee writes, 'Nehru's vacillations on Kashmir were mirrored in his relations with Sheikh Abdullah. It had a long-lasting bearing on India's postcolonial relationship with Kashmir.'[15]

As Nehru's confidence in his friendship with Abdullah dwindled, his policies towards Kashmir went from being democratic to manipulative. He was also under pressure from the growing influence of the Hindu right-wing party Praja Parishad in the Jammu region as well as the Hindu right-wing leaders in his cabinet like Dr Syama Prasad Mookerjee who 'accused Abdullah's regime of divided loyalty'.[16]

The Indian government's missteps in Kashmir continued to mount, starting with the arrest of Abdullah. And to offset those, it sought to buy over as many Kashmiris to its side as it could. As Arun Prakash wrote in *FORCE*, 'Ironically, the crores that India blindly poured into Kashmir were the biggest cause for resentment against it amongst the populace. The reason was simple: the state was a nest of corruption and nepotism, and possibly up to 95 per cent of Indian funds went to line the pockets of the ruling politicians.'[17]

What money could not buy was suppressed through brute force. The history of the Kashmir Valley is pockmarked with events of state violence on the restive population starting 1931, when the Dogra troops opened fire on unarmed protestors killing twenty-two people.[18] The first martyrs' graveyard came up in the Valley to honour these protestors. Since then, innumerable martyrs' graveyards have cropped up in the region to remind the people that nothing must be forgotten. With the start of the insurgency in 1989, these graveyards have multiplied. In the ebb and tide of violence over the last thirty-four years, peace has remained elusive.

Interestingly, despite mainstream Kashmiri memories of unending persecution since 1931, officially, violence began with the insurgency in 1989. Hence, the oldest insurgency in India belongs to the Naga rebels who took up arms in 1954 to wrest independence from New Delhi. The Nagas trace the origin of their nationalism to the thirteenth century when the Ahom kings tried to conquer their land. In modern times, even as the Indian freedom movement was underway, the Naga leadership was also seeking independence, both from the British as well as the possible inheritor state, India. As early as 1929, the Nagas submitted a memorandum to the Simon Commission, seeking independence.[19]

During World War II, the fiercest eastern battles were fought in Naga territory. While the bravery of the British Indian troops in pushing back the Japanese invasion as part of the Allied effort is well recognized (and honoured), the contribution of the local Naga population has mostly been glossed over. Unlike the Allied forces, who were fighting for colonial territory and the amorphous notions of liberalism and democracy, the Nagas were fighting for their homeland. Hence, once the Japanese fell back, they expected the British to vacate their land too.

The British, however, bequeathed their problems to independent India, which inherited not only a restive and conflict-ridden region dotted with huge caches of unclaimed arms and ammunition—the residuals of World War II [20]—but also the oppressive mindset of the former colonial rulers with regard to a people and customs it neither comprehended nor respected. The newly independent India had another problem. Even in a truncated form, because of Partition, the British had left behind a huge landmass as one nation, which the Government of India wanted to consolidate under a strong central control. There was fear that parts of the nation, especially at the periphery, might break free or get nibbled at by hostile neighbours if the central control became even a little tenuous. This made it sound the nationalistic bugle, and thereafter conflate it with territorialism.

'Mookerjee's nationalism was focussed on territoriality. Territory poses a limited situation and determines the reason behind the nation's paranoia. The paranoia of nations is territorial,' writes Bhattacharjee,[21] referring to Syama Prasad Mookerjee, who was pushing the notion of Akhand Bharat on the government in 1950, which entailed invading Pakistan to undo Partition.

When territory becomes paramount, people inhabiting that territory become inconsequential, and in some cases, obstacles. All the violence in India, from Kashmir to left-wing extremism affected areas to Nagaland, has been a consequence of this mindset. The was evident in the epochal manner in which the Naga people were pushed into armed resistance seven years after Independence.

Journalist Harish Chandola, who was based in Shillong, reported extensively from the Northeast in the 1950s. He recounts the beginning of the armed struggle in great detail in his book *The Naga Story: First Armed Struggle in India* (2013). He describes how, on 30 March 1953, Naga people of all tribes lined the road from Imphal to Kohima, dressed in their best traditional attire, to welcome India's first prime minister, Jawaharlal Nehru, who was visiting Kohima accompanied by the prime minister of Burma.

Before the prime ministerial cavalcade could arrive, Indian intelligence agencies informed the deputy commissioner of Kohima, Satyen Barkataki, that the welcoming Nagas also wanted to present the prime minister with a memorandum urging him to recognize the independent manner in which the Nagas have always governed themselves, and that they would like that to continue without interference from India.[22]

Barkataki regarded this as an insult to the prime minister upon his watch. Hence, in the traditions of the training he received under the British India government, which entailed disdain for the population and loyalty to the masters, he ordered the police to disperse the welcome party by force.

'The news of the police assault on Nagas standing on the road spread like wildfire through Kohima. Among those come to welcome him were members of the only Naga organization, the Naga National Council (NNC). Their...leader and general secretary Theo Sakhrie...decided that the people need not bother to wait to hear Nehru after the police's barbaric behaviour.'[23]

Sure enough, as Nehru and the Burmese prime minister entered the stadium, the people collected there started to walk out in protest. Despite repeated appeals by the prime minister of India, people continued to leave the stadium, much to his embarrassment in the presence of a foreign guest.

The Assam administration, which governed the Naga Hills District then, did not take kindly to this affront. Police and the army were sent to the villages to arrest the mischief-makers, including Sakhrie, and punish the rest. People were beaten, houses were burnt, and some were killed. To subdue the tribals into silence, two of the killed persons, 'Beechatami of Meema, near Kohima, and Lopeelu Tami, were tied with ropes by the police and dragged through streets, to put fear in the minds of the onlookers.'

'Not fear, but rage rose in people's minds. They wondered, what kind of people are these new rulers, who humiliate even the dead?'[24]

Thereafter, state violence against the Naga tribes, including women, continued to escalate, forcing more and more people to go underground—to train for armed resistance. By the end of the year, future Naga insurgents, including Angami Zapu Phizo, had trekked across the Cachar hills of Assam and crossed into East Pakistan. 'It was from there that Naga militants began bringing small arms, explosives, and funds.'[25] Full-blown insurgency started the following year and on 18 September 1954, the NNC declared the setting up of an underground Naga government. An insecure and anxious government responded in the only way it understood. More force. In 1958, the government enforced the Armed Forces Special Powers Act (AFSPA) and deployed the army to quell the uprising. Like in Kashmir, the AFSPA remains in force in Nagaland till date.

In 1967, the tallest Naga leader, Thuingaleng Muivah, accompanied by over hundred followers, trekked across northern Myanmar (then Burma) into the Yunnan province of China for succour and support to fight the Indian Army.[26] 'Once a secure connection was established, other insurgent groups from Assam and Manipur flocked to China.' Even after China closed the Yunnan facilities, it 'continued the supply of arms through private players based in Yunnan'.[27]

Interestingly, the Naga tribes are believed to have originally come into India from the Yunnan province of China, just as the Ahoms of Assam came from the region between Myanmar and Yunnan. Nandita Haksar writes, 'Some claim they were forced to leave during the construction of the Great Wall of China.'[28]

As money from Indian government poured into the restive Northeast in the name of development and small arms from across the border, more and more tribal groups in the region, some as small as a few thousand, took to arms in the garb of insurgency. At one point, every state of the Northeast, from Assam to Nagaland, with Mizoram, Meghalaya, Tripura, and Manipur in between, had two or more insurgencies raging with multiple groups involved. Some causes were xenophobic, some communal, and some reactionary—basically in response to another group. Becoming an underground ultra became a career option because then one could extract money. It was no longer an ideological cause. Except for the Naga insurgency, which remains the most sustained campaign, others have either run out of steam or have been co-opted into mainstream politics.

Colonial Heritage

Many years ago, a retired banker and historian-columnist by hobby, Akhilesh Mithal, told me that the reason for all the violence in India can be traced back to the colonial legacy of the administration and law enforcement agencies. 'They still regard themselves as masters or rulers as they did during the colonial period. They have not been able to understand that in a democracy, they have to serve the people, not push them into servility,' he had said.

It wasn't until I started paying attention to the left-wing or Maoist violence in central India that I truly understood the depth of his words. I also discovered a devastating consequence of this mindset—a mission to civilize the tribal and the forest dwellers as they didn't conform to mainstream notions of education and modernity. Hence, using the excuse of development, just as the British did, successive governments of India have destroyed traditional habitat, religion, and culture.

To perpetuate its authority and superiority, the Indian ruling class—both political and feudal—has systematically dehumanized and demonized vulnerable sections of society. Dehumanization takes away the guilt of treating fellow citizens as less than human beings. And demonization justifies the use of violence against them in the civilizational mission. This has been poignantly recorded by Hansda Sowvendra Shekhar in his writings. In his short story *The Adivasi Will Not Dance*, he writes, 'They pinned me to the ground. They did not let me speak, they did not let me protest, they did not even let me raise my head and look at my fellow musicians and dancers as they were being beaten up by the police. All I could hear were their cries for mercy....

'I only said, "We Adivasis will not dance anymore"—what is wrong with that? We are like toys—someone presses our "ON" button, or turns a key in our backsides, and we Santhals start beating rhythms on our tamak and tumdak, or start blowing tunes on our tiriyo while someone snatches away our very dancing grounds. Tell me, am I wrong?'[29]

The story reminded me of an old article on tribal tourism. It spoke of how the Jarawa tribal people of Andaman and Nicobar Islands were being used as exhibits for tourists who came to gawk at them and throw food at them.[30] What was true of Jarawas has been true of the Santhals, Gonds, Nagas, and Mundas and everyone else who is regarded as different from the urban mainstream. They are fit for exploitation for the natural resources they sit on and for the entertainment of the visiting elite, political or otherwise.

In this two-pronged outreach of the powerful lie the roots of what has repeatedly been regarded as India's biggest internal security challenge—left-wing extremism (LWE). In the popular narrative, LWE is referred to as Naxalism—the name comes from the 1967 farm labourers' revolt against their landlords in the Naxalbari village of West Bengal. The revolt caught the fancy of many students across India, fired up with the communist ideology of total revolution. Though the West Bengal government brutally crushed the revolt in three months, the sparks spread to other states, such as Bihar, Madhya Pradesh, Orissa, Maharashtra, Karnataka, and Andhra Pradesh.[31]

Under government pushback, it remained dormant for almost a decade. Then it gradually started to coalesce into local issues of injustice and disaffection; after all, Indian society is neither just nor equitable. In Andhra Pradesh, it sprung up as the People's War Group (PWG), fighting for the rights of the peasants against cruel landlords. In Bihar, it took the form of the Maoist Communist Centre (MCC), fighting for the rights of Scheduled Castes against upper-caste landholders, or the Bhumihars, who had formed their own militia, Ranvir Sena (through tacit support from select police and politicians).[32] In 2004, the PWG and MCC merged into the Communist Party of India (Maoist), and the Indian government woke up to the internal security threat it had so far dismissed as a localized law and order problem.

The CPI (Maoist) took up the cause of the tribals in central India, a region that was the epicentre of industrial growth in India. The forest produce, and mining of minerals, mostly iron-ore, were big revenue churners. This assault by the government on the forests of India to exploit its resources has not just been captured evocatively in Shekhar's book but has also been the subject of a few Indian films where tribal women are presented as exotic and promiscuous creatures for whom sexual profligacy doesn't have the same meaning as it does for 'educated, urban' women—this absolved the officials of sexual criminality.

However, this was not the beginning. In 1946, peasants from several villages of the erstwhile region of Telangana (then part of the Hyderabad state which post-independence became Andhra

Pradesh and recently saw the carving out of the Telangana state) mounted a series of revolts against the landlords, leading to much bloodshed. This revolt was one of the inspirations for Shyam Benegal's 1975 movie *Nishant*, which focussed on the sexual exploitation of peasant women at the hands of the landlords. Eventually, with the support of the Communist activists, the rebels managed to seize control of some villages, especially in the areas of Nalgonda and Warangal and establish self-governance in the form of gram rajyams (village communes) in several villages. The government was finally able to overcome the revolution through military force in October 1951. In the face of military brutality, the Communist Party of India urged its cadre to lay down arms.[33]

But even this was not the beginning. If one were to look beyond the communal aspect of the 1921 Moplah massacre in Kerala, then even that was the horrific culmination of the series of peasants' (in this case, Muslim) revolts over a few years against the upper-caste Hindu landlords.[34] It acquired communal overtones only when Muslim religious leaders likened it to jihad.

Landlordism was understandable during the colonial period as the British Indian government had no interest in the welfare of the people. It only cared for the revenue it could generate. The zamindars, talukdars, forest officers etc., were the conduits for that. They promulgated laws, such as the Land Acquisition Act (1894) and Forest Act of India (1927), which took away the ownership of the land from the tiller or the forest dweller and arrogated it to the government, and through the government to its appointed feudal overlords. This meant that the tribals who had been living in the forests for generations were now encroachers. Their centuries-old economic activity of plucking leaves or chopping wood for trade was now a crime. Similarly, the farmer who had been tilling the land for generations and bartering its produce for other goods was now either a tenant or a bonded labourer on his ancestral property.[35]

Independent India should have abolished these acts. Yet, it took over fifty years to do so, either because Indian bureaucracy was happy to step into the shoes of the British, or successive Indian governments found these laws lucrative means of generating revenue. In a conversation with me in September 2005, a senior official in the Ministry of Panchayati Raj said that the roots of the anger and discontent which eventually manifested itself in the form of violent Naxalism could be traced to the unfair and archaic Forest Act of India (1927). 'The Act made tribals, who had always lived in the forests, encroachers and criminals. They were displaced and robbed of their livelihood as these people traditionally lived off the forest produce.' Even as they were deprived of the primary source of livelihood, they were not given any alternate means of subsistence. Worse, they had no rights, as spin-offs of democracy also didn't reach them. In most case, they ended up as pawns in the hands of vested interests, poachers, forest officers, contractors, and other petty government officials.[36]

It was this realization that made the chief minister of Karnataka, Dharam Singh, demand an amendment in the Forest Act of India in the first meeting of the standing committee of state chief ministers on 19 September 2005 in New Delhi. He said that an amendment would reduce the disaffection of the tribal groups in his state.[37] It took the government another year to pass the Scheduled Tribes and Other Traditional Forest Dwellers (Recognition of Forest Rights) Act 2006.[38] The Land Acquisition Act was amended in 2013 as Right to Fair Compensation and Transparency in Land Acquisition, Rehabilitation and Resettlement Act, 2013.[39]

Perhaps the change in laws helped. Perhaps the government's

policy of hard policing and hard development has eliminated the committed insurgents and created vested groups amongst the fence-sitters. Perhaps people have become tired of the relentless violence and of endlessly living a fugitive's life in the forests. Perhaps it's a combination of all of these that has caused the Maoist violence to ebb consistently over the last decade. One can only hope that the reduction in violence will lead to the emergence of peace. With honour and justice, and not ordered under the gun.

The Peacemakers

When my editor Pujitha Krishnan proposed an anthology on people who have risked life and limb to bring about peace in the midst of violence, I thought compiling a book on the peacemakers would be an easy matter. After all, violence is an escapist's excuse to avoid addressing his or her own prejudices, and peace, a realist's abiding faith in the idea of collective and interdependent future. How difficult would it be to find peacemakers in a country as diverse as India?

Sure enough, finding the peacemakers was not difficult. However, it was disconcerting to see how few they were despite our long history of violence. And even these numbers have been progressively depleting. That alone is a reason to celebrate each of these individuals whose collective optimism hopefully will be able to pierce through the darkness that seems to have engulfed our society.

Despite our national assertion of being a non-violent people, India has, at best, experienced only piecemeal peace. Even when there has been no physical violence, cruelty has manifested itself in non-kinetic ways, through marginalization, denial of justice, and sometimes by simply ignoring the plight of the weak.

Perhaps this is the reason Indians remain among the unhappiest people in the world[40]—because in some kind of a symbiotic connection, the oppressor suffers too in some measure, if not as much as the victim. And neither is happy.

Perhaps these stories of ordinary people standing up against the powerful to help the helpless will inspire others. But even if that does not happen, they will act as reminders of invincibility of hope. And courage.

This anthology begins where it rightfully should, with an essay by Rajmohan Gandhi chronicling the closing years of his grandfather's life. Disillusioned and heartbroken by the acceptance of the two-nation theory by those from whom he expected better, Gandhi didn't celebrate India's independence; he mourned the bloodshed that accompanied it in parts of Bihar and Bengal. Rajmohan Gandhi evocatively captures his anguish, as well as his awareness of the challenges ahead.

Human rights lawyer and activist Nandita Haksar, who was informally and voluntarily involved in the Naga peace process for decades, writes about the challenges in fostering peace in a conflict zone. Her essay chronicles the many roadblocks to peace in an area where conflict has spawned vested interests, both among the insurgents as well as the law-enforcers. Haksar underscores the truism that good intentions mean half the battle is won; and manipulative half measures undo all the progress made.

One of the worst massacres in India was the violence unleashed on the Sikh community in Delhi and some other parts of north India after the assassination of Prime Minister Indira Gandhi in 1984. Rahul Bedi was not only a witness to, but also the reporter of, the grisly massacre in East Delhi. In those harrowing couple of days, there were more killers than saviours. Bedi recalls both in his essay.

Journalist Uttam Sengupta tries to resolve the mystery of a peaceful Bihar after the demolition of the Babri Masjid in 1992, when other parts of north and western India were up in flames. Peaceful Bihar was particularly noteworthy given its history of some of the worst communal conflagrations in post-Independence India, including the horrific Bhagalpur violence of 1989. Sengupta connects the dots from chief minister Lalu Prasad Yadav, the state administration, to the civil society members who walked the talk of communal harmony.

Bombay (now Mumbai) saw one of the worst fallouts of the Babri demolition. Jyoti Punwani covered the violence as it unfolded in her capacity as a journalist. Subsequently, as a conscientious citizen, she compiled and published accounts of witnesses to the violence. In her essay, she profiles the civil society members who risked their lives to ensure pockets of sanity and peace in the midst of communal madness. In recording the courage of ordinary citizens in 1992–93, Punwani also makes the point that this is a declining tribe. A disturbing truth in these troubled times.

In 2002, when several cities and villages in Gujarat went up in flames after the killing of karsevaks inside the *Sabarmati Express* near Godhra railway station, journalist-activist Teesta Setalvad was among the first to record both the violence and efforts at peacekeeping. Thereafter she provided legal assistance to the victims and till date is pursuing those cases. Her essay records how even in the darkest of moments there were people in Gujarat who rose against violence, many of them, at personal cost. Her compilation of small stories of courage belies the perception of total communal polarization in the state.

Sunil Kumar is a journalist and a long-term observer of the rise, and now decline, of Maoist violence in the state of Chhattisgarh. In his essay, he profiles the people committed to peace and justice in the restive heart of India, and in doing so he also dwells upon those who have impeded the multiple peace processes through their short-sightedness and sometimes a misplaced sense of infallibility.

Teresa Rehman's heart-warming essay shows what good intentions and earnest efforts can achieve. She writes about a non-government organization working towards empowerment of women in the once conflict-ridden districts of Assam. Through her essay, Rehman shows how women, irrespective of their religion and history, can be the enablers of change, coexistence and interdependent lives.

In my essay on Kashmir, I recall the halcyon years of 2005–08 when all was in the realm of possibility. This was a time when everyone was on the side of peace, making their contributions, no matter how small, to the process that promised to change lives forever. However, that possibility shattered. And even though violence resumed, those committed to a peaceful and just future continue to work towards that. I record their efforts and their sacrifices.

The 2013 riot in Muzzaffarnagar district of western Uttar Pradesh had been in the making for a few years. Shivam Mogha, who grew up in the district, witnessed how the city slowly and deliberately slid towards communal insularity and hatred. He chronicles the divisive politics and growing insecurity of the people before all of it culminated in vicious violence. In the midst of this, he shines a light on people who rose above the hatred and pulled others out of darkness.

The 2020 violence in the national capital of Delhi was not only shameful but shocking too, in the way select politicians exhorted their footsoldiers to teach Muslims a lesson. Natasha Badhwar and Oishika Neogi show in their essay how it is possible to not rise to the vilest of provocations and do what is right.

Through their profile of the work of Dr Mohammad Ahtasham Anwar, they reflect upon the brutality of the violence and complicity of law-enforcement agencies.

This volume ends with the luminosity of love and hope. Ramani Atkuri walked with Rahul Gandhi's Bharat Jodo Yatra for a few days in Karnataka and later in Rajasthan. Her essay shows us how there are many people invested in the idea of India as a nation for all who call it theirs. It's a heart-warming story of resilience and optimism. A fitting end to the book on peacemakers.

I am deeply grateful to everyone who has contributed to this anthology. But more than that I am grateful to those whose stories of courage feature here. They are the ones who are protecting and nurturing the idea of India at a time when personal aggrandizement takes precedence. More power to you and your spirit.

Of course, this is by no means a complete book. It is probably just a beginning. There are a lot of aspects of our society which are missing here. For instance, peacemaking in the face of caste-based, gender-based, and class-based violence. These deserve a book of their own.

1

BEFORE AND AFTER THE PARTITION
FOUR YEARS IN GANDHI'S LIFE

Rajmohan Gandhi

Nine days before he was killed in Delhi, Gandhi was told by an influential Punjabi leader, Giani Kartar Singh, that 'afflicted men cannot be balanced men. Everybody cannot be a Mahatma Gandhi.' Replied Gandhi: 'Mahatma Gandhi is neither an angel nor a devil. He is a man like you.'[1]

In the year 1944, as World War II moved towards its end in Europe and the Far East, India witnessed more than one longing. One unstoppable wish across all of India was for the country's independence. That desire had been strengthened by the fact that Gandhi and thousands of others were still in prison for their Quit India struggle of 1942.

Another sentiment, growing in India's Muslim-majority areas, was that these areas should have a state of their own. Voiced in Lahore in March 1940, the sentiment was championed by Mohammed Ali Jinnah, president of the All-India Muslim League.

In May of 1944, Gandhi, by then the British empire's prisoner for twenty-one months, was released. He was seventy-four and ill. His wife, Kasturba, who had been detained along with him, had died in February. The empire's guardians didn't want to strengthen the freedom tide by letting Gandhi too die in prison.

Two months later, in July 1944, making a broadcast from 'somewhere in Southeast Asia', Subhas Chandra Bose called Gandhi 'the father of the nation'.[2] Others had employed similar expressions, but Gandhi had never assumed a right to tell others what they should do. Yes, he had exercised his own liberty to speak, act, and persuade. For example, he had secured acceptance for his 1942 Quit India campaign from his younger colleagues, many of whom were hesitant at first.

Slowly regaining strength, Gandhi made a bold move in September 1944. In order to forge a Hindu–Muslim alliance, he conferred fourteen times with Jinnah in the latter's home on Bombay's Malabar Hill. If, said Gandhi to Jinnah, the League joined the Congress in demanding independence, he, Gandhi, would persuade the Congress to agree to post-independence plebiscites in West Punjab, Sindh, the Frontier Province, and East Bengal. If the plebiscites favoured separation, India and a newly created Pakistan should enter into a treaty of friendship.

Jinnah rejected Gandhi's offer. He wanted his Pakistan to include western Bengal and eastern Punjab, regions where non-Muslims constituted a clear majority, and he wanted the plebiscites confined to Muslims—conditions Gandhi could not accept.

While he talked with Jinnah, Gandhi's principal colleagues, all younger than him, were behind bars. From August 1942, Abul Kalam Azad, who was the Congress president, Jawaharlal Nehru, Vallabhbhai Patel, and other Working Committee members had been confined in Maharashtra's Ahmednagar Fort. Gandhi had not been allowed to contact them.

Inside the Fort, as one dreary month followed another, Nehru (twenty years younger than Gandhi), Azad (only a year older than Nehru), and Patel (six years younger than Gandhi) had concluded, privately in each case, that after release, whenever that came, they would act independently of their mentor. In reaching this conclusion, they had been influenced by imprisonment, by the passage of time, and by imperial policy. Physically separating Gandhi from the Congress leadership had worked. When word of the Gandhi–Jinnah talks reached the Fort, its inmates were not pleased.

In June 1945, with the war effectively over, the Fort's prisoners were let out. Greeted as heroes, they were more popular than ever, if also thin and tired. Patel insisted that India's cause 'would have been lost forever' had the Quit India resolution not been adopted.[3] However, in a letter to Gandhi, he argued that approaching Jinnah was a mistake. Gandhi wrote back disagreeing, but he added that Patel should feel free to 'condemn him from the house-tops'.[4]

Clear decisions were made at this juncture. Gandhi would continue to offer his counsel, but active leadership would henceforth belong to his younger colleagues. Azad, Patel, Nehru, and others like Rajagopalachari and Rajendra Prasad constituted a highly gifted and capable group. They were ready to take charge, and Gandhi was ready to hand over.

It wasn't just that he had become older. His close aide Mahadev Desai—described by Kasturba as Gandhi's 'right hand and his left hand'—had died in front of him during their detention together. Kasturba herself had gone. He was no longer what he had been in August 1942. The world had changed in other ways too.

A change in his role was required. Subhas Bose and others might call him the nation's father, but henceforth he would merely advise younger associates with whom he had worked for close to thirty years. But he wasn't retiring. He would remain active. Including as a ground-level peacemaker.

East Bengal

From November 1946 to April 1947, Gandhi immersed himself in two regions where horrible Hindu–Muslim conflict had just occurred: East Bengal and Bihar. In each place mobs belonging to the preponderant majority (Muslims in East Bengal, Hindus in Bihar) had attacked helpless individuals and families of the minority community. Aiming to instil courage in victims and remorse in attackers, and taking a small band of co-workers with him, Gandhi reached out to people in their villages. In a span of two months in East Bengal, he halted overnight in forty-seven different villages, where his hosts included washermen, fishermen, cobblers, and weavers.

Individuals or pairs from Gandhi's team went to live in half a dozen different villages in Noakhali district. Only one in this team, Bibi Amtus Salaam, was Muslim. The rest were all Hindus. Even Amtus Salaam, born in eastern Punjab, was a non-Bengali 'outsider' in Sirandi, the village she adopted.

Although Bengal's Muslim League ministry deployed a small posse for Gandhi's security, his safety, and that of his peace-making team, depended almost entirely on the goodwill of East Bengal's Muslims. Gandhi and his team befriended many of them.

In Srirampur village, where Gandhi spent six weeks, Professor Nirmal Kumar Bose (whose aid Gandhi had solicited) gave Bengali lessons to the old man. Gandhi rose at or before four, read and wrote (on the bedstead) by the light of a kerosene lamp, spun on his charkha, conducted two prayer meetings a day, walked to adjacent villages, and practised natural cures (mud packs on the forehead and abdomen plus sunbaths) on himself and the villagers.

At a prayer meeting that Gandhi held in village Paniala on

22 January 1947, his co-worker and grandniece, Manu, sang a verse she had heard in a temple in Porbandar, where Gandhi was born. The verse included the line: 'Ishwar Allah tero naam', (Ishwar and Allah are names for the same God). Finding that Paniala's Muslims, listening in large numbers, had liked the verse, Gandhi asked Manu to sing it 'daily from now on'.[5] The verse that millions in India and across the world would later sing was thus launched in a village in eastern Bengal.

Much of Gandhi's time in Noakhali was spent with Hindu women assailed by fear. His translator, Professor Bose, noticed Gandhi's 'daily ministrations on behalf of love' and 'the extreme tenderness with which he regarded each individual' relating woes to him.[6] But Bose also recorded how during one meeting with bereaved women 'Gandhiji's face hardened, and he said that they must recover their courage.'[7]

Some Muslims objected to Gandhi, a Hindu, reciting verses from the Quran, but Muslims in village Navagram defended Gandhi's right to do so, and in the village of Sadhurkhil, an influential Muslim, Salimulla Saheb, invited Gandhi to hold multifaith prayers on his grounds, adding that he would not mind if the Hindu verses about Ram were chanted to the clapping of hands.[8]

Amtus Salaam, who never missed a Ramzan fast and always slept with the Quran near her, went on a fast in Sirandi when her call for the surrender of a sword used in attacks against Hindus was not heeded. While she fasted, Gandhi wrote her a letter or two every day. After twenty-five days, although the sword was not returned, Gandhi persuaded Salaam to end her fast.

Eleven Muslims of Sirandi took the pledge, 'with God as witness', that they would defend the right of Hindus to practise their faith and continue to search for the missing sword. Although the weapon was never found, 'things were altogether different in and around Sirandi after that fast'.[9]

In August 1947, five months after Gandhi left, East Bengal became East Pakistan. In 1971–72, East Pakistan became Bangladesh. In the year 2000, I made two visits to some of the Noakhali villages where Gandhi had walked. I wanted to find out if that fifty-three-year-old peacemaking effort was still remembered.

Much of the time I simply accosted people walking on village paths and, with a Bangladeshi translator's aid, asked questions. In Srirampur, Abul Kalam Bhuiya, a farmer who seemed around seventy in age and spoke some English, replied:

> I am the son of Hyder Baksh Bhuiya. I attended [Gandhi's] prayer meeting. He went to Muslim homes, offered them [medical] treatment. He took goat milk and a red leaf vegetable. Was punctual about his time, wore pocket watch at the waist, a dhoti that went down to his knee, advocated peace, love, and brotherhood.

Also in Srirampur, Fazlul Huq Patwari, again around seventy, a farmer and son of Jalauddin Patwari, recalled: 'I saw him. We sat together possibly at a prayer meeting. He said, "Let us Hindus and Muslims live side by side." He was a good man. He walked a lot, and we were running behind him. He distributed toffees for the children. Muslims took and ate what he gave.'

Most interviewees were in their teens at the time of Gandhi's visit. A day labourer, Aamir Husain Shaikh, seventy-five years of age in 2000, said: 'When he came, it was total chaos. He brought peace. I saw him many times. He wore khadi clothes.'

Md. Akhtar uz Zaman of Srirampur, son of Maulana Abdul Majid (who may have been an imam in a mosque in 1946–47), recalled: 'He came to our home, showed my father the Quran, and asked where the holy book authorized wrongdoing.

Dr Ali Ahmed, around seventy, a homeopathic doctor in Madhupur near Srirampur, son of a government servant, said: 'I attended many prayer meetings. He asked for Hindu–Muslim unity. He told the Hindus, "No revenge".'

Madhusudan Chakravarti, a seventy-five-year-old grocer in Paniala, son of late Anada Charan Chakravarti, a priest, said: 'I saw him. He stayed in Mazumdar badi.... He got the whole village to sit together and have khichri—Hindus, Muslims, Harijans. It had not happened before.'

Sirajul Islam Majumdar of Kamalpur, in his late fifties, son of Dr Khaleelur Rahman Majumdar, said: 'My father told us of "Raghupati Raghav Raja Ram, Ishwar Allah tero naam". My grandfather protected Hindus on his roof.'

Usha Rani Das, a widow, aged around sixty-five, living in a house between Kamalpur and Bangsha, said: 'There was a meeting in the fields. Hindus and Muslims all came. I was very young but married. He asked us to put on the bindi and the sindoor that we had taken off. We obeyed the advice and were not attacked.'

In Chandipur, Ayub Ali, a day-labourer in his late seventies who owned a little land, said: 'He told us what has happened has happened. He came close to my house. He went to every house for peace, spoke to all. He spoke in Hindi, but there were translators. He knew the kalima.... If he had not come, troubles would have continued.'[10]

On 19 January 1947, during Gandhi's stay in East Bengal, Calcutta's *Amrita Bazar Patrika* reported that 'a number of Muslim youths' who were walking alongside Gandhi in Bhatialpur had assured him that 'they would stand guarantee' against a recurrence of attacks on Hindus. The Bombay-based writer, D. G. Tendulkar, who joined Gandhi in Noakhali, wrote that on 4 February 1947, four young Muslims in Sadhurkhil challenged

Gandhi to say publicly that fewer people were killed in East Bengal than in Bihar. Agreeing to do so, Gandhi gave his estimate that less than a thousand had died in Noakhali, and that 'the murders and brutalities in Bihar eclipsed those in Noakhali'.[11]

Bihar

Gandhi was in Bihar for most of March 1947, half of April, and about a third of May. Among those who had pressed him to visit the province was Syed Mahmud, a minister and a Congressman. Most of Gandhi's nights in Bihar were spent in Mahmud's home on the banks of the Ganga, but he managed to visit several other villages and towns, at times on foot. It was summer; Bihar's roads were dusty and walking was hard.

In the previous November, more than 7,000 Bihari Muslims had been killed and nearly 10,000 homes destroyed. Six districts—Saran, Monghyr, Bhagalpur, Santhal Parganas, Patna, and Gaya—were the worst hit.[12] In some places, Hindu neighbours protected defenceless Muslims, and there were people like Sakal Babu, the headmaster in Gaya district, who, supported by students and friends, took all the Muslims of Daulatpur, Nagama, and Rasalpur villages to safety in the town of Jehanabad.[13]

Yet the record of Bihar's Congress government was appallingly inadequate.[14] Except for a few instances when attackers were confronted, the state police had merely looked on. When Gandhi arrived early in March, Bihar's Muslims, comprising less than 13 per cent of the population, were still frightened.

Telling Premier Shrikrishna Sinha that the killings in his province were 'like the Jallianwala massacre',[15] Gandhi was equally candid with Congress workers. On 19 March he said to them:

'Is it or isn't it a fact that quite a large number of Congressmen took part in the disturbances?... I wish to ask you, how could you live to see an old woman of 110 years being butchered before your eyes? ...I will not rest nor let others rest. I [will] wander all over on foot and ask the skeletons [what] happened.'[16]

There was, he said, a way out for Bihar:

'The Hindus of Bihar have committed a grave sin. They will raise the head of Bihar much higher if they do honest reparations, greater in magnitude than their crimes.'[17]

'Abducted women, stolen goods, and illegal arms should be returned,' Gandhi said, to the police—or, he added, to him, or Rajendra Prasad, or Syed Mahmud. If Bihar wanted its fame back, Biharis should 'rebuild what you have destroyed'.[18] The government should catch the culprits and award due punishment.

After his arrival there were signs of remorse among some of Bihar's Hindus, and Gandhi was given confessional letters, stolen goods, and arms by a few of the November attackers. Pyarelal recorded a scene from the village of Masaurhi, where fearful destruction had occurred:

'After the prayer address, Gandhiji stayed on to collect money for the Muslim relief fund. There was a stampede as everybody pushed forward to be the first to put his or her copper into the Mahatma's hands. As he bent forward with outstretched hands, he read in those faces, aquiver with emotion, the unmistakable evidence that repentance had at last crept into their hearts.'[19]

Yet Bihar's killings had strengthened the urge for India's partition. Photographs of the killings were displayed to Muslims in Punjab and to the Frontier Province's Pashtuns as warnings against remaining in Hindu-majority India.[20]

Out of the Box Idea

Early in March 1947, 2,000 or more Sikhs and Hindus were killed in or around Rawalpindi and Multan in western Punjab, where Muslims were an overwhelming majority. Punjab's non-Muslim leaders responded by demanding their province's partition, and the creation of an East Punjab where Sikhs and Hindus would comprise a majority and feel safe. When, on 8 March, a resolution of the Congress Working Committee endorsed this demand, and implied that Bengal should be similarly partitioned, India's division was clinched.

Replacing Lord Wavell as viceroy, Lord Mountbatten quickly produced a scheme for Partition. Our peacemaker was in Bihar when word of the Congress's 8 March resolution reached him. In letters he asked Patel and Nehru why they had gone that far.

He also came out with an out of the box idea for preserving India's unity: a Jinnah-led, Congress-supported ministry in New Delhi. Such a ministry, he thought, would arrest Hindu–Muslim polarization across India, including in Bengal and Bihar. To this idea Gandhi added a demand for disbanding the gangs of armed Hindus, Muslims, and Sikhs that were surfacing menacingly in Punjab.

On 1 and 2 April in New Delhi, Gandhi discussed his idea with Mountbatten and also with Nehru, Patel, Azad, and company, including Acharya Kripalani, the new Congress president.

Although Mountbatten, for one, and Maulana Azad, for another, thought that Gandhi's unexpected proposal was sensible and also practical, the viceroy was so attached to his own Partition scheme that he lobbied actively against Gandhi's last-minute solution.

The easily accessible *Transfer of Power* volumes (published in London in the 1970s and 1980s) show that on 2 April the viceroy admitted to his staff, to quote from Mountbatten's own notes, that 'basically Mr Gandhi's objective was to retain the unity of India and basically he was right in this,' adding that 'it would not be very easy for Mr Jinnah to refuse Mr Gandhi's offer'.[21] The viceroy also recorded Gandhi's willingness, if his plan was adopted, to 'tour the length and breadth of the country getting all the people of India to accept the decision'.[22]

Half an hour after his 2 April meeting with Gandhi ended, the viceroy received Abul Kalam Azad. Mountbatten recorded the gist of their conversation:

'I told [Azad] straightaway of Gandhi's plan, of which he already knew from Gandhi that morning. He staggered me by saying that in his opinion it was perfectly feasible of being carried out, since Gandhi could unquestionably influence the whole of Congress to accept it and work it loyally. He further thought that there was a chance that I might get Jinnah to accept it, and he thought that such a plan would be the quickest way to stop bloodshed.'[23]

A week later, on 9 April, when Mountbatten had a three-hour meeting with Jinnah, the viceroy tested the waters. As the viceroy would record right after this talk, he began the conversation by claiming that 'it was a daydream of mine to be able to put the Central Government under the prime ministership of Mr Jinnah himself'. Thereafter, it seems, Jinnah 'once more appealed' against 'a moth-eaten Pakistan'. He still wanted all of Bengal and all of Punjab.

Then, 'some thirty-five minutes later', to quote again from Mountbatten's record of the discussion, 'Mr Jinnah, who had not referred previously to my personal remark about him, suddenly made a reference out of the blue to the fact that I had wanted him to be the prime minister. There is no doubt that it had greatly tickled his vanity, and that he had kept turning over the proposition in his mind. Mr Gandhi's famous scheme may yet go through on the pure vanity of Mr Jinnah!'[24]

An alarmed viceroy now redoubled his effort against Gandhi's proposal, but his energies were not greatly required. For by now leaders including Nehru, Patel, Rajendra Prasad, Rajagopalachari, and Kripalani had not only reconciled themselves to Partition; they thought that other options, including Gandhi's idea, were worse than the Partition plan that Mountbatten was drawing up.

Among the leaders, Patel was the most enthusiastic about concentrating attention on 'four-fifths of India' while also freeing himself, and India, of the Jinnah/Pakistan headache. The other leaders too felt that the chance to guide a free if truncated India was preferable to supporting or watching an unrepresentative Jinnah-led ministry govern undivided India.

On 11 April, Gandhi conceded defeat. In a letter to Mountbatten, he wrote:

'I had several short talks with Pandit Nehru, and an hour's talk with him alone, and then with several members of the Working Committee last night about the formula I had sketched before you, and which I had filled in for them with all the implications. I am sorry to say that I failed to carry any of them with me except Badshah Khan....'

Telling the viceroy that the leaders he had failed to persuade were 'stalwarts' and 'seasoned servants of the nation' who fully represented the 'the Congress point of view,' Gandhi prepared himself to return to peacemaking in Bihar.[25]

The conversations regarding a possible Jinnah-led ministry in an undivided India would not enter the public record for some time. However, one Delhi newspaper reported on 12 April that Gandhi was leaving Delhi because he had 'fallen out' with the Working Committee. Calling the report 'sheer nonsense', Gandhi pointed out that Azad, Rajagoplachari, Patel, Nehru, and Kripalani had seen him during the day. 'We have our differences,' Gandhi said, but he added that he would be back 'the moment' the leaders summoned him.[26]

His solution for retaining India's unity had been rejected by Nehru, Patel, and company, but our peacemaker was not going to break his bond with them.

Calcutta

On 9 August 1947, Gandhi arrived in Calcutta on his way to Noakhali, where he wished to spend Independence Day. India would be split in six days, but our peacemaker felt he belonged to both halves. In Calcutta, meanwhile, the Muslim League's Hasan Suhrawardy, premier of undivided Bengal, was on his way out, and the Congress's Prafulla Chandra Ghosh was about to take over as chief minister of West Bengal. Many Muslim police officers had been replaced by Hindus.

'Calcutta's Muslims are terrified,' Gandhi was told, and Suhrawardy urged him to spend some days in Kolkata before proceeding to Noakhali and 'pour a pot of water' over the city's 'raging fire'.[27] He would put off his Noakhali visit, said Gandhi to Suhrawardy, provided 'you and I are prepared to live together under the same roof.'

He added, 'I don't want you to come to a decision immediately. Go back home, and consult your daughter....'[28]

Suhrawardy accepted the offer. Hindu friends who warned Gandhi that Suhrawardy was 'not to be relied upon' were told that some Muslims imagined him (Gandhi) 'to be an enemy of Muslims'.

'Both of us (Gandhi added) will live under the same roof

and have no secrets from each other. We together will see all the visitors. People should have the courage to speak out the truth...in the presence of those against whom it has to be said.'[29]

On 13 August, Gandhi and Suhrawardy moved to Hydari Manzil, 'an old abandoned Muslim house' in Beliaghata, a run-down Hindu-majority locality.[30] 14 August was a happy day. The people of Calcutta embraced one another. Hindus were taken to masjids, Muslims to mandirs.[31]

At midnight, India became independent. At 3 a.m., Gandhi opened his eyes in a free India in a Muslim house in one of Calcutta's humble localities. In the evening, at his request, he was driven quietly through the city. He found that Calcuttans were joyous, excited, and peaceful. Eid day fell on 18 August. 5,00,000 Hindus and Muslims attended Gandhi's prayer meeting, held on the grounds of the Mohammedan Sporting Football Club.

On the night of 31 August, however, angry Hindus smashed Hydari Manzil's windows, doors, and ceiling fans. With his aides—Abha Gandhi, Manu Gandhi, and Shiv Balak Bisen—Gandhi came out to meet the demonstrators. Bricks and a lathi were thrown at Gandhi, at an unidentified Muslim who was present, and at Bisen, who the crowd thought was a Muslim.

With Abha and Manu, 'two very brave girls', as Gandhi called them, at his side, Gandhi instructed the Muslims in the house and two policemen who were present to remain calm. He asked the crowd to disperse, which they did, though only when a police officer arrived.

Going to sleep at 12.30 a.m., Gandhi was up again in three hours. He wrote to Patel, now India's home minister, described the incident, and added that he was being asked to visit Punjab, where violence had risen dramatically, crossing the marks left by Bengal and Bihar. Saying that he felt 'totally lost,' Gandhi added, referring also to Nehru, 'I pin my hopes on you two.'[32]

After writing to Patel, Gandhi learnt of other killings in Calcutta. He went to the affected areas and saw 'two dead bodies of very poor Muslims'.[33] In the afternoon of 1 September, a telegram arrived from Nehru suggesting a visit to Punjab 'as early as possible', whereupon Gandhi thought he would do that, giving up Noakhali,[34] even though Patel had written to him, 'You will not be able to put out the conflagration in Punjab.'[35]

When visitors brought more news of Calcutta's violence—around fifty had been killed—Gandhi again changed his mind. At about 8 p.m. on 1 September, he decided he would go neither to Noakhali nor to Punjab: he would stay put in Hydari Manzil and fast until peace returned to Kolkata. To Nehru he wrote, 'If the fury (in Calcutta) does not abate, my going to Punjab will be of no avail.'[36]

Announced at 8.15 p.m. on 1 September, the fast had an immediate impact. That day, young Sachin Mitra had been martyred in Calcutta while leading a peace squad. Two days later, on 3 September, another young Hindu, Smritish Banerjee, lost his life while protecting a peace march.

However, violence died down. Hindus and Muslims marched jointly for peace. Processions of young women and girls of both communities demanded peace. About 500 members of the North Calcutta police force, including a few Britons and Anglo-Indians, went on a twenty-four-hour sympathy fast while remaining on duty. University students gathered weapons from streets and homes and gave them to Gandhi.[37]

Ram Manohar Lohia, who was in Kolkata, brought a band of young Hindus who handed over an arsenal of arms. Members of another gang turned up, asked for 'any penalty', and pleaded, 'Only you should now end your fast.' Gandhi asked them to go 'immediately among the Muslims and assure them full protection'.[38]

At 6 p.m. that day, 4 September, a citizens' deputation of Hindu, Muslim, and Sikh leaders, headed by Suhrawardy, went to Gandhi's bedside and urged him to end the fast. When Gandhi asked if they would risk their lives to prevent a recurrence, they withdrew to another room, from where they returned with a pledge that they would. Reminding them that 'above all, there is God, our witness,' Gandhi agreed to break his fast.

'Gandhiji has achieved many things,' Governor Rajagopalachari observed, 'but in my considered opinion there has been nothing, not even independence, which is so truly wonderful as his victory over evil in Calcutta.'[39]

Delhi

On the morning of 9 September, Gandhi arrived in Delhi by train, on his way, he thought, to Punjab. Meeting him at Shahdara station, Patel took Gandhi to where he would stay, Birla House. In the car, Patel told him of killings that had started in Delhi. Gandhi went the same morning to a camp near Humayun's Tomb where Mewatis from Alwar and Bharatpur had taken refuge, another camp at Jamia Millia, where many of Delhi's Muslims were huddled together, and later that day to three camps filled with Hindu and Sikh refugees from West Punjab.

'Whole day long' he listened 'to the tale' of Delhi's suffering.[40] At Jamia, Zakir Husain told Gandhi of his escape on a train a few days earlier. Had a Sikh army captain and a Hindu railway officer not helped, Husain would have been killed. Gandhi learnt, too, that Saifuddin Kitchlew had been forced to flee from his Delhi home to Kashmir, the land of his forebears. In April 1919, Dr Kitchlew and Dr Satya Pal had organized the anti-imperialist protest that was followed by the Jallianwala Bagh massacre.

Hindu and Sikh refugees from Pakistan told Gandhi that he 'had not undergone the hardships they did...he had not lost kith and kin...[he had] not been compelled to beg at every door'. Gandhi's hosts at Birla House said the city was in such disarray that even they, belonging to one of India's richest families, had not been able to obtain fruits and vegetables.[41]

Talking to P. C. Joshi, a Communist leader, Gandhi said: 'I do not remember an occasion in my life...when I have felt [as] baffled as I am today.' But at the end of the day, Gandhi found clarity: he would not go to Punjab but remain in Delhi until the capital 'regained its former self'.

The next morning a Sikh taxi driver told Brij Krishna, Gandhi's associate and aide in Delhi from the 1920s: 'If Gandhiji had waited some more days before coming to Delhi, all the Muslims here would have been eliminated.'[42]

Three days after arriving in Delhi, Gandhi confronted the Rashtriya Swayamsevak Sangh (RSS) chief, M. S. Golwalkar, with reports of the RSS's hand in the Delhi violence. When Golwalkar said that the RSS did not stand for the killing of Muslims, Gandhi asked him to say so publicly. Golwalkar said Gandhi could quote him. This Gandhi did in his prayer talk that evening, but he told Golwalkar the statement ought to come from him.[43]

Four days later, at Gandhi's instance, a group of RSS activists met him. One of them asked Gandhi, 'Doesn't Hinduism permit killing an evil-doer?' Gandhi answered: 'Can a sinner claim the right to judge or execute another sinner? Only a properly constituted government is entitled to punish an evil-doer.'[44]

Day after day, Gandhi spoke to the people of Delhi through his prayer meeting talks, which were broadcast by All India Radio and carried by most newspapers. Thus he said:

'I have seen the terrible plight of the Hindus and Sikhs of Pakistan. I have lived in Lahore. Do you think I am not pained?

If any Hindu or Sikh from the Punjab comes and tells me that his anguish is greater than mine because he has lost his brother or daughter or father, I would say that his brother is my brother, his mother is my mother.

'I had gone to Jama Masjid today. I met the residents of that area. I also met their womenfolk. Some of the women wept before me and brought their children to indicate their sad plight. Should I narrate to them the plight of the Hindus and Sikhs in West Punjab and in the Frontier Province? Will that mitigate the sorrow of Punjabi Hindus and Sikhs?'[45]

In another talk, referring to the kirpan, he said:

'I speak freely and frankly because I am [the Sikhs'] true friend. A sacred thing has to be used on sacred and lawful occasions. A kirpan is undoubtedly a symbol of strength, which adorns the possessor only if he exercises amazing restraint over himself and uses it against enormous odds....'[46]

'Ram' was constantly on Gandhi's lips. On 18 November, he wrote: 'My Ram is not a man with two hands and two feet. But if I am perfectly fit it is due to Ram's grace.'[47] Everyone understood that Gandhi's Ram was a synonym for Krishna, Shiva, Allah, Khuda, Waheguru, and God....

That month, November 1947, Gandhi spoke candidly to the All India Congress Committee:

'I know what some people are saying. "The Congress has surrendered its soul to the Muslims. Gandhi? Let him rave as he will. He is a washout. Jawaharlal is no better. Sardar Patel? Yes, there is something in him. A portion of him is sound Hindu, but he too is after all a Congressman." Such talk will not help us.... Hinduism cannot be saved by orgies of murder. You represent the vast ocean of Indian humanity.... [T]here are many places today where a Muslim cannot live in security. There are miscreants who will kill him or throw him out of a running train for no reason other than that he is a Muslim....

'[S]uch things should never happen in India. We have to recognize that India does not belong to Hindus alone, nor does Pakistan to Muslims....'[48]

To the AICC, Gandhi spoke, too, of reports that the Mewatis were being coerced to go to Pakistan.

'I understand that a lakh and a half Muslims are about to be pushed into Pakistan... How shameful that we want to force them to trudge three hundred miles on foot!'[49]

Gandhi's intervention thwarted the plan. It was no longer possible for anyone to ask for the Mewatis' expulsion. And the AICC renewed its commitment to an India for all, with equal protection to all.

On 14 January, one day after starting what would be his final fast, Gandhi said:

'Delhi is the capital of India.... It is this city which was Indraprastha, which was Hastinapur.... It is the heart of India.... All Hindus, Muslims, Sikhs, Parsis, Christians, and Jews who people this country from Kanyakumari to Kashmir and from Karachi to Dibrugarh...have an equal right to it.'[50]

On 18 January, after six days of fasting, Gandhi accepted a glass of orange juice from the hand of Maulana Azad, and dictated this statement:

'The leaders and people of Delhi have assured me that from now on Hindus, Sikhs, and Muslims will live as brothers and under no conditions and on no provocation will the residents of Delhi, including the refugees, become enemies of each other. This is not a small thing.....

'[W]e must pledge that once we have turned our face towards God we shall never turn away. When that happens India and Pakistan will unitedly be able to serve the world and make the world nobler. I do not wish to live for any other purpose.'[51]

On 21 January, a day after those who had come to the Birla House lawns to kill him had failed in the attempt and slipped out, although one of them who had exploded a grenade was caught, this is what Gandhi said:

'Let me first deal with the bomb incident of yesterday. People have been sending me wires congratulating me and praising me. In fact I deserve no congratulations. I displayed no bravery. I thought it was part of army practice somewhere. I only came to know later that it was a bomb and that it might have killed me if God had not willed it that I should live.....

'You should not have any kind of hate against the person who was responsible for this. He had taken it for granted that I am an enemy of Hinduism. Is it not said in chapter four of the Gita that whenever the wicked become too powerful and harm dharma, God sends someone to destroy them? The man who exploded the bomb obviously thinks that he has been sent by God to destroy me. I have not seen him. But I am told that is what he said when questioned by the police.

'But...if we do not like a man, does it mean that he is wicked?.... If someone kills me, taking me for a wicked man, will he not have to answer before God?.... When he says he was doing the bidding of God, he is only making God an accomplice in a wicked deed.....

'Those who are behind him or whose tool he is, should know that this sort of thing will not save Hinduism. If Hinduism has to be saved it will be saved through such work as I am doing. My nurse, who literally brought me up, taught me to invoke Ram whenever I had any fears.....

'[H]aving passed all the tests, I am as staunch a Hindu today as intuitively I was at the age of five or six.... Do you want to annihilate Hindu dharma by killing a devout Hindu like me? Some Sikhs came to me and asked me if I suspected that a

Sikh was implicated in the deed. I know he was not a Sikh. But what even if he was? What does it matter if he was a Hindu or a Muslim? May God bless him with good sense....'[52]

Nine days later Gandhi was killed. But thanks to him and other peacemakers, the tide of hatred died down. The Constitution was created, and a democratic republic was launched that belonged equally to all in India.

2

THE INDO-NAGA PEACE PROCESS
CONFLICT AND CONVERSATION

Nandita Haksar

The Naga insurgency is the oldest armed resistance in India, having started in 1950. The Naga people inhabit parts of the northeastern states of India and Myanmar. The international boundary that divides India and Myanmar actually cuts the village of Longwa into two, with one half of the village chief's home in Myanmar and the other in India.

The objective of the Naga national movement was to create an independent, sovereign nation state by combining all Naga-inhabited areas in India and Myanmar. In many ways, it was shaped by the Cold War. Even as the Indian government worried that China could use the resistance to influence the people in the Northeast, the Naga insurgents took the opportunity to travel to China in 1967 for training in the People's Liberation Army. They returned with sophisticated arms and ammunition.[1]

This essay is neither the history of the Naga movement nor of the Indo-Naga peace process; it is an account of an Indian citizen's involvement in the Naga question in her capacity as a human rights lawyer.

My involvement with the Indo-Naga conflict began in 1979 when I met Naga students at the Jawaharlal Nehru University (JNU) in Delhi. The insurgency was at its peak then, and even to speak of the Nagas was considered anti-national. Though I did not support the cause for independence, I was drawn to the soft-spoken, polite students who laughed easily. Their radiant smiles were always warm and welcoming. Despite my political misgivings, it was love at first taste. I fell totally in love with Naga cuisine.

Like most Indians, I had no understanding of the insurgency or the history of the region. I did not even know that Naga-inhabited areas had been declared 'disturbed'[2] by the Government of India, and the Naga people had been living under virtual army rule for decades.

Gradually, I learnt that the Nagas were not one tribe but a community of more than thirty (even today there is no agreement on the exact number) tribes, each speaking their own distinct language and having their own territory. These Naga tribes were spread across four Indian states—Nagaland, four districts of Manipur, parts of Assam, and Arunachal Pradesh[3]—and parts of Burma, as Myanmar was then called.

Around this time, a powerful human rights movement had emerged in India. The Naga students too were engaged in forming a human rights organization dedicated to documenting violations committed by Indian security forces against the Nagas. This is was the first time I had heard of the Armed Forces (Special Powers) Act which had been passed in 1958 to enable the Indian military to carry out counter-insurgency (CI) operations as it deemed fit, without worrying about prosecution by the state on the basis of complaints by citizens affected by those operations.[4]

In 1982, I joined the first fact-finding team led by Pramila Dandavate to Ukhrul in Manipur to document the alleged human rights violations committed by the Indian armed forces. In February that year, the newly formed Naga insurgent group, the National Socialist Council of Nagaland (NSCN), led by Thuingaleng Muivah and Isak Chishi Swu, had announced its arrival on the scene by laying an ambush on an Indian Army convoy, killing nearly twenty-two soldiers of the 22 Sikh Regiment.[5] In the counter-insurgency operation that followed, there were allegations of widespread human rights violations.[6]

This was my first encounter with military rule. It was the beginning of my awareness of how brutal and violent the state could be against its own citizens. But I was still young and idealistic and had faith in Indian democracy. I thought if I worked hard, it would be possible to use the law as a weapon for justice, especially since the Supreme Court was evolving a special jurisprudence for reaching justice to those who did not have access to the courts: Public Interest Litigation.

This faith in Indian democracy was strengthened when I won my first case in the Supreme Court in February 1983. I had filed a writ petition challenging the constitutional validity of the AFSPA enforced in Nagaland. The court ruled in my favour, issuing an interim order directing the security forces not to use churches and educational institutions in Naga-inhabited areas as detention centres.[7]

The next year, following another petition, the Supreme Court awarded ₹1 lakh each to two Tangkhul Naga women whose husbands had been picked up by Indian security forces and not returned.[8] The women insisted that their husbands had been tortured to death. This time the petitioner was a fellow student from JNU, Sebastian Hongray. I had no premonition then that ten years later we would be married.[9]

However, in the midst of celebration of our victories in court, three successive events made me see that the reality of the Indian state was far more complex than I had imagined.

First, the documents relating to my cases mysteriously

disappeared from Hongray's hostel room. And then at the court hearing the next day the solicitor general asked the judges to direct me to produce the documents. I do not know if he knew that they had been stolen; but it was most unusual to ask the counsel to produce the original documents. Luckily for me, the judges refused the request.

Second, the Union of India claimed in counter affidavits that I was linked to the NSCN. Until then, I had neither met anyone from the underground nor did I have any sympathy for the Naga cause.

Third, the fledgling human rights movement was dubbed as anti-national and against national security, thereby putting human rights activists at risk of persecution by the state. All that activists like me were saying was that military repression could never be a solution; that the Indo-Naga conflict, like any other conflict, was a political issue and the resolution could come only through talks.

However, I had no idea what peace talks entailed or how complex they could be. At the same time, I also did not realize that my efforts at exposing human rights violations were contributing to what would now be called 'confidence-building measures'. The result of our fact-finding mission, our victory in courts, and media publicity was that many Naga students started to feel that there was a possibility of dialogue between the Indian state and the Naga people.

The Peace Accords

Much before the Narendra Modi government signed the Framework Agreement in 2015, several attempts at peace had been made and at least three major accords signed. These were:

- The June 1947 Nine Point Agreement, also called the Hydari Agreement;
- the July 1960 16 Point Agreement, which led to the creation of Nagaland state and the incorporation of Article 371(A) in the Indian Constitution; and
- the 1975 Shillong Agreement signed during the Emergency.

The history of these accords is well documented by both the Indians and the Nagas, hence I will not go into the political differences which fuelled the controversies plaguing the signing of these agreements and their aftermath. But it is true that these peace accords did not lead to any lasting peace. On the contrary, they have led to the conflict becoming more intense and deeply entrenched. There are two features of the past accords which have bearing on the present Indo-Naga peace process.

The first was the creation of the Nagaland state. I was in school when the state was created in 1963. It was an amalgamation of the Naga Hills District of Assam and Tuensang area of the North East Frontier Agency (NEFA), present-day Arunachal Pradesh.[10] The man who was regarded to have been the architect of the Nagaland state and the 16 Point Agreement was the head of the Naga People's Convention (NPC), Imkongliba Ao.

During the Naga Students' Federation Conference in 1989, where I was invited to speak, someone gave me a book called *Nagaland Church and Politics* (1986) by Reverend V. K. Nuh. The book included a document which was marked secret. It was called 'Joint Directive for Counter Insurgency Operations in Nagaland'. Reverend Nuh described the document as a part of the programme 'to wipe out all traces of patriotism among the Nagas.'

The document had a section on Psychological Operation. This included:

- divide, disorganize, and induce defections of members of the hostile elements;
- reduce and ultimately eliminate civilian support and hostile elements;
- dissuade civilians from participating in covert activities on the side of the hostiles;
- win the active support of non-committed civilians;
- preserve and strengthen the support of friendly civilians; and
- win popular approval of the local presence of security forces.

The document also instructed the intelligence agencies to promote the idea that the creation of the state of Nagaland had fulfilled the major demand of the Naga insurgents, which was the creation of a Naga homeland, thereby conflating the state of Nagaland under the Union of India with independent Naga homeland.[11]

The consequence of this was that on 22 August 1961, the Naga underground assassinated Imkongliba Ao for agreeing to the establishment of the state of Nagaland.[12] Ao was shot in Mokokchung and died from his wounds two days later. Accusing the Indian government of genocide, the president of the Naga National Council (NNC), Angami Zapu Phizo, who was living in exile in the UK, referred the matter to the International Commission of Jurists (ICJ) on 11 February 1962.[13]

The Naga movement under Phizo's leadership did not tolerate any dissenting voices, even though there were distinguished Nagas who felt it would be wiser to make peace with the Indian government and come to an agreement which would allow the Nagas political autonomy and social freedom. For instance, the general secretary of NNC, T. Sakhrie, favoured a negotiated settlement. He was credited with writing all the NNC speeches. He was assassinated in 1956, and there were strong allegations that Phizo was behind the killing.[14]

Then there was R. Suisa, a Tangkhul Naga and a member of the Indian parliament. He gave a set of proposals to the Indian government and asked them to negotiate with the NNC on that basis. But his ideas were brushed aside.

In the first Indo-Naga talks, which led to the signing of the Shillong Accord, the interlocuter was Harish Chandola, a journalist married to Phizo's niece. He was appointed by Prime Minister Lal Bahadur Shastri to assist the peace mission comprising the missionary Michael Scott, Congress leader Jayaprakash Narayan, and chief minister of Assam Bimala Prasad Chaliha to broker a peace deal between the Indian government and the Naga insurgents. The peace mission was undermined and Chandola was thrown out of Nagaland, which he has recorded in his book, *The Naga Story: First Armed Struggle in India* (2013). B. K. Nehru, who was the Nagaland governor at that time, has written his version in his autobiography *Nice Guys Finish Second: Memoirs* (1997).

The Shillong Accord was signed between the members of the NNC and the Government of India in 1975 in Shillong where Governor B. K. Nehru lived. At the time of the signing of the accord, Thuingaleng Muivah and many of the leaders of the Naga underground were in China.[15] They condemned the accord as a betrayal of the Naga cause. They waited for Phizo to condemn the accord, but he did not. This was the beginning of bitter rivalries and divisions within the Naga national movement. It ultimately led to Thuingaleng Muivah and Isak Chishi Swu establishing the NSCN on 31 January 1980.

This was the second feature of the peace process. From 1982

to 1988, the NSCN was one of the most powerful insurgent groups with a highly trained and well-equipped cadre. They also trained and supported dozens of other armed groups and encouraged them to fight for their imagined homelands all over northeast India. The NSCN also formed alliances with other insurgent groups and lived together in bases in Bhutan, Bangladesh, and Burma.

The first major ambush of the NSCN was at Namthilok in Ukhrul district of Manipur in 1982 as mentioned earlier and the last major attack was at the Assam Rifles post in Oinam village in Senapati district of Manipur in 1987. In the aftermath of both attacks, the Indian armed forces led counter-insurgency operations which led to widescale alleged human rights violations.

I was instrumental in documenting the violations and taking up the case on behalf of the villagers who had allegedly suffered at the hands of the Indian security forces during these operations. I have documented much of the work in a book co-authored with Sebastian Hongray called *The Judgement That Never Came: Army Rule in Northeast India* (2011). The book chronicles the history of Naga challenges to the AFSPA from 1982 to 1991.

I believed my work as a human rights activist taking up cases on behalf of the Naga people would be a way of building a bridge between mainstream Indians and the Nagas. In many ways, it did that. However, there were three factors which undermined the efforts of the human rights movement:

- The courts delayed giving any judgment at all, perhaps, under pressure from the Indian state. The writ petitions filed in the Supreme Court lay before the Constitution Bench from 1983 to 1997. For instance, the final hearing in the Oinam case was in 1992, but the judgment was delivered in 2019;[16]

- the state attack on the human rights movement portraying it as anti-national undermined the legitimacy of the issues we tried to focus upon; and
- various foreign agencies started pouring money into the human rights movement, using them for their own foreign policy objectives.[17]

By 1997, I came to the conclusion that it was not possible for me to work in the human rights movement, including the Naga human rights movement. I could see that the influx of foreign money had ensured that the agenda was no longer dictated by the needs of the people but by western states and perhaps corporations. In other words, the human rights discourse had been weaponized and used as a tool of foreign policy rather than as an instrument for liberation.

The demand for the repeal of AFSPA had, for a short time, brought communities together but now the human rights movement itself became a pawn to identity politics, with each community taking up the issue on behalf of their own particular agenda. This was especially true with the way activists showed their support for Irom Sharmila who went on a hunger strike for more than sixteen years.[18] While Irom Sharmila became a symbol of Meitei nationalism in Manipur, in the rest of India she became a symbol of non-violence. Ultimately the campaign turned into 'Save Irom' and not the repeal of the Act for which she had gone on this long hunger strike. The campaign was not even linked to the political conflict and the need to resolve it.

Ceasefire and Peace Process

In the mid-1990s, rumours were rife that the NSCN (Isak-Muivah) led by Thuingaleng Muivah was willing to negotiate but the other group, led by S. S. Khaplang, a Burmese Naga, was opposed to the talks. Since Muivah was still underground, several journalists were looking for ways to get an interview with the famous insurgent who had spent ten years in China.

The editor of the weekly *Northeast Sun*, Deepak Dewan, was also trying to get the interview. One evening in 1995, he was having dinner with the senior Naga policeman Peter Chiphang when he met the Naga contractor Grinder Muivah. It turned out that Grinder's father was Thuingaleng Muivah's elder brother.

Grinder and Deepak became friends and Deepak got the interview with Muivah. Grinder showed the published copy to his uncle who then allowed Grinder and Deepak to go ahead with making arrangements for the peace talks.

Rajesh Pilot, then minister of state for Home Affairs in Prime Minister P. V. Narasimha Rao's government, was instrumental in setting the stage. Thereafter, Thuingaleng Muivah and Isak Chishi Swu of the Isak-Muivah (IM) faction met Prime Minister Rao in Paris. This was followed by a meeting with Rajesh Pilot in Bangkok. The two sides agreed to a ceasefire and to begin peace talks. On 3 February 1997, Prime Minister H. D. Deve Gowda met the two Naga leaders in Zurich, Switzerland and, on 4 March, he announced during the budget session of the parliament that the NSCN had agreed to peace talks.

Over the next decade, successive Indian prime ministers met Naga leaders who were across the globe—New York, Tokyo, Bangkok, Zurich, and Amsterdam—as peace talks got underway.[19] The two sides agreed on three points which would become the basis of future talks. These were:

- The talks would be held at the highest level. This meant the Indian side would be represented by an officer deputed by the Indian prime minister and from the Naga side the chief negotiator would be the general secretary of the NSCN, Thuingaleng Muivah, who also held the post of ato kilonser or prime minister in the Government of People's Republic of Nagalim (GPRN).[20]

- The talks would be unconditional. This meant that India would not insist on talking within the Constitution and the Nagas would not insist on sovereignty.
- The talks would be held outside India.

The government did not agree to the demand of the Nagas that there be a foreign observer. However, they allowed Michael van Walt van Praag, a Dutch jurist, to facilitate the Indo-Naga peace talks by playing the role of mediator.

Michael van Walt was the executive president of Kreddha, a conflict resolution organization and the first General Secretary of the Netherlands-based Unrepresented Nations and People's Organization (UNPO). Michael has been the legal advisor to the Dalai Lama in the negotiations with the Chinese. The NSCN became a member of the UNPO in 1991.

Ceasefire Monitoring

The government of India and the NSCN also set up an elaborate ceasefire monitoring system. To begin with, it had four tiers:

- The Ceasefire Monitoring Committee was headed by a former Indian Army general;
- the committee was to make the ground rules;
- the Ceasefire Supervisory Board included representatives of both, the Government of India and the NSCN; and
- the NSCN ceasefire monitoring cell.

The Naga army was allowed to carry arms in designated camps and some officers were allowed to carry arms, discreetly, outside the camps. This was for protection not from the Indian security forces as much as it was from rival Naga insurgent groups.

Meeting Thuingaleng Muivah and Isak Chishi Swu

When my husband and I heard of the ceasefire and that NSCN (IM) would begin the peace process, we thought one way to contribute would be to interview the NSCN leaders and make their views known through a book.

In 1984, I co-edited a book titled *Nagaland File: A Question of Human Rights*. It was the first book to publish the various documents on the Indo-Naga conflict. I could take little credit for the book because I knew little of the history of the Naga insurgency, and it was my co-editor, Luingam Luithui, one of the founders of the Naga Peoples Human Rights Movement (NPMHR), who had collected the documents. This time I wanted to write a more detailed account of the Naga national movement from the point of view of the insurgents. I believed it was important for Indian citizens to listen to the voices of people whom they would otherwise never hear.

Sebastian and I managed to send a message to the two NSCN leaders who were then in Bangkok. They had heard of our work, especially the fight for the victims of Operation Bluebird[21]. They agreed to meet us but were intrigued by our request of one months' time for the interviews. They were used to the usual one-hour interviews.

In 1998, we spent one month in Bangkok recording the stories the two leaders had to tell. They gave us several hours a day and we would record from morning to evening with a short break for lunch. We followed up these interviews with those of other men and women who had been a part of the movement in the early stages. These interviews were possible only because a ceasefire was in place.[22]

Unfortunately, we could not publish the book till many years later. The book, entitled *Kuknalim, Naga Armed Resistance: Testimonies of Leaders, Pastors, Healers and Soldiers* finally came out in 2019. By then Isak Swu was no more. He had passed away in a Delhi hospital in June 2016. However, we were able to give the first copy of our book to Thuingaleng Muivah. It was also the last time we met him.

Thuingaleng Muivah's Arrest

One of the reasons why the book could not come out earlier was that Thuingaleng Muivah was arrested on 19 January 2000 in Bangkok when he travelled there for another round of talks.[23] He was travelling with a Korean passport.

From media reports it seemed that the arrest was at the behest of the Research and Analysis Wing (R&AW), which did this in pique.[24] Being an external intelligence agency, it wanted to lead the talks since the NSCN leaders lived abroad. However, the Intelligence Bureau (IB) asserted its right to lead the peace process since it was a matter internal to the country.

I was in Delhi when I read the news of the arrest and was rightly confused. Did this mean that the Indo-Naga peace talks had been put on hold or was there some other agenda?

Meanwhile, the anthropologist B. K. Roy Burman turned up in Bangkok. When Thuingaleng Muivah appeared for the hearing in court, Burman presented to him the article he had published in the July 2000 issue of *Mainstream* on his ideas of resolving the Indo-Naga conflict. He was inspired by the Sami council comprising Sami tribes living across Norway, Sweden, Finland

and Russia. It was very odd for an anthropologist to try and get Muivah to approve of the plan while he was in court in shackles. Muivah threw away the papers Roy Burman handed to him.

Subsequently, Muivah's nephew Grinder, who had been appointed as the official go-between the NSCN and the Government of India, was arrested in Calcutta on 4 March 2000 while returning from meeting his uncle in the Bangkok jail.[25] However, he managed to slip a note to someone with the phone numbers of his wife Sonia and his lawyer (me).

What unfolded thereafter was not only inexplicable but also underscores the Indian reality that conflict creates its own vested interest groups. Of all the cases that I have handled so far, this was the weirdest. The FIR (First Information Report) No. 116 dated 21 February 2000 stated that one K. Ranju Ranjan had confessed that he posed as a director of the ministry of civil aviation and inspected the Lengpui airport in Mizoram to help Grinder Muivah hijack a plane to rescue Thuingaleng Muivah from the Thai jail.[26]

Even though the FIR was registered, it was said the story was concocted by director inspector general of police, DIG (Range), at Aizawl, Deepak Misra. Ranju Ranjan was from Kerala, brought up in Mizoram, and had been living in Mizoram House in Delhi. He had struck up a friendship with Pam Shimray, a cousin of Grinder Muivah's. The story planted in the media was that Grinder had told Ranju that if he helped in the hijacking, he could marry Pam.

Sonia and I flew to Kolkata where Grinder was in jail. As some sort of a security cover, I asked a journalist friend to do a story on Grinder's incarceration, lest they simply make him 'disappear'. The next day, they (I cannot say who, because several intelligence agencies were involved in the arrest) were going to take Grinder to Mizoram. The airlines denied us a ticket on the same plane. However, we did meet Grinder in jail.

Since I needed an Inner Line Permit, we had to stop at Silchar to get one. By the time we reached Aizawl it was dark. I straightaway went to the police station to be present during Grinder's interrogation. In Aizawl, rumours were rife that the NSCN was coming to Mizoram to hijack a plane. Before coming to Mizoram, I had called the leaders of the Northeast Students Organisation (NESO) for contacts of student leaders in Mizoram; I had also asked a lawyer friend to give me contacts of a local lawyer without which it would be difficult to proceed.

Luckily, with all these contacts, Sonia and I managed to stop the attempts to create tensions between Mizos and Nagas. Ranju Rajan was clearly an imposter. But who used him to get Grinder arrested and what the motive was, I still do not know. I managed to get Grinder out on bail on 14 March 2000.

After this harrowing experience, Grinder resigned as mediator. The IB also persuaded him to withdraw the petition I had filed asking for compensation for wrongful arrest. Following this, the Government of India case against him also disappeared. But Thuingaleng Muivah was still in jail and the deadline for the ceasefire was approaching. Indo-Naga talks were floundering and this could affect the prospects of peace in the entire region.

Thuingaleng Muivah's Release

Deepak Dewan suggested that I speak with Prime Minister Atal Bihari Vajpayee about the release of Thuingaleng Muivah. I finally managed to reach Home Minister L. K. Advani and met him at his office on 19 February 2000. His first question was:

'How are you involved in Indo-Naga talks?'

The honest answer was that I wanted to play a role in the

peace process so that Indians and Nagas could live in peace. But I knew this answer would not resonate. So, I opted for second best.

'I am married to someone from Thuingaleng Muivah's tribe,' I told him.

'A Naga bahu!' He seemed to think it was a good enough reason.

His second question was: 'What kind of man is this Muivah?'

'All I can say is that if he says he is interested in the peace talks, he is interested,' I replied truthfully.

Thereafter Grinder and I went to three former prime ministers to get them to sign a statement asking for the release of Thuingaleng Muivah so that the peace process could be resumed. V. P. Singh was undergoing dialysis, but he signed the statement in the hospital. Chandrashekhar and Deve Gowda also signed it.

The next step was to place the statement on record in the Bangkok criminal court. That is how I found myself appearing as an expert witness and placing the appeal from three former prime ministers on record.

When we came out of the court, Thuingaleng Muivah thanked me warmly. He was released from the Thai prison in September 2000.

But there was another difficult problem. Muivah needed travel documents and he had applied to the United Nations High Commission for Refugees (UNHCR) to be accepted as a refugee. However, the UNHCR at Bangkok rejected his application on the grounds that he was involved in war crimes. This was very serious. It meant that no country in Europe would give him a visa.

I truly believed that unless he was involved in the peace process, there would be no resolution to the Indo-Naga conflict. I had been handling refugee cases in India, so I had contacts in the UNHCR. Grinder said I should try and sort out the problem by going to Geneva, the UNHCR headquarters. So, on 12 January 2001, Sebastian and I flew to Geneva.

We stayed with friends from JNU. I managed to get Thuingaleng Muivah an under-consideration certificate from the UNHCR, following which Michael van Walt organized his visa and travel documents. However, Indian intelligence agencies ensured that Muivah was forced to take an Indian passport. From then onwards, talks took place in India. More recently, in April 2022, the latest interlocutor, A. K. Misra, went to the NSCN headquarters in Camp Hebron near Dimapur and held talks inside their camp.

From 1997 to 2008, the talks made no headway because of one issue—the extension of the ceasefire to Naga-inhabited areas of Manipur. The Government of India promised to extend it several times, but there was always stiff resistance from the people and leaders of Manipur who oppose the Naga-inhabited areas of Manipur being integrated into Nagaland and other Naga-inhabited areas.

In 2001, I was invited by one of the television channels to give my views on the issue of integration of all Naga-inhabited areas as one entity. I said, according to the provisions of the Indian Constitution, it was entirely possible but politically it was opposed by the Meiteis, who spoke of the unity and integrity of Manipur state. Manipur had been a princely kingdom where the hill and plains people had lived together for centuries.

There was a sharp reaction to my interview. It was banned in Manipur. The Meiteis were so furious with the Government of India for appearing to concede the Naga demand that they set fire to the legislative assembly.[27] They also burnt effigies of the prime minister and some other Indian leaders as well as an effigy of a woman in a salwar kurta; one of my Meitei friend's daughters said: 'That is Aunt Nandita!'

Government of India Proposal

The first two interlocuters, Swaraj Kaushal (1997 to May 1999) and K. Padmanabhaiah (July 1999 to 2009), did not put forward any proposals and only discussed the issue of whether the ceasefire should be extended to Manipur. The peace process did not progress between 1997 and 2010. The only issue that was discussed was the issue of extension of ceasefire to Manipur, the presence or absence of designated camps in Manipur, and various cases of ceasefire violations on both sides.

In 2002, Sebastian and I went to Bangkok to meet with the two leaders, Thuingaleng Muivah and Isak Chishi Swu, to discuss the actual negotiating document. In the early stages they had taken advice from international lawyers who had no familiarity with the Indian Constitution.

I finally picked up the courage and told the NSCN leaders that they would have to understand the provisions of the Indian Constitution if they wanted to negotiate with the Indian government. In 2007, I had the privilege of taking classes on the Indian Constitution and discussing it with a group of senior NSCN leaders.

The one question that they repeatedly asked me was what happens if the Government of India goes back on its promises made in an agreement. My honest answer—they could do very little; India had sovereign power to do so. I am sure that watching the government exercise that power on 5 August 2019, when it repealed Article 370 for Kashmir, would have reinforced their fears.[28]

In 2010, the interlocutor of many years, Home Secretary K. Padmanabhaiah, was replaced by R. S. Pandey, who had been the chief secretary of Nagaland. He put forward a non-paper which had some concrete proposals for the consideration of the NSCN. A non-paper is an informal document usually without explicit attribution, meant for closed door negotiations. The NSCN decided to call a meeting of international lawyers from the United States, South Africa, and Australia to look at the document and give it a legal shape. The senior-most was Professor Yash Pal Ghai who had been involved in the drafting of a new constitution for Kenya in 2004. Sebastian and I were the only two people from India.

We met on 20–21 May 2011 for two days and thrashed out issues. It was really exciting to be involved in the process of concretizing the ideas in the document in terms of the law and Constitution. It was the first time I had hope that the Indo-Naga conflict could be resolved, and that it would be a just and honourable resolution. The basic idea put forward in the non-paper was the idea of a pan-Naga body. I am not at liberty to reveal the details of what we discussed, but Michael Van Walt told us that Thuingaleng Muivah had taken our proposals seriously and had included them in the NSCN's official response to the non-paper.

But there was one question that the NSCN persistently asked: what kind of agreement can we have that ensures that the Government of India does not go back on its promise? They had seen how India had promised Sikkim the status of associate state but then fully integrated it into the Indian union. Nobody had an answer to this.

After this I was no longer involved in the peace process for various reasons. I read that Prime Minister Modi had taken interest in the Indo-Naga peace process and had appointed R. N. Ravi as the interlocutor in 2015. Ravi was from the R&AW, India's external intelligence service.

Framework Agreement/Agreed Position

Like everyone else I too was surprised and excited to learn that the NSCN and the Government of India had signed a Framework Agreement on 3 August 2015. The contents of the agreement were kept secret by both parties allowing for endless speculation on the meaning and contents of the document.

We even got a call from a distant relative asking whether this agreement meant the Nagas had finally got their independence. The woman eked out a living by crushing smoked chillies and I wondered what she imagined independence would be like.

Sure enough, news of the Framework Agreement spread like wildfire across the Naga-inhabited hill villages. People started celebrating and some even believed that the Nagas had finally won their independence. The excitement was palpable. Even though I was living in Goa then, I could feel the beating of the pulse of a people as they watched the signing ceremony live on social media.

There was the image of R. N. Ravi, the interlocutor and member of India's external intelligence agency, the R&AW, handing over a signed agreement to Thuingaleng Muivah. Ravi was beaming, but Muivah's expression was grim. Just behind Muivah was National Security Advisor Ajit Doval. He was also not smiling. However, Prime Minister Narendra Modi, with a Tangkhul shawl draped over his shoulders, looked pleased and satisfied.

The contents of the Framework Agreement were not made public for many years, leading to much speculation and misinformation. Both the Indian people and the Nagas were kept in the dark about the true import of the Framework Agreement; both felt that the peace process was coming to a satisfactory resolution.

Two years later, in November 2017, there was another announcement that the Government of India had signed a document called the 'Agreed Position' with seven militant groups called the NNPGs (Naga National Political Groups). By this time there were sixteen different armed groups, which included seven breakaway groups of the NSCN. The rest were splinter groups of the NNC.

The contents of the Framework Agreement have been made public, and it appears to me that there was little substance in it. In 2019, Ravi was appointed the governor of Nagaland. There was controversy over whether a governor could act as an interlocuter. In 2022, A. K. Misra, former special director of the IB, was appointed the interlocuter and he went to the NSCN Camp Hebron for talks.

The talks and controversies have continued but they have no political direction. In 2020, I wrote that the Indo-Naga peace process was dead.[29]

Lack of Vision

While working on *Kuknalim, Naga Armed Resistance: Testimonies of Leaders, Pastors, Healers and Soldiers*, we interviewed hundreds of Naga national workers. I asked each one to tell me what they dreamt of as the future of Naga society. They looked at me askance. The question had never arisen in their minds.

The Nagas are proud of their unique culture, society, and history. But with globalization, much of Naga culture has been distorted, stolen, or destroyed. I have written about the devastating impact of globalization on Naga culture in my book *ABC of Naga Culture and Civilization* (2011). I had hoped that it would start a conversation on cultural self-determination as part of the conflict resolution. But the Naga national movement has never engaged with the issues of culture and politics. The movement has deteriorated to an identity struggle which places overwhelming emphasis on race and religion to define its nationality. With the motto 'Nagaland for Christ', Nagaland has become a part of what is often called the Bible belt of India.

But it is not only the Nagas who lack vision. The talks were an opportunity to broaden the idea of India and make it more inclusive. Conflict resolution has been looked upon as a part of counter insurgency and not nation building based on democracy and federalism rooted in justice—social, economic, and political.

The Indian intelligentsia and political parties too have not engaged with the Indo-Naga question which is ultimately about Indian federalism—the challenge of making India inclusive so every community develops a sense of belonging to the Union of India. Lasting peace needs both pragmatism and magnanimity.

3

THE ANTI-SIKH POGROM OF 1984
THREE DAYS OF HORROR

Rahul Bedi

The anti-Sikh pogrom that raged unchecked for nearly three days across several parts of India, but especially in New Delhi, after Prime Minister Indira Gandhi was shot dead by two of her Sikh bodyguards on the morning of 31 October 1984, ended only with her cremation on 3 November.

During these seventy-two hours, droves of Sikhs, including women and children, were hunted down and corralled by Hindu mobs on the streets, their homes and workplaces in the capital, and slaughtered like animals. Some Sikhs were even 'necklaced' by pinioning them with rubber tyres drenched in kerosene oil or petrol around their chests and arms and setting them on fire.[1] By the time some semblance of order was enforced in the city by the Indian Army, the organized massacres had led to the killing of some 2,733 Sikhs in Delhi alone[2]—though human rights organizations put this number closer to 4,000.

Thereafter, a mix of some fifteen inquiry commissions, committees, and special investigation teams (SITs) over the following thirty-four years, determined variously beyond reasonable doubt that these killings had been engineered by Congress party loyalists.[3] These slayings were duly supervised, in many instances, by Delhi Police personnel.[4] Yet, a token few of those eventually deemed guilty were convicted, and even fewer ultimately sentenced and jailed.

These probes also determined that the extended slaughter was executed by a cross section of largely Congress party minions along with their underlings, sympathizers, and especially dragooned bands of criminals. Reportedly carrying voter lists to identify Sikh households in Delhi neighbourhoods and armed with crude swords, scimitars, cleavers, scythes, kitchen knives, and even scissors, these groups executed their retribution without let or hinderance.[5]

Significantly, the latter implement was wielded widely over these three murderous days to shear the kesh (hair) of thousands of Sikhs[6] in a gratuitously sacrilegious and heretical endeavour at demeaning and humbling this proud and outwardly distinctive community, for whom uncut hair is one of the five symbols of their faith ordained by their tenth and last guru, Gobind Singh, in 1699. Kesh not only symbolizes faith for the egalitarian Sikhs, but also manifests the denial of all vanity and pride in their appearance.

Justifying this slaughter, if such were possible, the assassinated prime minister's son and political successor Rajiv Gandhi complacently declared at a public rally at Delhi's Boat Club on 19 November that 'Jab bhi koi bada ped girta hai, to dharti thodi hilti hai'—when a big tree falls, the earth shakes a little.[7] The new prime minister had fittingly delivered the Congress party's metaphor for the pogrom, even though in officialese and in media reports at the time—and even now—it continues to be euphemistically referred to as the 1984 anti-Sikh riots.

And whilst unbridled chaos and mayhem proliferated unimpeded across the capital, the calculated slaughter of some 300 indigent Sikhs in the trans-Yamuna resettlement of Trilokpuri Colony in East Delhi[8] was, without doubt, the most brutal. The charred and hacked remains of the hundreds that perished in Trilokpuri's Block 32 over forty-eight hours between 1 and 2 November depicted an implausible tale of state-sponsored carnage, the memory of which continues to haunt me nearly four decades later.

Face to Face

On the morning of 2 November, around 11.30 a.m., one Mohan Singh, who had sought refuge in our office canteen, told me and my *Indian Express* colleague Joseph Maliakan of the Trilokpuri massacre, which was then ongoing. He himself had shaved his head and beard only hours earlier. Terrified of the police and local officials, who were obviously complicit in these killings,[9] he had feebly hoped that a paper like the *Express* may somehow, through its influential pages, assist in ending the bloodbath that had been raging uninterrupted along two narrow, adjoining alleyways in Trilokpuri's Block 32. Each of these lanes was no more than seventy metres long and five metres wide. They were lined on either side with one-roomed tenements that were inhabited largely by poor Dalit Sikh families, many of whose menfolk wove string beds for a living.

Vacantly, Mohan Singh told us how scores of Sikhs in Trilokpuri had unhurriedly been butchered in these twin streets by bands of sword, axe, and chopper-wielding men who went about their task with gory determination. In between their killing spree, they found time to rest and take breaks for meals, before resuming their butchery with renewed vigour.

Unlike Mohan Singh, there was no possibility of any other resident of the two streets bolting to safety, as an impenetrable cordon of locals armed with lathis had girdled the area to block any runaways. Neither was there hope of succour from surrounding Hindu households in the colony, or from local police and block officials, many of whom, it later transpired, were in varying degrees of omission or commission complicit in the Block 32 slayings.

Almost immediately, along with Maliakan and Alok Tomar of *Jansatta*, the Express Group's Hindi newspaper, we rushed to Trilokpuri—one of numerous resettlement colonies established in East Delhi during the twenty-one-month long Emergency imposed by Indira Gandhi in 1975. The entrance to it was blocked by massive concrete pipes, with lathi-wielding men standing guard above. They stared menacingly at us but made no move to hinder our progress further into the labyrinth of Trilokpuri's criss-crossing alleys, providing us the first indication that something horrific and sinister was underway within.

A short distance from Block 32, our way was blocked by a lathi-wielding mob, also armed with bricks and rocks. But before they reached us, two policemen astride a motorcycle burst through them, coming from the direction opposite to where we were headed. We flagged them down. Has any unrest been reported in Block 32, we asked the head constable riding the bike.

Smiling mockingly, he said shanti (peace) prevailed in the area. However, on insistent questioning, he gruffly admitted that two people 'may' have died there. Before they could be quizzed further, they sped away. We did not realize it then, but over the next few days as we witnessed the mayhem in Delhi, mostly in East Delhi, a host of similarly conniving police officials would use the word 'shanti'[10] to define the surrounding chaos. We also did not comprehend at the time that these two policemen from the local Kalyanpuri police station were in reality a reconnaissance team for mid-level local Congress party functionaries[11] who had been tasked with determining whether the retaliatory Sikh killings in Block 32 were progressing as planned.

As we proceeded down the narrow brick-tiled road towards Block 32, our car was stopped by a mob that turned nasty and began stoning us when we asked to be let through. A spokesperson for the crowd, a short vicious-looking man dressed in a grubby white blood-splattered kurta and pyjamas, told us to leave or 'face the consequences' if we insisted on moving any further.

Block 32, he said ominously, was out of bounds.

Hurriedly reversing our car amidst a barrage of projectiles, we headed for the nearby Kalyanpuri police station and asked its duty officer whether any trouble or unrest had been reported from Block 32. Impassively, he too echoed what his motorcycle-borne colleagues had said earlier: the area was 'shant' (peaceful). No violence had been reported.

A truck parked nearby attracted our attention, principally because of the canopy of flies and insects hovering over it. Inside lay three charred Sikh bodies. Lying on top of the corpses was a half-burnt but still alive Sikh youth. In his half-conscious state, the young man in his mid-twenties mumbled that he had arrived from Punjab a day earlier to visit relatives in Trilokpuri's Block 32. Soon after, news of Prime Minister Indira Gandhi's assassination by her Sikh bodyguards had swept through the colony. A few hours later, a mob, armed with machetes and lathis had burst into his hosts' house and started hacking off their hair and beards with scissors and blunt knives.

It then proceeded to beat them with lathis. Thereafter they were stabbed. Their inert bodies were then lined up on the ground, doused with kerosene, and set on fire. The horribly scorched youth couldn't remember how he had arrived at the police station or how long he had lain atop the corpses in a semi-comatose state, life slowly ebbing out of him.

He died shortly after, we later learnt.

When we questioned the duty officer about the burnt bodies and the barely alive Sikh man in the truck, he brazenly denied their existence. Contact sahib, or the station house officer Soor Veer Singh when he returns from central Delhi later that evening, he said, before busying himself with the paperwork he was occupied with when we arrived, as if it were just another day.

Convinced that something murderous was afoot in Block 32, we combed the deserted trans-Yamuna area seeking police assistance. Eventually we came across an army unit led by a Sikh colonel. It had just driven in from its headquarters in Meerut and was one of several random army details similarly summoned by the federal government from nearby areas to assist civil authority in restoring order. But like all the others, it too was lost and disoriented as the local police who were supposed to be its guides were missing. The commanding officer assured us that he would dispatch help to the beleaguered Block 32 despite being ignorant of its location, but never did.

We returned tentatively to the area contiguous to Block 32, only to discover that no troops had arrived. Over the next few hours, we pleaded in vain with several other military detachments we encountered, including a truckload of soldiers at the ITO bridge and another comprising Indian Air Force personnel, to intercede and somehow end the turmoil in Trilokpuri. Both declined. The former was preoccupied with finding their equally adrift formation somewhere in North Delhi, while the latter was on its way to assess VIP seating arrangements at Prime Minister Gandhi's cremation site, adjoining Mahatma Gandhi's Rajghat samadhi that later came to be known as Shakti Sthal.

Both units advised us to proceed to the nearby Delhi Police headquarters for help, where we arrived at around 5 p.m. and informed the additional commissioner of police Nikhil Kumar, the officer in-charge, of the goings on in Trilokpuri. To our amazement Kumar, who went on to head the elite counter-terrorism National Security Guard, helplessly asserted that he was a 'mere guest artist' at the police headquarters.[12]

Kumar plaintively pleaded that he was on transfer out of Delhi and in the interim, had been hastily summoned as an emergency measure to oversee the police control room, tasked with fielding distress calls from across the lawless city. In short, the high profile and politically well-connected policeman pathetically stressed his abject helplessness[13] in providing any support or backing to Trilokpuri's terrorized residents, despite his high rank.

Other equally senior police officers, including those in charge of Trilokpuri, many of whom were present at the police headquarters despite the enduring turmoil raging around them, too expressed indifference and their inability to be of any assistance.

One such was the additional commissioner of police Hukam Chand Jatav.[14] He told us that he had returned from a tour of the trans-Yamuna colonies, particularly Trilokpuri, and nothing was unduly amiss. Or, in keeping with what by now had become a set piece, shanti prevailed in his district. It later emerged that sketchy details were available from the police log regarding Jatav's movements, as for inexplicable reasons, his wireless operator had broadcast his locations infrequently and often inaccurately. However, arriving at Block 32 well after sundown the same evening, Jatav refused to walk more than five metres down the corpse-filled alley.

I have seen enough, he snapped at us and left. But more later of the horror and bloodshed this police officer witnessed and simply could not stomach. It was, without doubt, far from the shanti that Jatav had nonchalantly ascribed earlier to Trilokpuri.

Jatav's deputy commissioner of police Sewa Dass too seconded his boss, mouthing the same inanities about shanti in Trilokpuri. These two policemen were eventually amongst just three senior Delhi Police officers to be prosecuted for dereliction of duty.[15] Unsurprisingly, like numerous other policemen, officials, political workers, and others directly or indirectly involved in Delhi's bloodbath, they served out their service tenures, with Jatav retiring in 1992 with the rank of Director General of the Delhi Home Guards. Their prosecution was repeatedly deferred till the statute of limitations for any inquiry and action against them eventually expired.

Equally sanguine about the situation in Delhi was its lieutenant governor P. G. Gavai, who also parroted the by-now familiar line that shanti 'more or less' prevailed in the capital. Addressing a press conference at the Delhi Police Headquarters on the evening of 2 November, Gavai maintained that no more than twenty people had died in 'rioting' in Delhi.[16] Gavai was replaced as lieutenant governor two days later by former federal home secretary M. M. K. Wali, but he too proved inept, not only in managing Delhi's violence and its aftermath, but also in prosecuting police officials under his charge, for either their active abetment or dereliction of duty in the Sikh massacre.

Men of Honour

However, one Delhi Police officer and a handful of his platoon were exceptions. On the morning of 1 November, additional deputy commissioner of police Maxwell Pereira led a band of some twenty-odd police personnel armed with lathis to protect Sikhs who had sought shelter in the Sis Ganj gurdwara in Delhi's walled city in the Chandni Chowk area. Armed with just a handgun, and with no backup nor hope of any, Pereira and his small group of policemen prevented the mob from storming the historic gurdwara, where the ninth Sikh guru, Teg Bahadur, had been beheaded by the Mughal emperor Aurangzeb in 1675. A day earlier, on 31 October, accompanied by a rag-tag police posse Pereira had spent the entire night escorting Sikhs to safety in his North Delhi precinct.

Some thirty-three years later, in late 2017, Pereira admitted to the BBC that the paralysed Delhi Police, awaiting 'clear cut' orders from a confused and 'shell-shocked' government and police leadership had ended up looking the other way when atrocities against Sikhs had occurred before them. But, defying the odds and peer behaviour, the brave officer said he was 'duty bound' to save any Sikh being attacked, even if it meant taking the aggressor's life by opening fire.[17]

'I firmly believe that no policeman needed orders from above to act correctly as warranted in times of such need,' he said. 'If the concerned policeman had dithered and procrastinated, he was guilty of dereliction of duty, if not of actively conniving with the perpetrators,' the officer told the BBC.[18]

Pereira, who surprisingly never ended up deposing before any of the multiple state-appointed inquiry commissions into the 1984 killings, went on to state that none of the police officers and men from North Delhi, who saved many Sikh lives, received recognition or reward for maintaining order amidst grave unrest. This, he added, was in stark contrast to some of his colleagues, elsewhere in Delhi, who even received gallantry medals for killing scared and petrified Sikhs who had opened fire on mobs in self-defence.[19]

There were also innumerable instances—too diffused and too scattered to enumerate—of Hindus, and in some instances, Muslims, either smuggling Sikh families to the safety of gurdwaras or of providing them shelter in their homes from marauding mobs. In many cases, some of these chance benefactors also prevented rioters from burning Sikh homes and workplaces but could not prevent them from being looted. Conversely, there were also shocking accounts that emerged much later of affluent and supposedly secular Hindus guiding mobs to Sikh homes in upmarket South Delhi localities like Maharani Bagh and Panchsheel Park but, expectedly, none were ever charged or prosecuted.

Senior advocate and human rights activist Harvinder Singh Phoolka deserves special mention for relentlessly waging one of the longest and most arduous legal battles—which still endures—to secure justice for victims of the 1984 pogrom against Sikhs. His doggedness and perseverance unambiguously revealed the Congress party's role in the genocide, especially the involvement of three of its prominent Delhi members of Parliament—H. K. L. Bhagat, Jagdish Tytler, and Sajjan Kumar.[20]

Phoolka was singlehandedly responsible for securing the conviction of Sajjan Kumar, who was sentenced to life imprisonment by the Delhi High Court in late 2018, some thirty-four years after he masterminded attacks on numerous Sikh households in Sultanpuri and Mangolpuri that were then part of his outer Delhi parliamentary constituency.[21] Sikh survivors, deposing later in court, claimed that Kumar had provided each attacker ₹100 and a bottle of liquor to attack Sikhs to exact revenge for the assassinated leader.[22]

As recently as November 2022, Phoolka told a television channel how diabolically the Sikh killings had been planned in advance, in all likelihood during Indira Gandhi's lifetime, and possibly with her connivance. He demanded the institution of a Truth Commission to determine whether this was so. He said the murderous mobs were carrying voters lists, precisely listing

Sikh households across Delhi along with an 'inflammable white powder' not available in the market, which they used freely on Sikhs.[23]

On the same programme, Justice S. N. Dhingra, who was appointed in 2018 to head the SIT to re-look at 186 cases related to the 1984 pogrom, stated that the entire effort of the Congress party government was to ensure that none of the perpetrators were punished. Hence, the government appointed Justice Ranganath Misra to head the commission inquiring into the killings, he said, fully aware that he was in line to become India's twenty-first Supreme Court chief justice and, therefore would be 'cautious' in his findings. Expectedly, Justice Misra's findings decreed that it was not an organized Congress party massacre and that just a handful of its members had been involved, Dhingra pointed out.[24]

Night of the Dead and Living Dead

Meanwhile, on returning to Trilokpuri an hour later in the darkness, at around 6 p.m. on 2 November, we found the local station house office (SHO) S. V. Singh and two constables surveying the sea of Sikh bodies strewn around, encircled by thousands of onlookers, many of whom were likely responsible for the carnage.

The headlights of their official Matador van pierced the darkness, as power to Block 32 had been disconnected two days earlier when the ethnic cleansing had begun, throwing up terrifying silhouettes that swayed ghoulishly in the dank November night.

The most chilling aspect of that horrific and gruesome setting that still sends a disquieting shiver up my spine after thirty-eight years was the total and complete silence and stillness that hung over the area, despite the large crowd. The macabre scene, which would be difficult even for a talented and imaginative film director to duplicate, seemed to have stunned the vast throng into mutedness.

We walked wordlessly, as if in a trance, in the light of a few hurriedly procured hurricane lanterns, down the two alleyways littered with bodies and body parts. It was impossible to place one's foot flat on the ground for fear of stepping on either a dismembered body or hacked head or limb, all of which were swathed with the kesh of the dead. Both lanes were awash with blood, most of it a black coagulated mass by now, over which flies and winter insects laconically buzzed. It could not even flow into the drains, inefficient at the best of times, as they too were choked with human remains and clumps of hair.

Halfway down the lane sat a young polio-afflicted mother on the doorstep of her two-roomed tenement tightly clutching her infant daughter in numb silence, all emotion drained from her face and sightless eyes. Her blank, uncomprehending gaze took us in unseeingly, in what we took to be a plea for help. And, as one of us bent down to lift up her child, her emotionless look momentarily changed to one of unmitigated terror, and her paralysed limbs too seemed to recoil in sheer panic and alarm.

She probably mistook us for one of the butchers who had massacred her entire family, piled up high in the room behind her. In all likelihood, her obvious incapacity had somehow permeated even the slaughterers' conscience, resulting miraculously in her life and that of her child being spared, but not the rest of her household. Without a word, we quietly lifted her and her child and placed them in the waiting police van, never to see or hear of them again, even though we tried tracking her down later.

A faint whimper from inside the same house led us to a

young Sikh man whose stomach had been slashed open two days earlier. He had managed to survive by tying a turban around his ghastly gaping wound before crawling under a pile of bodies and playing dead. All that the handsome scooter rickshaw driver craved for was water.

He died hours later.

Some doors down the same street, an infant girl, stepping over the bodies of her father and three brothers and countless others lying in the street, clung helplessly to one of us reporters, pleading mutely for assistance.

'Please take me home,' she wailed, standing uncomprehendingly, thigh-deep in corpses.

There was nowhere for her to go. She was already home; but it was one littered with the bloated bodies of her parents and older siblings, killed and partially burnt several hours earlier.

The police arrived in large numbers, hours after the Trilokpuri massacre was exposed by the *Indian Express* in its 3 November edition. It was the only paper to have reported this butchery in detail, despite a reporter from one of Delhi's largest circulated, albeit pro-Congress party newspaper, having accompanied us to Block 32. Even the media, it seemed, was culpable in validating the mass revenge on Sikhs, no doubt convinced that the entire community was to be blamed and needed to be taught a lesson it would not forget.

The death toll in Block 32 alone was over 300. In police records, it was logged as ninety-five. No further questions asked.

The State Wakes Up

Once Prime Minister Gandhi's funeral pyre was lit on the afternoon of 3 November, the state galvanized itself into action by empowering the army to restore order, even though the force had been summoned two days earlier, as international media coverage of the pogrom had become untenable for spokespersons of Prime Minister Rajiv Gandhi's Congress Party-led government to defend or rationalize.

But the little-known reality regarding the army's deployment in Delhi, even years later, was a little more complex. The army's Internal Security (IS) Brigade in Delhi, earmarked to backup civil authority in dire emergencies, had shortly before been shifted to the Western Front with Pakistan for winter exercises, compelling the authorities to hastily mobilize reserve units from nearby cantonments. The first such contingent rolled in from Shahjahanpur in Uttar Pradesh, after an overnight drive, sometime in the early hours of 2 November, followed by others from contiguous locations in Meerut and other stations in Rajasthan.

But deplorably, the army which four months earlier had so seamlessly cordoned off Punjab during Operation Bluestar, executed to flush out armed Sikh militants fighting for an independent homeland of Khalistan or Land of the Sikhs from inside the Golden Temple in Amritsar, had no specific instructions regarding its deployment in Delhi. All that the force knew was that it was authorized to act in conjunction with the Delhi Police, which was rudderless and for all practical purposes, leaderless. And in many instances, as emerged later, conniving with the murderous mobs.

In short, the army's placement in Delhi during the first three days of chaos and killings was simply a confused and disorderly non-deployment. Army units that were told they would be provided liaison officers on arrival in Delhi to help in their employment in curbing violence were left to fend for themselves. Using decades-old maps of Delhi colonies, particularly of the trans-Yamuna belt, where many roads and colonies were not even marked, as they simply did not exist then, the army was expected to end the violence, detect, evacuate, and safely billet Sikh refugees. Further complicating matters was the delineation of its jurisdiction; it merely had loose sanction to impose curfew, but not enough force, or more importantly, the authorization to implement it.

The first two days of the army's IS operation in Delhi, ironically codenamed Shanti, particularly in the trans-Yamuna and West Delhi areas, were something that concerned jawans and officers would, no doubt, choose to forget. Mobs dispersed as army officers drove impassively through vast crowds in East Delhi, with their junior commissioned officers (JCOs) announcing the imposition of curfew through bullhorns and calling for crowds to clear the streets. But once these details had passed, the crowds reassembled and resumed violence in a direct slight to the army which ended up being widely perceived as little more than toothless law-enforcers in olive green.

We witnessed one such incident on 3 November. A house in Gandhinagar in East Delhi was surrounded by a hysterical mob, which claimed that a group of armed Sikhs inside were sporadically firing upon them. We rushed for assistance to the nearby police station and the army's major rank officer in-charge, accompanied by his JCO and a deputy commissioner of police, immediately accompanied us to the besieged residence.

Anticipating gunfire, we gingerly made our way up the staircase of the ransacked three-storeyed home, shouting all the while that we were press reporters and accompanied by army and police personnel. Nothing happened and no one emerged, leave alone gun-toting Sikhs, as we gingerly tiptoed our way up the stairs to the terrace.

Instead of the supposed group of armed Sikhs, we found a single octogenarian Sikh grandmother who, it transpired, had refused to leave along with the rest of her family, which had taken refuge in a neighbouring Hindu household. Bombarded by a constant barrage of bricks and stones, the terrified old lady was huddled in a corner of the terrace, unable to speak. Once the agitated crowd spied us on the roof, it surged forward to storm the house, unmindful of the token army presence. It took all our agility and deftness to safely extricate ourselves along with the aged Sikh lady, who we deposited with her family in a nearby house.

In Retrospect

For the first three days of the pogrom in Delhi there was simply no centralized law and order machinery to manage the chaos. At a time when landline telephones were the only, albeit tenuous, means of communication, the Delhi Police commissioner operated from his office at Indraprastha Estate, the lieutenant governor, the capital's executive head, was based at Raj Niwas in North Delhi, while the army's headquarters were in Dhaula Kuan in southwest Delhi. In between them were murderous mobs, fires, and bedlam.

Distress calls to the army headquarters were mandatorily directed to the Delhi Police control room, on the plea that the army was authorized to act only on information furnished by the police. The police and the local administration, for their part, provided the army little or no information on the violence, often misleading it in many instances, making a complete mockery of the superior force's deployment.

To make matters worse, the army was also not issued the deterrent 'shoot-on-sight' authorization to quell the mobs till well after Indira Gandhi's funeral pyre was lit around 3.30 p.m. on 3 November. Thereafter, within hours it managed to effectively restore order, after resorting to firings on several occasions, although for many days thereafter there were innumerable instances in which local police and municipal officials deliberately kept the army ignorant about pockets of fearful Sikh refugees holed up inside gurdwaras and makeshift camps across East Delhi.

The joint report prepared later by the People's Union for Civil Liberties (PUCL) and the People's Union for Democratic Rights (PUDR) was blunt in its assessment of the army's overall helplessness. 'The entire nature of using the army...compels us to suspect whether there was not a deliberate design to keep the army ineffective even after it was called in, and that too following a long interval in which arson, looting, and massacre were allowed to continue, sometimes with the connivance of the local police force,' the report stated.[25]

The trigger for Indira Gandhi's assassination was without doubt, Operation Bluestar.[26] Heavily armed and trained Sikh terrorists—many of them former soldiers—had barricaded themselves inside the Golden Temple with the aim of waging war on the Indian state to secure the independent state of Khalistan.

They were dislodged after three days of fierce firefights inside the temple in early June, necessitating the eventual deployment of T-72 tanks to conclude hostilities. Some eighty-three soldiers died during Bluestar, whilst another 243 jawans and officers were injured.

For generations, the Sikhs have been a highly respected community; rough and irreverent but dependable, honourable, and generous; dogged and enterprising but imaginative; fiery but humorous. And, in inverse proportion to their small number—just under 2 per cent of India's population—Sikhs have occupied important jobs in the country, including India's ceremonial presidency, in addition to top posts in the security forces, especially the military. Sikh regiments and soldiers have ably distinguished themselves in both World Wars and in many battles and skirmishes with neighbouring Pakistan and China and with armed insurgents after Independence.

Yet, selfish political motives to undermine the Shiromani Akali Dal, a Punjab-based political party which had singlehandedly opposed Mrs Gandhi's imposition of the Emergency in 1975 in the state when her continuance in office was threatened by a court ruling, led her and the then Punjab chief minister, Zail Singh, to nurture and patronize the little-known Sikh preacher, Jarnail Singh Bhindranwale.[27] Soon after, Bhindranwale slipped his Congress Party leash and independently began furthering the Khalistan movement he had founded at the Congress's behest to discredit and upstage the Akalis.

Consequently, through the early 1980s, Punjab was enveloped in a virulent armed insurgency in which state control almost completely evaporated. Radical Sikh militant groups emerged as arbiters of Sikhism, openly dictating Punjab's social, linguistic, and moral mores. Totally subverting state authority, militant kangaroo courts dispensed justice in Punjab's villages and small towns where, in many instances, summary executions were the sentence for prostitution, adultery, and excessive dowry demands, in addition to cattle rustling and even misappropriating canal water.

Total anarchy gripped Punjab, with periodic massacres of train and bus passengers. This savagery often spilled over into Delhi with serial bomb blasts claiming scores of civilian lives. Matters exacerbated after the Khalistan movement was seized upon and strategically furthered by Pakistan's military junta, adding a worrisome external dimension to a hostile and volatile internal security situation.

The climactic, possibly avoidable, storming of the Golden

Temple generated a wave of turbulence amongst Sikhs, culminating in Gandhi's assassination and the ensuing genocide principally in Delhi but also to a lesser extent in towns like Kanpur and Bokaro. From then on, a far more virulent armed insurrection perpetuated by Sikh terrorist groups suffused Punjab. It was eventually stamped out around 1993 through counter insurgency operations by the state police backed by the military.

Manmohan Singh's elevation to prime ministership in 2004 was looked upon by the Sikh community as the collective vindication of its destiny of being born to rule. His Congress party's previous genocidal transgressions were buried, but not forgotten, and Singh's casually tied trademark Oxford Blue turban represented a collective crown for the enterprising but horribly persecuted and wronged Sikh community.

Singh—went the refrain when he became prime minister for the first time in 2004—was king, an appellation that all Sikhs also applied individually to themselves and continue to do so even now. In 2005, Singh tried mitigating his party's previous transgressions when he told the parliament that he bowed his head in shame over the 1984 killings and apologized, not only to his community, but also to the country.[28] Reacting to the findings of the Nanavati Commission instituted in 2000 to investigate the 1984 killings—the tenth such inquiry committee in sixteen years—Singh went on to state that the horrific incidents needed to be viewed from a 'wider perspective'. The past, he said, could not be undone or brought back and the Sikh community needed to move on.

'But let us, as a unified nation, find new pathways to ensure that our nation will never again go through such traumas, whether they are in Delhi or Gujarat or in any part of the country,' Singh said in an emotional speech imbued with quotations from the Guru Granth Sahib. All of us should ask for forgiveness of those who have suffered in this tragedy, he declared and promised in the parliament that the rehabilitation of all widows and orphans of the 1984 massacre was his government's 'solemn obligation'.[29] Singh also stated that action would be taken against culpable police officers, but ironically, he was whistling in the wind as twenty-nine years had elapsed by then and all such guilty personnel would have long since retired, well beyond any prosecution.

Regrettably, the Nanavati Commission also revealed that of the original 587 FIRs registered after the 1984 violence, only twenty-five had resulted in convictions, of which merely twelve were for murder. And of the 440 overall convictions, many cases featured the same person being found guilty of as many as seven counts each. Subsequently, the Supreme Court monitored SIT was formulated in 2018 and continues to ramble on, inconclusively adjudicating appeals on dozens of cases.[30]

In the meantime, compensation to the survivors too fell prey to officialdom which required the production of certificates and proof from an uncooperative, almost hostile administration, loath to register cases of murder, arson, or looting, or even to issue death certificates. No explanations were given, but it seemed that being Sikh was reason enough not to comply, with the result that scores of illiterate widows, who comprised the bulk of compensation seekers, were now forced to add penury to their overwhelming woes. And, despite grandiosely announced compensation schemes, hundreds of victims were handed cheques for ₹2,000 and asked to leave.[31]

The state has absolved itself cheaply for its genocide.

More recently, the 2022 film *Jogi*, released on Netflix, was centred on Trilokpuri as the leitmotif of the 1984 Sikh massacre. It had the potential of being a powerful narration of the horrendous and sickening events that transpired there, but unfortunately cinematic licence and box office compulsions reduced it to a pedestrian Bollywood production, ridden with inaccuracies.

And so, almost two generations after the 1984 pogrom, and independent India's first instance of ethnic cleansing, in which the government was found complicit to some extent, the axiom that there is no greater tyranny than that which is perpetrated by the state under the shield of law still holds good.

4

BIHAR/JHARKHAND, 1983–94
A FEW GOOD MEN

Uttam Sengupta

I was yet to rent a house in Patna and was working out of a hotel, when there was a knock at my door at midnight on a cold December night. It was Dr Vinayan.[1] An associate of Jayaprakash Narayan's, Dr Vinayan was briefly associated with one of the Maoist groups and was on the run. There was a reward for his arrest since the Arwal Massacre in 1986 in Jehanabad when police had opened fire at a peaceful meeting of villagers that he was presiding over.[2] The villagers had whisked him away to safety but several villagers had died and the trigger happy police came in for widespread criticism. The government banned the overground organization he was heading and declared a reward for his arrest.[3]

As an aside, he was finally arrested in 1988 when a policeman recognized him at the Jehanabad railway station.[4] The policeman actually greeted him, apologized for sounding the alert, and explained that he needed the money. Unfortunately the reward had apparently lapsed! Vinayan spent some time in prison before he was granted bail.

That night when he visited, I was delighted to see him. His sharp intellect and the reading he had done made him very interesting company.

He asked me how I was doing in the state capital and about the people I had met. Not too many, I replied candidly, and rattled off names of sundry political leaders. Visibly irritated, he asked if I had called on some of the bureaucrats, academics, and police officers he had mentioned to me. I confessed I had not.

'You journalists spend all your time chasing rogue politicians but have no time for good people in the system,' he said. 'No matter what we do in life, we must support good people in society. Do remember that good souls are lonely souls, and they need our support. The bad guys always flock together and will always have support,' he had declared as a parting shot before melting away into the dense morning fog that used to engulf the city in winter. Ironically or not so ironically, Vinayan himself was a 'good man' for whom I had developed great respect. But more on him later.

One of the 'good human beings' I was introduced to was Ram Sevak Sharma. Sharma turned out to be an exceptional officer and a good human being. We hit it off and I have followed his career closely and often admired his versatility. A techie at heart, he is happiest when he is looking for technological solutions. He was computerizing official data in the 1980s in Bihar at a time when most people had no clue about computing. He relinquished his charge as the first chairman of the National Health Authority in 2023; earlier he was the TRAI chairman for two terms after his retirement around 2015 and is better known as the first DG of UIDAI to have helmed Aadhaar between 2009 and 2015.

Sharma was the deputy commissioner of Dhanbad in 1990 when he called me up in Patna one evening, where I was the *India Today* correspondent. He was on his way to the railway station to board the overnight train for Patna. Could he have breakfast with me the next morning, he asked. His train would reach very early at 5 a.m. and he could be at my home by 7.30 a.m. or so. I readily invited him.

What is your impression of the chief minister, he asked as he was settling down. Lalu Prasad Yadav had taken over as chief minister some weeks ago and had summoned Sharma to the state capital. The chief minister, Sharma disclosed, had called him the previous morning and asked about the communal tension brewing in Bokaro in the Dhanbad district—an hour's drive away from the district headquarters. Taken aback, the DC had replied that to his knowledge, all was well, prompting an irate chief minister to tell him to go out and enquire. If sitting in the state capital, the chief minister was aware of the tension brewing, how was the DC so oblivious to it, Lalu Yadav asked and ordered him to reach Patna the next morning.

Sharma admitted that he had been upset by the call. He didn't like the chief minister's tone. But following the conversation he did call up Bokaro and was reassured that neither the police nor the administration there had any clue about any communal tension brewing. However, not wishing to take a chance, he rushed to Bokaro to figure out what could have upset the new chief minister. It took a few hours before he stumbled upon a minor dispute between Hindu and Muslim neighbours in a locality in the sprawling but otherwise thinly-populated steel city. He went to the spot, spoke to the people, sorted out the issue and returned after asking police and civil authorities to remain alert.

The new chief minister clearly had his ear to the ground. He was possibly extra-sensitive to the communal situation because riots had ravaged Bhagalpur just ahead of the assembly elections in the state in 1989. The riot made headlines nationally and was the last nail in the coffin of the Congress government in the state. The previous five years had seen four Congress chief ministers in Jagannath Mishra, Bindeshwari Dubey, Bhagwat Jha Azad, and Satyendra Narayan Singh, the first three being Brahmins and the last one a Rajput—also upper caste.

A socialist and protégé of Karpoori Thakur and Devi Lal, Lalu Yadav was an OBC[5] chief minister after a long time. He was new to the job and quite possibly did not want to take any chances. He may also have been extra sensitive because Yadavs, the community the chief minister belonged to, had been accused of leading the rioting in Bhagalpur.[6] He must have been aware of the razor's edge he was walking and had overreacted to an incident that others might have overlooked. A more seasoned chief minister would have asked the chief secretary to enquire and report. But Lalu Yadav may have been suspicious of the bureaucracy that was dominated by the upper castes.

A relatively young IAS officer then, Sharma was yet to meet the new chief minister. He wanted to learn as much about him before his first meeting. That was the reason he had landed up at my place early in the morning. After I shared the little I knew about the chief minister, he appeared to relax. He also slipped in a word of praise. 'If the chief minister himself is so alert, the rest of the administration too have no choice but to remain on their toes,' he quipped before leaving to call on the chief minister.

Lalu Prasad Yadav's MY (Muslim-Yadav) coalition did ensure a prolonged period of relative peace when Bihar remained free of communal riots; although, during his initial days as chief minister, attempts were made to whip up communal passions. When there were communal clashes in Biharsharif, Yadav was quick to rush to the place. He berated the officials publicly, a tactic he would use often to show people who was boss. A nun, Sister Sujitha from the congregation of Notredame Sisters, who was then engaged in relief work, recalls seeing the new chief minister supervising relief efforts. He insisted on delivering the cash component to the victims immediately and ensured that the first lot of cash was handed over in his presence.

It was nice to see the administration on their toes, she confided, and to find officials complaining that the new chief minister was in the habit of calling them at odd hours, sometimes in the middle of the night, to demand specific pieces of information. The flare-up in Biharsharif was controlled quickly.

Police officers and officials I have had the opportunity to speak to since then have been unanimous that riots cannot get out of control without complete indifference or complicity of the police. Poor governance, lax supervision, and mixed signals given by political masters often dictated how the police would act. The first term in office of Lalu Yadav as chief minister of Bihar was proof, if any proof was needed.

The man at the top matters and Lalu Yadav, in his own political interest, had built up direct contact in the districts. A. R. Kidwai, governor of Bihar in the 1990s, told me that while he could instruct the state's director general of police (DGP), the chief minister could speak directly to any SHO he liked. One wonders if the 'system' will work for all time to come though.

The Maverick

Dr Vinayan hailed from Agra, studied in the medical college there till his final year before deciding to drop out and become a sanyasi. He disappeared to the Himalayas and when his family members finally tracked him down and brought him back home, he had been on a forty-day fast to demonstrate that he could indeed become a sanyasi. The ascetic he had reached out for 'deeksha', however, was not convinced, it appears, and sent word to the family to force him to return.

He never appeared for his final MBBS examination but had picked up enough about medicine to treat minor ailments and advise villagers later in life. He was particularly popular among village women to whom he would patiently explain the genesis of various diseases.

A chance meeting with Jayaprakash Narayan (JP) in Delhi sometime in 1974 brought him to Bihar. JP asked Vinayan to go to Jehanabad and work among the people there. He did. He went underground during the Emergency and was a fringe player in the 'Baroda Dynamite Conspiracy Case'.[7] He would later recall hilarious accounts of his attempts along with his accomplices to blow up railway lines and the gas pipeline coming all the way from Assam. All the attempts failed because the amateur ultras had no experience using explosives and did not have the equipment to drill through the thick pipeline. They also didn't know how to muffle the sound of the hammer striking the railway track every time they hit it.

It was during this time that Vinayan came in contact with the 'Party Unity' faction of the CPI (Maoist-Leninist). Later an overground organization, Mazdoor Kisan Sangram Samiti (MKSS), not to be confused with Mazdoor Kisan Shramik Sangathan (MKSS) in Rajasthan, came up in Bihar and Vinayan served as its president for several years. In course of time the MKSS was also banned, and a reward was declared for the arrest of Dr Vinayan. It was during this time in 1986 that I first came in contact with him. Impressed with his wide-ranging knowledge of issues and with his articulation, I kept seeking him out to clear the cobwebs in my own mind. I also wanted to understand better what the underground movement was all about.

I had initially expected that Dr Vinayan would be armed when I first met him in 1985–86. I had also expected him to travel in disguise. But it was disconcerting to find that his jhola contained only books, his diary, a blanket, and a lungi. I had once asked him why he didn't wear any disguise—a false beard perhaps, a pugree, or at least a pair of sunglasses. That would be more reassuring as I had to often give him a ride on my scooter whenever he visited the city. I remember him laughing heartily at my naivete and telling me that it was best to be himself. 'The day I try to disguise myself, I will be caught', he had explained.

Shyamal Dutta, who was joint director (JD) of the Intelligence Bureau at Patna once casually told me that I should be more careful while meeting Dr Vinayan. I was taken aback because I did not suspect he would know about my closeness with the underground leader. Dutta, who later went on to become director of the Intelligence Bureau and governor of Nagaland after his retirement, smiled and quipped that I underestimated his organization.

He had been to a meeting with the DGP that morning (in late 1987 during the winter) at the police headquarters, he said and during a presentation a police officer named the journalists who were in contact with Dr Vinayan. My name and house address were also shared and it was suggested that the journalists should be placed under surveillance. Dutta was alerting me to be careful.

I was in a quandary. There were no mobile phones those days and I had no way of alerting Dr Vinayan. I had no idea when he would suddenly appear at my house either. I was also apprehensive that if he got arrested from my house, how the comrades would react! But there was nothing that I could do but keep my fingers crossed and wait. A few weeks later he did turn up at night and declared that he was hungry and would like to make khichdi for us all. I firmly told him that he would be leaving with me immediately and spending the night at a friend's place, where he would be safer. I quickly told him of my conversation with the JD.

He laughed off my concerns while making a dash to the kitchen. The IB had a lot of secret funds, he told me. 'Ask your friend to buy some blankets for my people in the village. I need at least thirty of them,' he added seriously. The next morning, I dropped him to the railway station on my scooter. I conveyed, half in jest, his request to Shyamal Dutta. To my surprise, Dutta not only bought the blankets but drove in his private vehicle to drop them off to my house. Dr Vinayan and he met several times and developed mutual respect for each other.

Though associated with Maoists, Vinayan believed violence was counter-productive. He had tried to convince the underground group to give up violence, he claimed. Talking of the party's armed squads, he said that the party would hold 'people's court' and sentence one or more 'enemy of the people' to death. The armed squad would execute the poor man and overnight they would disperse in three adjoining districts and would be 100 miles away before the police could reach the village. Most of the menfolk would also disappear, which would allow the police to ransack houses, molest the women, and then file named FIRs against all the missing men.

The families would be ruined, he recalled. The men would spend months in jail before getting out on bail. The women would be forced to sell jewellery, utensils, land, and animals to pay the lawyers and the cases would go on for years. Not surprisingly, he had his detractors within the underground organization and we feared for his life. But he would laugh off the threat.

Early Lessons

The other good man that Dr Vinayan introduced me to was Arvind Verma. I had heard of Arvind Verma, who was superintendent of police (SP) of Palamu in 1984. During the anti-Sikh riots in Daltonganj, he dealt with the rioters firmly and prevented escalation. Another friend, Meghnath, a young left-leaning filmmaker from Calcutta, had good words to say about the Palamu SP, whom he had seen in action during the riots.

Both R. S. Sharma and Arvind Verma had graduated from IIT Kanpur and were friends. It was a privilege to know them and their work. But both were shunted around in Bihar till Sharma took the first opportunity to leave on a central government posting. Verma took a sabbatical and went to the US to study. He returned with a PhD in criminology but within months of joining the IPS decided that he could not work there. He quit the service and went back to the US to work in academia. Sharma, luckily, was allowed to utilize his computing and mathematical skills to do some useful work.

During the 1984 anti-Sikh violence, my neighbour in Ranchi was M. Khan, the suave regional sales manager of Grindwell Norton, a multinational company. As curfew was imposed late on 31 October, I could see him getting restless. He had several Sikh friends and so did I. Both of us were worried about their safety but with no mobile phone or social media, and landlines not being answered or not working, we had little clue of their whereabouts.

But the next day I managed to get a curfew pass and a car sticker for Khan's Fiat car. We drove to the gurudwara on the Main Road, where several Sikhs had taken refuge. For the next two days we would turn up every morning at the gurudwara for information about Sikhs stranded in various places. We would then drive through the deserted streets and ferry them back to the safety of the gurudwara. Luckily, our friends had escaped the violence, partly, I suspect, because they were relatively well off.

A young Sikh couple we rescued had taken shelter in the

nursing home of Dr Shobha Chakravarty on Bariatu Road. The couple had been at the gynaecologist's office with their infant child when the rioting started. A mob reached the nursing home, looking for Sikhs. While the gate was shut and secured and the presence of any Sikh denied, the panic-stricken doctor hid the couple in a room and locked it from the outside. She was an influential doctor in town, and it is a mystery why she couldn't get the police to intervene. But she was clearly relieved to see us and hurriedly unlocked the door and asked us to drive the cowering couple away. We did so without uttering a word and without asking for the name of the Sikh gentleman, telling him merely that the couple should sit not on the seat but crouch on the floor of the car.

We were once stopped by an army jawan at Pepee Compound, a residential area predominantly inhabited by Sikhs. The machine-gun toting jawan asked for our curfew pass. While he was inspecting the pass, I tried to strike up a conversation with him and asked if all was well in the area. He looked up, made a face and returned the pass. 'These Khalistanis? We have warned that if we so much as see a window open or a turban, we will shoot first. They will not dare make any trouble.'

I was taken aback. I remember the look of utter shock on Khan's face. We drove away quietly and did not speak for several minutes. The army had been deployed there to protect Sikh lives and property but here was a soldier who was filled with hatred towards them.

This was an important lesson because the responsibility for the 1984 anti-Sikh riots has traditionally been placed on Congress supporters alone. That was simply not true. The media had as usual been irresponsible in reporting from Punjab and the government as usual was ineffective in communicating its point of view. Our Sikh friends would often tell us that the situation in Punjab was bad but not as bad as was being reported. They would invite us to visit Punjab with them and see things for ourselves. But the situation worsened progressively; so much so that Sikh boys started refusing to go to school in turbans. They were being bullied as Khalistanis and Bhindranwale. Large sections of people had bought into the narrative that Sikhs were traitors. It was therefore strange but not surprising to see the hatred being reflected by the army jawan. Everyone was complicit in their massacre.

Hope is Important

I looked up to Dr Vinayan, who was as passionate about the forest rights of tribals as he was about secularism and agriculture. A plain speaker, he would not spare any one and was intensely disliked by both politicians and bureaucrats. He was also active in the Narmada Bachao Andolan with Medha Patkar.[8] Some senior bureaucrats, however, admired and respected him and for some time during the 1980s and 1990s, he was also invited to Mussoorie to address probationers at the Lal Bahadur Shastri Academy for IAS.

When the Babri Masjid was demolished, Dr Vinayan disappeared for several weeks. When he surfaced, he confided that he was making arrangements for a long walk to Rajghat in the national capital. He would be leading a group of twenty-five villagers from Jehanabad to Delhi on foot. They planned to stop on the way to talk to villagers and explain the dangers of communalism and violence. Two bullock carts would carry provisions so that they could cook wherever they stopped.

I was excited. As the Resident Editor of *Times of India*, I could not afford to leave but I wanted a reporter and a photographer to accompany the 'yatra'. But the response was lukewarm and the wisdom of deploying scarce human resources on a minor yatra was questioned. Reporters showed little interest in accompanying him. Newspapers paid no attention to the long walk and after the initial reports when the walk started, no media outlet tracked their progress.

When Dr Vinayan finally returned after two months or so, the villagers having returned earlier by train, I worried that he would complain bitterly about the lack of media coverage and support. He did nothing of the kind. Instead, he bitterly complained about the difficulties pedestrians faced while walking on the Grand Trunk Road. Are highways meant only for vehicle owners, he fumed, recalling how the group had found it difficult to negotiate speeding vehicles on GT Road. After he had calmed down, I asked if the fast at the end of the long walk had garnered any media coverage in Delhi. He laughed and commented that journalists were the same everywhere—indifferent to people.

I remember asking him about the impact on people along the way. He was sombre, recalling that while most villagers they spoke to condemned the demolition and endorsed the need for communal amity, he sensed a certain degree of insincerity. It would take many more long walks, he said, to change the mindset. I last met him when I was Resident Editor of *TOI* at Lucknow between 1997 and 2000. He wanted to undergo some medical tests and stayed with me for some time. In 2000, I was transferred to Kolkata to launch the *TOI* edition there. I had introduced him to a fine cardiologist in Patna who had become a family friend. It was Dr Chatterjee, I learnt, who had received the SOS from the ashram in Jehanabad where Vinayan lived and had rushed with an ambulance from Patna. But by the time he was brought to Patna and admitted in the hospital, it was too late. He apparently succumbed to dengue. It was not diagnosed in Jehanabad and I suspect he neglected his health. He left too soon.

Rajeshwar Mishra, a well-known name as a trainer in the NGO circuit, was a social science researcher associated with AN Sinha Institute at Patna in the 1990s. A good soul, Mishra was secular to the core and was disturbed by the demolition of the Babri mosque. We met to discuss what we could do. It was decided that some of us like-minded people could meet once a week at the AN Sinha Institute, preferably over the weekend, and visit a village on Sundays to talk and explain to the people the dangers of communalism and understand their points of view. The meetings were attended by people we knew and was 'by invitation'.

We were, therefore, surprised one Saturday afternoon when a young man, Shashank Shekhar, walked in, introduced himself as a budding musician and sought permission to attend the meeting. We were suspicious and quizzed him on how he had learnt about our meetings and what he was up to. What he said continues to ring in my ears.

'I have been learning Hindustani classical music and want to make a career in music. All my ustads happen to be Muslim and all of them begin their riyaaz with Saraswati Vandana. I am, therefore, puzzled at this Hindu–Muslim divide and want to understand why there is so much animosity,' he told us.

Shashank Shekhar bowled us over with his sensitivity. At this very first meeting he told me that he was a cricket buff and found the cricket coverage in the *Times of India* both pedestrian and error-prone. He readily came up with examples and accepted my request to do a post-mortem of our sports pages for a week. He later joined the sports desk of *TOI* and went on to become one of the sports editors in *TOI*, Delhi. His foremost passion, music, was unfortunately sidelined and I do feel guilty at times for pulling him away from this.

Our visits to the villages on Sundays were tougher than we had imagined. Villagers were invariably suspicious of strangers and more so of city slickers casually visiting the village for a few hours to give gyaan. There was a wall between us that we could not penetrate. It was also impossible to interact with women. The women, we were told, felt no such inhibition with saffron-robed and bearded saints and sadhus. They would flock to the satsangs and even call on the babas alone.

We were bemused. The villagers clearly did not take us seriously. We toyed with the idea of taking a saffron-robed swami with us because we sensed that that is how the bigotry had infiltrated the villages. But none of us was particularly religious and the idea merely triggered jokes and laughter. Regrettably, the project was a non-starter, and we gave up after a few weeks.

Old Prejudices Run Deep

How and when Muslims began to live in herds is something I seldom paid attention to while growing up in Ranchi in the 1960s and 1970s. But even as children we were conscious of 'Pakistan' or Muslim-dominated areas in our towns and cities. There were other, even more more insensitive and shocking ways, for Muslims to learn of the divide. A Muslim woman, accomplished and educated, once confided that it was in school that she learnt she was different, that she was Muslim. Her Hindu 'friends' had pointed to black ants, and said those ants were Hindus. The red ants, they insisted, were Muslims. She could not recall if any teacher had put an end to this bullying. Similarly, we grew up being told that the 'border' began at Muslim localities like Hindpirhi.

Growing up in Ranchi, we were also familiar with the slurs

'jolha' and 'kolha'. Muslims were called jolhas and Adivasis were called 'kolhas', but I still have no idea why. Was it because they were generally dark complexioned (although contrary to popular belief many Adivasis in Jharkhand are fair complexioned) or was it because many of the Adivasis worked in coalmines (koyla khadan)? Jolha, of course, stood for weavers or Julahas, the traditional occupation of many Muslims in the region.

The slurs were generally used by older boys, as we younger boys merrily played football or cricket with both jolhas and kolhas on our teams. Their religion or occupation did not matter and made no difference to any of us. We also took it in our stride because it seemed like an innocuous stereotyping as some of us Bengalis were contemptuously referred to as 'saral Bangali' or rotten Bengalis. The impression that most Bengalis consumed rotten fish (dried fish that had a strong smell is indeed a favourite with some Bengalis) was so strong that we took the abuse sportingly. Our Muslim and Adivasi friends also did not seem to mind the occasional barbs coming their way. We were, I guess, too busy with ourselves.

Communal hatred, in retrospect, should have come naturally as my parents were refugees from East Pakistan. They had to leave everything behind. My maternal grandparents refused to leave and stayed till 1964 when they were also advised to escape from East Pakistan. My grandfather died in Kolkata, lamenting that he had been forced to leave his library behind. My mother too would betray some emotion and clearly missed the place she grew up in. But possibly because both my parents were 'communists', their concerns were different, and they never betrayed any bitterness.

My parents got married during the Kolkata riots and the registrar was driven to the wedding venue by my father in an ambulance. Jyoti Basu, later chief minister of West Bengal, was one of the witnesses and travelled in the same ambulance. Decades later, after my only interview with him for *India Today*, I joked over tea that he was partly responsible for my existence. Jyoti Basu was flummoxed and looked quizzically at me. I explained that I had heard he was a witness at the marriage of my parents. I mentioned their names. Photojournalist Saibal Das who was accompanying me got upset asking why I didn't speak to the chief minister about my parents before the interview. 'I would have got a much better photograph because he actually smiled at the memory and the lines on his face softened,' he complained.

At Partition, the Communist Party was banned in Pakistan. My mother, who was expecting her first child, managed to go underground while my father, who was a more prominent leader, was arrested. He, however, managed to escape from the court, played hide and seek with the police for a month, met up with my mother and both of them stealthily crossed into India with less than hundred rupees.

They had lost their ancestral home and struggled to make a living in India. They could not bring any documents either and hence received no compensation. For millions of refugees like them, there was no rehabilitation, no plots of land, no subsidized housing as was provided to many from West Pakistan. But they never betrayed any bitterness, never complained and rarely spoke of the Partition riots or the traumatic post-Partition days.

I have often wondered why my parents never had any hatred towards Pakistan or Muslims. They always welcomed my Muslim friends. Showkat, Irfan, and Afzal ate food from the same plate as me. Refugees from West Pakistan, I believe, continued to harbour much more hatred and bitterness because they were possibly far better off. My parents, though both belonged to well-off families, had become communists early in life and were more egalitarian in their outlook.

My mother was actually fond of talking about the village she had left behind and her Muslim neighbours. A name I remember she took was that of Enayet and how difficult it was for his mother to find a bride for him. Enayet seemed to have been a fussy young man who needed everything and everyone to be perfect. If he approved of the bride, he would find something repugnant about her father, brother, or sister. Full of mirth, my mother would recall the time when Enayet approved of everyone but the match broke down because he did not approve of some strange habit of his prospective mother-in-law!

The communal riot in Ranchi in 1967 therefore came as a rude shock. Ranchi was then a small one-street town. But the rioting took its toll. My father was a lawyer, but his first love was journalism. In pre-independence days he had worked for one of the two revolutionary groups in Bengal, then spent fifteen years in prison or internment during which he became a communist. I was too young to follow the joke my father's friends shared of Vakil sahib trying to douse the fire with his black coat and handkerchief. It seems he had rushed out to control the rioting in Ranchi and had managed to save some of the fruit stalls which had been set on fire by the rioters. Within twenty-four hours of the rioting, a peace committee was formed. My father, the Vakil sahib, was part of it, and community leaders from both sides were called and asked to behave. Good administration and prompt steps brought the situation quickly under control.

The trouble had started when a group of students of the Birla Institute of Technology, Mesra, 18 kilometres from Ranchi, had an altercation with some Muslim taxi drivers over fares. The students were beaten up. The next day, busloads of BIT students landed up with hockey sticks and smashed the taxis parked at the taxi stand and beat up whoever they could. In retaliation, some shops owned by Hindus were set on fire and the owner of Kashmir Vastralay was stabbed.[9] Rumours spread, shops downed their shutters, and both Hindus and Muslims barricaded themselves and prepared to defend their localities. My elder brother remembers the rioting in Ranchi was a relatively tame affair. But he does remember that 1967 was the year when a Bharatiya Jana Sangh candidate won an assembly seat for the first time from Ranchi.

Minor riots did keep occurring in the town and one of the flashpoints every year was the Ram Navami procession. Started ostensibly in response to Muharram processions (most Hindus, I later realized, had no idea of the different sects in Islam but found Muharram violent), my suspicion is that the Ram Navami akharas were patronized by the traders as their private militia. The akharas would all converge on Ranchi's Main Road. The town would shut down by noon and armed processions, with participants carrying traditional weapons, would pass through town with flags, chariots, bands, and musical groups besides pageants.

Muslims would invariably shower rose petals and rose water as the procession reached the daily market. They would also serve sherbet and the community elders would greet those participating in the procession and embrace the organizers of the Ram Navami celebrations. But there was always tension and the police would patrol the area and deploy static forces and even erect watch towers at various points. Peace committee meetings would be held before Ram Navami. Yet it remains a mystery why violence would break out every now and then over the routes of such processions.

In sharp contrast, the processions taken out by the Sikhs were more organized, colourful, and more peaceful; in short more pleasant. Could there be a lesson in that?

5

BOMBAY RIOTS 1992–93
MONTHS OF MADNESS

Jyoti Punwani

Anil Ingle was just sixteen when the 1984 Mumbai-Thane-Bhiwandi communal riots broke out. He remembers seeing a bakery near his home in Dharavi, Mumbai's largest slum, being attacked, and thinking that he should do something as he had often bought bread from there. What he and his friends finally managed to do through those days of violence was to go from one narrow lane to another, dispelling rumours about mobs coming to attack the residents.

'I understood at that time what a riot does. It makes everyone fearful and creates a chasm between communities,' Anil says.

Interestingly, this chasm didn't exist in Anil's home. With his father in the leather trade, Muslims were regular visitors to his house; they would often leave animal hides for his father there. He remembers Muslims reading the fatiha in his home during Muharram and his family hosting iftars and celebrating Eid with them. The Muslim visitors would also attend the Lakshmi puja on Diwali and other pujas to which his father invited them.

Anil wasn't religious. By the time he finished school, he was attending study circles on Dr Ambedkar and Bhagat Singh. When the 1992–93 riots broke out in Mumbai hours after the

Babri Masjid was demolished on 6 December 1992, Anil was personally affected. He'd just got married, but the curfew imposed throughout the city on 7 December prevented him from attending his own wedding reception scheduled for that evening. At this time, he was working with the NGO YUVA (Youth for Voluntary Action) in a sprawling settlement of slums and chawls in Jogeshwari East, one of the areas worst affected by the riots.

Once again, Anil became active in his own area of Dharavi, trying to dispel rumours. YUVA too was engaged in countering rumours in Jogeshwari by tracing them to their source, informing the police of impending trouble through information received from the local youth it worked with and distributing rations during curfew. Anil witnessed Hindus and Muslims attacking each other and even got trapped in one such clash. He was recognized as a Hindu because of his pierced ears, but Anil told them: 'I'm not a Hindu, I'm just a human being (insaan).' Earlier too, he'd been assaulted by a group of Muslims who identified him as a Hindu by the Marathi newspaper he was carrying.

However, once the Radhabai Chawl incident took place on the night of 7–8 January, wherein six Hindus (of whom one was a man, and two were children), were burnt alive in a room in Jogeshwari, Anil found he could do little. After the violence ended, he went back to Jogeshwari to work with YUVA in distributing relief as well as in attempts to bring communities together, especially children. He still recalls a nine-year-old telling him that her friend no longer came to play with her.

Anil has stayed with YUVA since and continues to hold workshops with young people. 'They often ask me, "What's wrong in reciting the Hanuman Chalisa?"' The recitation of Hanuman Chalisa became an issue in Mumbai after Maharashtra Navnirman Sena (MNS) chief Raj Thackeray threatened in April

2022 that his followers would recite the prayer outside mosques if the practice of relaying the azaan on loudspeakers wasn't stopped. Some MNS workers were arrested when they tried to recite it on the streets of Mumbai.[1]

Anil tells these youngsters that there's nothing wrong in reciting the verse, but they should judge for themselves which of their problems would be solved by doing so. He remains committed to dialogue rather than confrontation. As Ambedkarites, he and his wife do not contribute to their housing society's Ganpati festival celebration, though he accepts the prasad his neighbours send him. He painstakingly explains to them why it is a sensitive issue for him. In return, he invites them over on Ambedkar's birth anniversary.

Anil feels YUVA has changed hundreds of lives through its range of activities. '75 per cent of those we work with remain untouched by the hatred being spread,' he says confidently.

Sajeed Akbar Sheikh vouches for this. Sajeed, who now heads his own fledgling political party after having worked with the Samajwadi Party and the Aam Aadmi Party, became involved with YUVA when the 1992–93 riots singed his neighbourhood of Jogeshwari East, a mixed settlement of Hindus and Muslims that had previously seen riots in 1990 and 1991. Sajeed and his friend, Javed, both just out of their teens, were members of a local group of Muslims called the Muslim Youth Association, which worked on educational issues.

The lanes of Jogeshwari are mini ghettoes; in only a few of them do Hindus and Muslims live next to each other. However, thanks to their association with YUVA, Sajeed and Javed came to know Hindus outside their own little ghetto. They were thus able to cross-check and dispel rumours about mobs of either community coming to attack. They would also inform YUVA if they saw any sign of trouble in their locality.

But then the Radhabai Chawl incident happened. The incident came to be known as the cause of the January violence, though later, the Srikrishna Commission would prove that it was not.[2] The Shiv Sena went to town over it, and even the police's and state government's affidavits to the Srikrishna Commission described the violence against Muslims that followed the incident as a 'spontaneous Hindu backlash'. The Srikrishna Commission showed that it was an engineered backlash.[3]

Muslims across the city were made to pay the price for the Radhabai Chawl incident. But Sajeed, who lived barely five minutes away from the Gandhi Chawl where the incident took place (it was wrongly identified as Radhabai Chawl by the police and the media, and the name stuck), recalls that even Muslims in the vicinity knew nothing about the incident when it happened. An old Muslim woman who went to buy milk very early in the morning on 8 January saw three truckloads of men coming towards Jogeshwari East from the highway, recalls Sajeed. 'It's only after she informed everyone about what she'd seen that we sensed something was about to happen that would be worse than all that we had seen until then.'

Like Anil Ingle, Sajeed too recalls that all coordination with Hindus stopped after the Radhabai Chawl incident. 'They were suspicious and we couldn't blame them. We were busy defending ourselves, not just against Hindus but also against the police,' he says. No Hindu entered Sajeed's ghetto, but the police did, and took away his younger brother.

Though YUVA had told him not to step out of his home, Sajeed thought it best to take his mother and sister-in-law to relatives in Kandivali, a suburb further north. He was sure no place could be worse than Jogeshwari; he had no idea that the violence had spread all over the city.

Unlike Jogeshwari, which had a strong Muslim presence,

Muslims in Kandivali were few and far apart, too insignificant thought Sajeed, to be attacked. However, their small numbers only made them more vulnerable to being targeted, and his relatives turned them away, saying they were in no position to shelter anyone. Finally, he deposited the two women in Jogeshwari West, a predominantly Muslim area.

Given all this, did the thought of revenge ever cross Sajeed's mind?

'Never,' he says, crediting YUVA for this. 'I wasn't involved with any identity-based or religious Muslim organization. Working with YUVA made it impossible for me to think of revenge.'

YUVA, he says, was indeed a friend in need. And not only because two of its senior-most members stayed in Muslim areas during the riots. The arbitrary arrests of Muslims for the Radhabai Chawl incident prompted Sajeed and Javed to get involved in arranging the defence of those arrested. Eleven of the seventeen arrested were sentenced to life by the TADA court[4] in 1996, only to be acquitted by the Supreme Court in 1998. Sajeed recalls carrying the bulky files related to the case to Delhi for every hearing. 'Though they did not officially get involved, YUVA advised us throughout,' says Sajeed.

Women in the Lead

Talking about those days, Mani Mistry, secretary, YUVA, says: 'Given the torture they faced from the police, we were worried that the youth we worked with would turn violent. None of them did.' After the riots, YUVA bought the tenement that had been burnt in the Radhabai Chawl incident and turned it into a 'Sadbhavana Sadan' (communal harmony centre). They did this, says Mani, to prevent two things: the place turning into a 'tourist spot' where Hindus would be brought to show what Muslims had done to them, and the owner having to make a distress sale as nobody would have been willing to buy it.

YUVA had been working with women in the area much before the riots happened. However, after the violence broke out, Mani and another YUVA member, Navtej, stayed in Jogeshwari off and on. Mani is a Parsi and Navtej a Sikh. They felt that they would be safe in both Hindu and Muslim areas. To make doubly sure, they wore sarees, which they felt was 'religion-neutral' attire.

Even after the Radhabai Chawl incident, when communication between the youth they knew broke down, they felt they needed to continue working in the area at least to distribute rations to those who couldn't go out to buy them because of curfew. They would do this in the police vehicle. They also informed the police whenever they were told that a dead body was lying somewhere. 'It was important for the body to be taken away immediately,' says Mani. They also visited the nearest municipal hospital to ensure that Muslims were being treated fairly; reports had started coming in of Muslim victims being ill-treated in municipal hospitals.

After 8 January, Muslims were at the receiving end of the violence. Both Mani and Navtej stayed in the homes of their Muslim members in Jogeshwari, though they also visited the local Shiv Sena shakha (branch). Significantly, some of their Hindu members bluntly told them not to interfere in what was going on. 'Earlier, we used to refuse to attend their Satyanarayan pujas whenever they invited us, telling them not to involve us in matters of religion,' recalls Mani. 'When the violence broke out, they threw that in our face. "You said you didn't want to get involved in religion,' they told us. 'Now it is a matter of our religion, so keep quiet.'

Once the curfew was lifted, YUVA took out a women's peace march through the narrow lanes of Jogeshwari, going through both Hindu and Muslim ghettoes. Both communities welcomed them. 'Everyone trusted women; it helped diminish the fear that had gripped both communities.'

Were they ever afraid?

'No,' says Mani. 'We trusted the people we worked with. They didn't let us down.'

This experience also brought home a few surprises for Mani. Some of her neighbours in the middle-class area where she lived were Kashmiri Hindus and vocal about their dislike of Muslims.

'But when we started a fund collection drive for the riot victims, they readily donated, though they knew the money would also go to Muslims,' she says.

When a Muslim lawyer in her building started receiving anonymous threats, the Hindu boys in the nearby slum vowed not to let anything happen to him.

'See, ordinary people are not normally consumed by hate for the other community. It's when they get brainwashed and instigated that they support violence,' she says.

This was the experience of activist Janki Prashant too, who had been working in the Shanti Nagar slum area with other colleagues of the Sarvodaya Movement, a movement inspired by Gandhian thought. She recalls how because of the work done by her and her colleagues earlier in the suburb of Dahisar, it wasn't too difficult for her to quell talk of retaliation among a few youngsters.

Janki and her colleagues even managed to convince the Hindus in the buildings around the slum to maintain peace. In several places, Muslim-dominated slums were attacked from the terraces of nearby buildings by residents of those buildings. 'We told them that once a fire breaks out in the slum, your building too will be affected,' recalls Janki. 'We used the same logic to convince hotheads in our slum that peace wasn't an abstract concept, but a necessity in daily life.'

As Shanti Nagar became a refuge for Muslims fleeing violence in Kandivali, it became a potential target. However, 'not a stone was thrown', says Janki with satisfaction. 'Because Sarvodaya activists had been working there for a long time, the local group already had a good understanding and local leadership had emerged. An organization run by local people is the best guarantee of safety,' she says.

The slum-dwellers decided that they would patrol the slum, not allowing any outsider to enter; not even the police, recalls Janki. 'We had heard what the police had done in other areas.'

Police in the Middle

According to Anil Ingle, when the riots began, the police were upbeat because Muslims were being 'taught a lesson'. 'I had seen them barge inside Muslim homes and beat up the residents (in Jogeshwari).' But as the violence showed no signs of ending, they grew tired. 'While the SRP (State Reserve Police) were provided lunch by their platoons, nothing was done for the police. By the end of the January violence, they were not just tired, but worried about the safety of their own families in their absence,' he says.

Interestingly, one of the leading peacemakers at that time worked closely with senior police officers throughout the violence. Indeed, had it not been for the backing of senior officers, some of her efforts may not have been successful.

Sushobha Barve, one of the founders of Mumbai's Mohalla Committee Movement, spent both phases of the riot in Dharavi. Her book, *Healing Streams* (2003), describes in detail the many occasions she managed to get Hindus and Muslims who were full of anger against each other to sit down and talk, air their resentments freely, and work out a solution. While most of these meetings were held on the initiative of the residents, with Sushobha acting as a bridge without any police presence, the fact that Sushobha was part of the governor's Peace Committee and available at all times in their area inspired confidence in people. She used her access to the authorities to the fullest—informing the police about the peoples' fears so that they could post forces there; calling them when an unexpected morcha (rally) spread panic; going to the police station to check whether boys who'd been arrested were in fact there; and even calling up the police commissioner when necessary.

Throughout the period, the officer she coordinated most with was Sanjay Pandey, then deputy commissioner of police in charge of Dharavi, an unusually secular police officer. It was his idea that Hindus and Muslims jointly repair a temple and a mosque that had been damaged in the violence. Later, after the violence had ended, a stormy meeting of Hindus and Muslims conducted by Sushobha, from which the police were kept out, resulted in Hindus guarding the same mosque to enable the imam to clean it and ready it for reopening. They also stood guard while namaz was taking place.

In her book, Sushobha describes the various ways in which she brought peace: from taking Hindus who'd heard that weapons were stored in the common toilet block by Muslims to the spot to check for themselves, to warning miscreants acting suspiciously near a dargah (she later discovered they'd planned to plant bombs inside it). Along with a few Hindus, she cleaned up the dargah that had been burnt and vandalized and collected money for its repair.

This gesture—one community atoning for the damage

done by its co-religionists to the place of worship of the other community—was tried in Bandra East too, but was met with rejection, probably because politicians, rather than ordinary people, were involved.

On the night of 6 December, a Ganpati idol was desecrated in Bandra East. Shiv Sena supremo Bal Thackeray lived in the area. Not far from where the idol was desecrated was the large slum of Behrampada, projected by the Shiv Sena as a den of illegal Bangladeshi immigrants.[5] Former Rajya Sabha MP (of the Congress party) and then the Maharashtra secretary of the Janata Dal, Husain Dalwai, who lived in the vicinity, met the local Shiv Sena MLA Madhukar Sarpotdar with the offer that Behrampada's Muslims would arrange for a new idol to be installed in the temple. Sarpotdar rejected the gesture.

A khadi-wearing socialist, Husain had tried other Gandhian ways already. Shocked by the demolition of the Babri Masjid, he had undertaken a fast the next day outside the Janata Dal office in South Mumbai, hoping that it would inspire other Muslims to join him in expressing their anguish. But by then, Muslims were already on the streets as were Hindus.

Gandhi to the Rescue

One Gandhian experiment at peacemaking did work. The stakes involved were high. Had it failed, the area could have descended into brutal mob violence.

The Muslims of Kasaiwada, in the densely populated Muslim-dominated suburb of Kurla, would normally come down the hillock on which their settlement was to shop at the Chunabhatti Market below, which was Hindu-dominated. There was a mosque there, which had remained unused through the December violence. The Kasaiwada Muslims wanted to start using it again by offering namaz on 1 January 1993.

Throughout December, rumours about the Muslims of Kasaiwada attacking Hindus from their vantage position on top of the hillock were rife, especially one about a pregnant woman being attacked. Activists working in socialist leader Mrinal Gore's women's group Swadhaar had done their best to trace this woman but could not find anyone who actually knew her. Intriguingly, the same rumour was spread in Jogeshwari East where YUVA members tried to trace the alleged victim in vain. At a meeting held by the State Women's Commission between the two phases of the riots, the socialist activist professor Shama Dalwai suggested that the commission set up a unit to counter such rumours, but her suggestion was ignored.

When it came to be known that Muslims from Kasaiwada would be coming for the Friday namaz, the Hindu settlement was gripped with fear. On their part, the Muslims were afraid of venturing into the Hindu area but keen to revive the masjid.

The socialist activists decided to try a Gandhian way of resolving this. Shama Dalwai joined them from Bandra East, where she was active. In Chunabhatti, it was decided that Professor Gopal Dukhande (also a socialist and well-known in the area) would accompany the Muslims from their homes to the mosque below. Shama, Fatima Khadas, Rekha Thakur, and others who'd already been working there would form a human chain around the mosque. The local police as well as senior officer P. S. Pasricha were informed, and Pasricha himself was at the spot throughout.

However, as the time for namaz approached, a crowd of angry Hindus led by local Shiv Sainiks began gathering near the mosque. As the crowd swelled, Shama and another colleague got separated from the rest of their colleagues. The Shiv Sainiks started questioning them aggressively. One of them recognized

Shama and asked her: 'You're Shama Pandit aren't you, from Yuvak Kranti Dal?' Yuvak Kranti Dal was a youth organization started in 1967 by socialist students of Pune University.

More Shiv Sainiks joined in: 'Don't you know what was done to the Congress municipal corporator a few days earlier when she had tried to intervene?' The corporator's sari had been torn off by the angry mob.

Luckily, someone else in the crowd also recognized Shama and managed to gradually take her and her colleague out of the circle that surrounded them. By that time the group of ten-odd Muslims had entered the mosque for namaz. Within half an hour, they emerged and were escorted back by Professor Dukhande, as the police stood guard.

'This one incident showed that when the police do their duty, no riot can take place,' says Shama. 'And if people in every lane decide they don't want violence, they can prevent one.'

Wasn't she afraid? After all, she was threatened even as police stood close by.

'Yes, the police remained unaware of what happened with us,' recalls Shama. 'But I knew that nothing serious could happen with a senior officer like Pasricha present.'

At any rate, Shama believed then, as she does now, that Gandhians should be willing to risk their lives if they want to intervene in situations of communal violence. Shama met Muslims who had fled their homes; they were too full of fear to return. She strongly felt that they should be encouraged to return, and only Hindus could do this. She suggested this at a relief meeting called by her husband Husain immediately after the violence subsided.

'There will be people who'll oppose us, but at the worst, what will they do to us? Rape us, kill us?' she asked. 'If this is to be a movement, we should be ready for such risks. Didn't Gandhians risk their lives when riots broke out pre-Independence?'

Not surprisingly, her suggestion found few takers.

In her book, Sushobha describes one such attempt by a Gandhian to get Muslims who had fled to their villages in Tamil Nadu to return to Dharavi. But it took the involvement of very senior bureaucrats and police officers of both the Maharashtra and Tamil Nadu governments for this to succeed.

Roadblocks to Reconciliation

Like Shama, Jayant Diwan, who'd been part of the anti-Emergency movement led by Jayaprakash Narayan and a member of the Chhatra Yuva Sangharsh Vahini, also rued the absence of politicians and Gandhians on the roads during the riots. 'Who worked for peace? Nobody,' he says cynically. 'Had Mrinal Gore, or trade unionists Datta Samant and Sharad Rao come out, all of us would have joined them.'

Jayant and his colleagues from the Mumbai Sarvodaya Mandal helped in relief work in the Tulsiwadi slum at Tardeo where they had been working since 1978. The predominantly Muslim slum was destroyed by fireballs thrown from the terraces of surrounding buildings. In the process, even the homes of Hindus got destroyed.

The Chhatra Yuva Sangharsh Vahini helped run a relief camp at the Janata Kendra near Tulsiwadi headed by veteran Gandhian Dr G. G. Parikh, and also rebuilt homes in Tulsiwadi for both Hindus and Muslims. They were surprised to see the slum-dwellers resist all their attempts to redesign their homes to provide better ventilation. 'They wanted their homes exactly as they had been earlier,' says Jayant. 'They wanted the same neighbours too. So, the homes we built had Hindus and Muslims staying next to each other as they did earlier.'

Jayant, who tried to help a few victims get back on their feet, discovered that governments didn't really care. The Pradhan Mantri Rozgar Yojna (PMRY) had just been launched, under which loans of up to ₹1 lakh to set up small businesses needed no collateral. However, when Jayant went with riot victims to submit loan forms, the bank managers simply placed the forms in their drawer and frankly told him that they already had too long a list of defaulters to take any more risks.

'Which riot victim can approach a bank official with a properly filled out form?' asks Jayant. 'Instead of making nationalized banks responsible for disbursing loans, the government should let credit societies or cooperative banks do so.' Jayant found it easier to take victims to informal employers such as Marwari merchants and small workshop owners who would give them piece work or tools of trade on hire.

Shama was more successful in getting bank loans for victims, but only because the New India Co-operative Bank was run by socialists. 'The loans were never repaid; bank chairman Ranjit Bhanu shrugged it off as the bank's contribution to the victims,' she recalls.

Individual Efforts

Not all peacemakers had well established organizations behind them or a history of political activism. But all of them had a tradition of social work. The late Fazal Sha'd was one such. The owner of Universal Book Depot, which sold Islamic religious literature, Sha'd was co-founder of the Bombay Aman Committee (BAC) which had been set up after the 1984 Mumbai-Thane-Bhiwandi riots. In the 1992–93 riots, he took it upon himself to sit in the morgue, helping those who came looking for their loved ones, sometimes even giving them money for some food, or the taxi fare home. The stench of decomposing bodies, the filth of oozing wounds—nothing deterred Sha'd.

The BAC set up a 'control room' at the office of another co-founder, the late businessman Wahid Ali Khan, in Musafirkhana, an area that marks the start of Mumbai's old Muslim quarter. As soon as they would get a distress call, BAC members would rush either with relief or to evacuate the victims. One of them, Mehboob Khan, recalls that the government hospital refused to part with their ambulance till he insisted that he was taking responsibility for it.

The most notable of these efforts were in Pratiksha Nagar, Antop Hill, a colony of transit homes for those whose buildings were being repaired by the state housing corporation. About 4,000 Muslims living scattered in Pratiksha Nagar were herded together in the open for three days by the local police, with Shiv Sainiks surrounding them. When the BAC sent relief, the Shiv Sainiks forced the truck to turn back and almost killed the driver.[6] A second attempt was made with the help of the army; even the army trucks were stoned, provoking the army to open fire. Finally, eleven army trucks took Pratiksha Nagar's Muslims to the Musafirkhana relief camp in South Mumbai.

After the riots, Sha'd was instrumental in bringing victims to testify before the Srikrishna Commission and accompanied Justice B. N. Srikrishna to some of the sites of police firing. He also filed an intervention petition in the Supreme Court for implementation of the commission's report.

Congressman Abdul Razzak Maniyar has been running the Public Complaint Centre, a place where matrimonial disputes are resolved, since 1989. He remembers confronting a group of Muslim boys who'd come to loot a locked imitation jewellery shop owned by a Hindu in a lane in Pydhonie, a predominantly Muslim area with pockets of Hindus. 'I told them to go away.

I explained to them that they would loot the shop and leave, but the police would come and arrest our boys. They left, but I heard them shoot someone after they left. I think they took out their frustration on a poor Hindu passer-by.'

Burhan Parkar, owner of a chemist shop in Mahim and a known social worker there, helped set up a makeshift medical centre in a local hall where injured Muslims could be treated without having to go to hospitals because any injured Muslim who went to the hospital was immediately listed as a rioter by the police.

Parkar understood the danger of this. Just a few months earlier, in September 1992, he himself had been hit by a police bullet while trying to help quell a potentially violent situation near the famous Mahim church on the occasion of Eid ul Milad ul Nabi, the Prophet's birth anniversary. The senior policemen knew him, so they rushed him to hospital, but a case of rioting was registered against him. It took him eighteen years to get acquitted.

In 1987, when the Shiv Sena had called a bandh over the killing of Hindu bus passengers by Khalistanis in Punjab[7], Burhan Parkar had, against the advice of his neighbours, refused to close his chemist shop in Mahim. Parkar hadn't forgotten the burning alive of thirty-one Muslims (and one Hindu) in nearby Bhiwandi just two years earlier—in the infamous Ansari Baug incident of the 1984 Bombay-Bhiwandi-Thane riots. The Sena had been on the offensive then.[8]

Confronted by the local Shiv Sena leader, Parkar refused to yield. 'Where were you when those thirty-one Muslims were being burnt alive in Ansari Baug?' he asked the Sena leader. He then turned to the police on duty there and asked: 'Is this an official bandh?'

By then the Muslim boys hovering nearby had pounced on

the Shiv Sena leader, who fell into a gutter and had to be rescued by the police. All shops down the road reopened. It was this reputation that made the restless Muslim youth of Mahim obey Parkar when a maha aarti took place down the road. Maha aartis, organized by the Bharatiya Janata Party (BJP) and the Shiv Sena all through January 1993 and attended by hundreds of Hindus, were marked by inflammatory speeches.[9] They were deliberately held on the road outside temples, ostensibly to get the government to ban namaz offered on the roads on Fridays. Despite many of them ending in attacks on Muslims, the government refused to ban them, terming them 'religious gatherings'.

Parkar lived in the Muslim part of Mahim. The maha aarti took place outside a temple just a few metres away in the Hindu part of the same road. It took all of Parkar's skills and standing to persuade the boys in his area to remain standing silently on the road while the maha aarti was on. When it was over, the participants saw a wall of young Muslims guarding their territory; they dispersed.

Parkar had got involved in peacemaking efforts on 7 December itself. That morning, he joined Mahim's most respected Muslim, the late businessman Amin Khandwani, a six-time municipal corporator and one time MLA, chairman of the Haj Committee of India and later, head of the State Minorities Commission. Khandwani had called some well-known Muslims from the area so that they could calm the situation the morning after the Babri Masjid demolition. Residents were agitated because their children had left for school early. No one had realized that violence had already broken out in the city. It was decided that an ambulance would be sent to fetch the children, but when police stopped the ambulance, some parents threw stones at the cops.

Khandwani was trying to manage the situation, but the

police, who were already angry because stones had been thrown earlier at two policemen on motorcycles further down the road, arrested Khandwani. All those who went to the police station to inquire after Khandwani were also arrested.[10] At the police station, Parkar witnessed the way the police addressed Khandwani, who had been put inside the lock-up. 'Ey idhar Amin kaun hai? Chal re, nikal'—Which one of you is Amin? Come on out!—a constable had shouted. Shocked and disgusted, Parkar decided he wouldn't let any Muslim youngster fall into the police's hands if he could help it. He set up a makeshift hospital for those injured so that they didn't have to go to government hospitals. He also tried to prevent agitated young Muslims from indulging in violence.

The story of Yasmin Shaikh is the most surprising. As a fresh law graduate, she and her two sisters were encouraged by her father to intervene to defuse the charged communal atmosphere in her area and help those being harassed by the police. No Hindus attacked Yasmin's Muslim area of Nagpada. In fact, the Muslims in her lane had worked out a perfect arrangement with the predominantly Hindu residents of the nearby Reserve Bank of India quarters: they would get their essentials such as milk, bread etc., from them. Her area became a refuge for Muslims fleeing violence; and Yasmin was active in arranging food and medicine for them.

As a lawyer, she would go to the police station to get those arrested out on bail, and even confronted cops who arrested boys shouting the slogan 'Naara-e-Takbeer, Allah o Akbar'. 'This is no crime,' Yasmin told the police. Yasmin and her sisters even led a demonstration of women against the indiscriminate arrests of innocent boys. That demonstration, however, ended in police firing in which a bullet barely missed her.

Mohalla Committees

Ironically, both Yasmin, who lost faith in the police during the riots, and Parkar who had done so even earlier, joined Sushobha Barve when she began her mohalla committee experiment. Yasmin remains one of its stalwarts even today.

'After I met Sushobha and saw how many Hindus were working with her, I realized there's nothing like Hindu–Muslim, there's only humanity,' says Yasmin. 'I saw Hindu professionals like me working for peace. Till today, I tell my community that we as Muslims must realize that there are Hindus who fight for us.'

The riots and then the bomb blasts of 12 March 1993 had left Mumbai scarred. F. T. Khorakiwala, owner of the iconic Akbarallys store and Mumbai's sheriff at the time, thought it would be worthwhile setting up committees on the lines of the mohalla committees in Bhiwandi that had ensured that the sensitive township, known for two major riots in 1970 and 1984, remained peaceful after the Babri Masjid demolition. Former police commissioner Julio Ribeiro was approached to head the movement.

'I accepted immediately,' says Ribeiro. 'I knew that with an alienated Muslim minority, it would be difficult to police a city like Mumbai. Crime comes with poverty, and Muslims and Scheduled Castes are the poorest sections in Mumbai. Where do the police get information from? Only from the petty criminals among them. After the riots, the police were worried; their sources had dried up.'

However, Sushobha, who was also among the first to be roped in by Khorakiwala, felt that the first thing that needed to be done for these committees to work was to restore the trust of Muslims in the police. It was she who suggested that first the police must listen to the Muslims' grievances against them.

As described in her book, these turned out to be highly charged meetings, with Muslims speaking freely against the police. One such meeting in Mahim went on till 10 p.m.; then continued again the next morning, recalls Ribeiro. The presence of Ribeiro helped; Muslims trusted him. And as Ribeiro says, Mumbai was lucky that the police commissioner then was Satish Sahney, another secular officer. In one meeting with Muslim women, he and Sahney were the only two men allowed.

At one of these meetings, writes Sushobha in her book, Sahney acknowledged the conduct of the police and sought forgiveness on their behalf.[11] 'That was the most important factor that worked,' recalls Ribeiro. It must be remembered that Sahney was not in Mumbai during the riots; hence he was not in the least bit responsible for the police's conduct during the period.

Sahney however, downplays his role, 'Mine was a practical approach. I knew we couldn't change minds, and I didn't even try. I just told the people that breaking each other's heads was no solution. You have to live together, not as brothers, but peacefully. Brotherhood etc. are big words. First learn to develop a working relationship, I told them, don't get irritated over small things. We gain nothing by harming each other, I explained, pointing out that it was poor people whose property gets destroyed. Attacking each other and committing breach of peace only harms you. I told them they have no option but to live in this city; it is a vibrant city and they must keep it so. I also told them they had every right to protest, but there were methods of protesting.'

Soon after the mohalla committees were set up, police in Jogeshwari organized a joint Hindu–Muslim celebration of Shivratri and Ramzan Eid, which fell just four days apart that year. They got Muslims to form a human chain for Shivratri, insisting they wear their topis to send out a message. They also held an iftar party before Eid.

One of the innovative ways of building trust between the two communities was the cricket tournaments held by the mohalla committees. The teams were made up of local Hindu and Muslim boys as well as policemen. 'Muslim boys found that they could, as captain of their team, tell the local policeman what to do as the latter would be an ordinary player in the team. That gave them a confidence they would never have otherwise got in dealing with the police,' recalls Ribeiro, who remains the head of the Mohalla Committee Movement.

The mohalla committee experiment worked well till Ram Dev Tyagi took over as police commissioner in late 1995 and changed the rules to allow members of political parties in the committee.[12] The entry of politically aligned people saw the movement degenerate, as police began to give them more importance than the original non-political members who had joined out of a genuine desire to keep their areas peaceful. However, a few of the committees set up right at the start of the movement have continued to function and also succeeded in keeping their areas peaceful during many sensitive situations, such as the arrest of Bal Thackeray in 2000 for his writings in his newspaper *Saamna* during the riots.

Reality Check

Significantly, some of those who joined right at the start, such as Sajeed, left in 2005—they found that their criticism of the local police was not welcome. However, he continues to try and bring the two communities together, holding inter-faith iftars, Eid milans, and sporting events through his Modern Youth

Association—'Muslim Youth' was changed to 'Modern Youth' on the advice of a sympathetic police officer.

Yasmin has remained in the movement, but she finds a sea change in the attitudes of policemen since the BJP came to power. 'Earlier, the police would be worried that we would complain against them for not being responsive to people's grievances or for being communal. Today, they don't care.' Other mohalla committee members, who are unwilling to be named, echo her view. Yasmin also feels a major failure has been the small number of Hindus the movement has managed to attract, while Janki acknowledges its failure in attracting young people.

What if such communal violence were to break out again in Mumbai? Would these peacemakers be able to play the role they did earlier?

Yasmin, who has prevented many a flare-up, is confident she could; she has a team in place. Shama Dalwai is pessimistic: 'The hatred against Muslims among Hindus in general is now more than in 1992, and only Hindus can counter it.'

Ironically, Ribeiro echoes Shama's feelings. 'The hatred has spread too deep among people like us,' he says. 'All that we achieved has been lost. The saving grace is that many Hindus still remain tolerant.' As far as the police is concerned, Ribeiro feels it all depends on the man at the top. 'If the commissioner sends a message that communal conduct will not be tolerated, the police will have to obey him.'

Sarvodaya ideologue Kumar Prashant is not convinced. He had worked in Dharavi during the 1992–93 riots and coordinated with Sushobha on occasion. The police are fundamentally communal, says Prashant. He finds their prejudice so deep-rooted that he has stopped going to the Hyderabad Police Academy as a guest lecturer. 'Until you change the role of the police in a democracy, they won't change,' he says. 'In fact, I believe you don't need the police to bring about peace in a riot; they make things worse.'

Prashant also feels that while being on official committees may give you considerable access and convenience, the best approach is bottom-up, to stand with the people and work with them. 'The administration is status quoist and communal,' he declares.

Prashant and his Sarvodaya colleagues, who have worked during riots in Bihar and Uttar Pradesh, followed Acharya Vinoba Bhave's model of 'Shanti Senas'. The concept, conceived of by Mahatma Gandhi, was expanded by Vinoba Bhave to mean 'An army which offers its services in perpetuity to all men without distinction. Its whole vocation will be to confront hatred with love.' The prerequisites of a Shanti Sainik were belief in non-violence, respect for all religions, and aloofness from power and party politics.[13]

However, Prashant points out that the new dispensation after 2014 has little place for civil society: 'People are unwilling to listen to you, they are too quick to react.' The space for Gandhians to intervene is even less, says Prashant. 'Earlier, even at the height of communal violence, Gandhians would be welcomed in riot-affected localities. The residents knew they meant well. But, today, Gandhians are reviled and abused.'

'All these years, our society managed to keep this communal ideology at the fringes. Today, it occupies centre stage. And instead of one riot, their goal is to keep communal tension alive all the time. We have to find new ways of countering this,' says Prashant.

Peacemakers have always become active after riots, and then, as things cooled down, so have their efforts. Today's situation demands continuous activity to counter the continuous hatred. For today's peacemakers, the experiences of these brave individuals who went out of their way to bring peace in 1992–93 could serve as inspiration.

6

GUJARAT 2002
A HERITAGE OF HUMANITY

Teesta Setalvad

'Parens patriae'—the Latin term literally means 'parent of the nation'. In law, it refers to the power of the state to intervene against an abusive or negligent parent, legal guardian, or informal caretaker meant to act as the parent of any child or individual who is in need of protection. In legal parlance, it is used to describe the principle of what a state in a constitutional republic, a welfare state, epitomizes—an overarching shield that protects every individual.

That principle has lain shattered in the western Indian state of Gujarat as of 2002, as expressions of solidarity, fraternity, and caring in the midst of targeted mob violence were met with open hostility by both state and non-state actors. The policeman who stayed true to his uniform incurred the wrath of his political master; the teacher who served her conscience was ostracized and ridiculed; the social worker who wanted to step into the breach was told to 'beware'; the businessman who wished to proffer economic assistance was threatened and abused; and doctors from the majority community, who risked life and limb to be true to the Hippocratic oath, were threatened by organized mob leaders who were tracking such normal, everyday moves, and asked to stop.

Parts of Gujarat's fractured cities that remained peaceful despite repeated taunts about their 'cowardice' and 'lack of manhood', were labelled 'locality of traitors' or 'mini-Pakistan'. In fact, some everyday courageous peacemakers who risked their lives were taunted as not male enough and even gifted the proverbial bangles in contempt!

This then has remained the narrative of a state that for twenty-one years has reeled under a mode of governance that is rigid in framework, that militates against the inherent lived reality of India, and the spirit of India if you will, enshrined so evocatively in the non-negotiable values and principles of the Indian Constitution.

Despite these heavy odds, individual expressions of human compassion that recognized no barriers and brave acts of defiance have not ceased; they carry on heedless of obvious obstacles. The issue is not, never was, the regular Gujarati—whether ordinary citizen or public servant. The problem was and continues to be a political dispensation with a worldview that perceives peaceful coexistence between diverse religious communities as a threat to its own existence. It is this political dispensation that has not allowed justice to be done and the wounds of 2002 to heal. So, they fester, unhealthily.

The sant of the Jagannath Mandir at Jamalpur, Ahmedabad, even today, decades after conflicts have arisen year after year over the route of the yatra, recognizes the contribution of the Muslim artisans who, for centuries, have worked with the beautiful idols and other materials that are vital for the July rath yatra each year. Kheda is one town where such idols are fashioned in marble, stone, and even wood. This procession and the politics construed systematically around its route etc., have led to tensions each year and brutal violence in 1969, when over 1,000 lives were lost, and then erupted in violence and deaths again in 1991.

Gujarat's famous poet and social historian Narmadashankar Lalshankar (who died in 1886) is remembered for his great poem 'Jay Jay Garvi Gujarat' (1873), in which he celebrated all the cultural icons that provided a sense of identity to those who lived in Gujarat. Asking 'Who does Gujarat belong to?' he lists all the castes, communities, religions, and sects; then he says, not just these, because Gujarat does not belong to any particular group; he continues: Gujarat belongs to all those who speak Gujarati; and then, not satisfied, goes on to say that Gujarat also belongs to non-Hindus, the Parsis, the Muslims, and the non-savarna (Dalits) communities. Narmad passionately believed that around such a cultural imagination—truly secular in spirit—a sense of belonging could be forged for the Gujarati people. Narmad followed a great Jain tradition of compassion and tolerance. Mohandas Gandhi followed Narmad, convincing a whole nation to espouse the idea of 'ahimsa'.[1]

Gujarat was once, for long periods that spanned centuries, one of India's windows to the world. It was from this historic western coast that a myriad fascinating exchanges and interactions took place through trade: of thoughts and ideas, technology, food, music, clothing, and handicrafts. Ironically, this exchange was often with West Asia which, after the seventh century CE, was hugely influenced by Islam and before that, Christianity and even Judaism. For the inhabitants of this land—Gujaratis—who prided themselves on travel and entrepreneurship, accepting exclusion and violence as the credo seems impossible.

Humanity Above All

The memory of Pushpabehn Bhatt, a social worker, also associated with our peace-building and constitutional values project in the northern town of Himmatnagar within the district of Sabarkantha, both inspires and haunts our work even today. She lives on in her valiant efforts at building bridges across communities. In her efforts post 2002, she brought eighteen years of social work experience, determinedly working to re-establish communication between communities fractured by targeted violence and hate. Her work previous to 2003 involved the education and training of rural women communities, but not having the opportunity or perspective (her words to me in 2004) with which to work on the issue of developing communication between two communities, Hindus and Muslims, she waded in with grace and vigour.

'February and March 2002 will be etched in our memories forever,' Pushpabehn told me. 'The strained relations and tensions, the violence, the fears, and insecurities that we experienced entrenched themselves deep into the soul of Himmatnagar where much interaction had existed before. When we volunteered to help dis-housed persons to rebuild their homes in three villages through relief agencies and even managed to complete some of them, our own relatives would tell us, "Do not risk your lives entering Muslim areas."'

During one such effort, the process had been especially painful for Pushpabehn. The compatriots of her own Hindu community adamantly refused to even think of letting the affected families, who had lived by their side for generations, back into the village. Political propaganda and hatred had seeped deep even into rural areas. She did not give up; she started building bridges fractured by suspicion through two programmes: one that worked with school children and teachers and the other through local communities.[2]

'We had close and intense discussions on how to even begin the work of dialogue and understanding within the parameters of Gujarat, given how deep the schisms ran. Himmatnagar had

had its bouts of violence in 2002 but they were not as prolonged and bitter as those in Ahmedabad,' she recalled.

'When we started this work in Himmatnagar, for the first few months we worked among separate groups of women—Hindu and Muslim. There were two kinds of sections and groups. One section was extremely poor, self-employed women from both the Muslim and Hindu community in Chhaparia, a really poor large urban dwelling that also suffers bitterly at the hands of the police. Setting up a mahila mandal and library, and beginning work on accessing government assistance and programmes (Below Poverty Line cards etc.) was a step to build camaraderie with and between the women while constantly speaking of the divide and schisms between the two communities,' she recalled.

'After several meetings we managed to establish the Pragati Mahila Mandal with a membership of thirty women in the Hadiyolpur Chhaparia area of Himmatnagar. Most women were domestic workers with a monthly income of ₹900. We opened a bank account for the mandal on 1 September 2003, and we have already affected savings of ₹11,000.[3] While the mandal chief was Madinabehn, Nasreenbehn and Sakinabehn were next in line.[4] To enable a vibrant and regular working relationship to emerge where the issue of communication and co-existence with different communities takes centre stage, we held meetings where we discussed the women's immediate problems and needs. The severe economic crunch they all faced was always a dominant issue.'

Intermingling with Hindu women of the same vocation and from the same area was easier in Chhaparia than in the middle-class areas of Himmatnagar. Among the domestic workers and the self-employed, there was a certain amount of intermingling and participation at the level of everyday needs, as well as symbolic sharing during festivals.

Over 300 villages spanning nineteen of Gujarat's twenty-five districts were scarred by the post-Godhra reprisal violence. From Sabarkantha in the north to Surat and Valsad in the south, valiant tales of bridge-building abounded even as hate governed the political sphere. Vadodara, Kheda, Anand, and even the more fractured environs of Ahmedabad, arguably most bitterly singed with hate and suspicion, recorded such valiant tales. With a ratio of 70 Muslim families to 700 Hindus, the Sandesha village in Anand district saw humanism shine through.

Risking Life and Limb

Sandesha is a village in the Anand taluk of Anand district. Hindus in Sandesha—including the valiant Motibhai and Sonubhai[5]—saved Mustafabhai Umerbhai Vora and Mohammadbhai Umerbhai Vora, traders and shopkeepers in this village, from a bloodthirsty mob. Soon after the tragic mass arson at Godhra on 27 February 2002, rumours started circulating that riots would take place here too. However, local Hindus dismissed these stories and tried to convince the Muslim residents that nothing would happen. Mustafabhai recalls that one Govindbhai Patel even avowed that he would chop his own head off if there was any trouble in the village. However, the Voras were not convinced and as a precautionary measure, sent their families to stay with their sister in Napa.

Two days later, a mob of 2,000 came for the Muslims. Govindbhai Patel himself was now tragically a part of this mob. The attack was sudden, unexpected, and vicious. Mohammadbhai was at his shop in the village when he realized that there was trouble. Motibhai saw him and realized his predicament. He asked Mohammadbhai to step inside his house—Mohammadbhai took refuge in Motibhai's house and survived. Five hours later, when the police arrived, Mohammadbhai left for Napa in the police van.

Mustafabhai was at his house when he heard the mob. Across the road, Sonubhai's family also heard them. His daughter-in-law, Roopabehn,[6] remembers that it sounded so menacing that her children and even she herself got scared and started crying. Sonubhai's immediate thought was for Mustafabhai's safety. The mob attacked Mustafabhai's house from the rear. This gave Sonubhai the opportunity to help Mustafabhai escape through the front door and take him to his own house. Realizing that Mustafabhai had escaped to Sonubhai's place, the mob followed him there, demanding that Mustafabhai be handed over.

Sonubhai and his family refused to yield to the hate mob. The mob then turned on Sonubhai's family and threatened to burn their house, burning the shed outside. Even then the family refused to give in and threatened to leave the village along with Mustafabhai until, finally, the mob turned away. Five hours later, when the trouble subsided, Sonubhai took Mustafabhai out of the village in his own car and dropped him off at Napa.

What does it take to stay so valiant in the face of imminent mob threat and violence when you and your family are identified and scarred with almost the same hate as the victims?

Similar was the experience of about seventy-five to eighty Hindu families living among 2,000 families in the Machchhipeeth, Rifaiya Dargah area, in the old city of Vadodara that held out against the hatred that the rest of the city fell prey to. None of them thought of moving out to 'safer' areas.

'We did feel slightly scared, but we trusted the Muslims in our area. Our relatives asked us to come and live with them, but we refused to move out,' said Truptibehn,[7] a resident of Machchhipeeth. The Muslims went out of the way to make them comfortable, and Hindus were assured that they would not be targeted. Most Hindus in this area were poor and worked daily wagers. They were badly affected by the violence in the town. Their Muslims neighbours pitched in to provide them with groceries and other necessities whenever possible. Within the mohalla, the Hindus felt safe enough to go out for their daily chores. In the areas where they felt insecure, the Muslims went and did their chores for them.

On their part, the Hindus pitched in whenever a Muslim neighbour needed anything from the Hindu-dominated areas nearby. Here, both communities helped each other and maintained peace and harmony within the area. Most major incidents that affected Machchhipeeth took place on the main road, between its Muslim residents and either the police or Hindu mobs from outside. Within the mohalla, there was no communal tension.

Similar tales flowed to me from the Mehboojpura area of Vadodara where Rameshbhai, a former politician in the erstwhile Congress government in the state, took charge and organized regular meetings of elders and influential members of both communities (there is a 50:50 ratio here) who would sit together in the chowk of the mohalla till late at night. They also talked to people from their communities and tried to control the fringe elements. By sitting together, they managed to quash all rumours and clear any misunderstandings as soon as they occurred. Though sporadic incidents of stoning did take place, the residents did not allow this to deteriorate further.

On the night of 3 March 2002, around 10.30 p.m., the Congressman got a distress call alerting him to the fact that the Rifaiya Dargah near Machchhipeeth was attacked. He was a regular faithful at this dargah and had very good relations with the caretaker, Baba Syed Kamaluddin Ahsamuddin Rifai.

When calls to the police did not get him help, Rameshbhai decided to go there alone in his car. On the way, he saw several armed mobs. At the dargah, Baba refused to leave the shrine, but he wanted his family to be moved to the safety of their family home at Tandalja. With the help of Baba's driver and another disciple, Rameshbhai took about a dozen members of Rifai's family to Tandalja, through the curfew and the mobs on the streets. This man, a beacon of humanitarian values, was also available for any kind of help, twenty-four hours a day. He managed to rescue many Muslims trapped in hostile conditions either on his own or with police protection as and when it was made available to him.

On the Same Side

Memdavad in Kheda district also saw tales of everyday heroism shine through the dark nights and days of 2002. A man from Versola village in Memdavad taluk, Kheda district, managed to escape the communal bloodletting, mainly due to the proactive efforts of its leaders. This village has a considerable Muslim population and is surrounded by Hindu villages on all sides.

After the incident at Godhra, rumours flew thick and fast in both Hindu and Muslim localities about impending attacks by the other community. The neighbouring villages drew up plans to target the only Muslim population in their midst, in Versola. Bipinbhai Bhoi,[8] then sarpanch of Versola, recalls the anonymous calls he received informing him about plans to attack the Muslims of his village and asking for his cooperation. Here, the Hindu leaders of Versola decided that they did not want to be party to any such attacks. They held a meeting with the Muslim leaders of the village to chalk out a plan for the safety and well-being of all villagers.

Desperate times call for desperate measures. When our team was documenting this tale months later, the district president of the Congress party and professor at the local commerce college recalled that at this meeting the Muslim leaders suggested that the Hindus of the village should themselves demolish the two village mosques so that outsiders would not be tempted to attack the village. The Hindus would not hear of it. They assured their Muslim neighbours that they would protect the Muslims and their properties, including the mosques and the dargah, with their lives if need be. Accordingly, outsiders who were keen to attack the Muslim villagers were informed that the Hindus of Versola would oppose any such move. It was such unity among ordinary residents that scotched rumours and suspicions and held the hate mongers at bay. There was tremendous pressure from 'outsiders', but the Hindus of the village did not cave. They received numerous phone calls and, as was the pattern, even bangles were sent to Versola to ridicule them. But the villagers stood firm in their commitment to their Muslim neighbours. They told the callers that this was the village's internal matter, and their interference was not welcome.

There were at least three more such tales of heroism from Kheda. One was that of Dr Nitinbhai B.,[9] a medical officer at the municipal hospital in Memdavad town. Uniquely placed to help those most affected during the riots in March 2002, he used his position to provide aid to members of both communities in a number of creative ways. During the riots, Dr B. worked day and night to provide relief and help to those who needed him, irrespective of their religion. He had two hospital ambulances at his disposal. Aware that most people trust ambulances and hence they could reach places that ordinary vehicles couldn't, he used these vehicles to rescue many trapped Muslims in the area. One such incident occurred in a village near Chhapra where some

Muslims were holed up in the sarpanch's house. When Dr B. found out about the Muslims trapped there, he sent the ambulances to rescue them and bring them to the Memdavad relief camp.

The good Samaritan doctor walked the extra mile when he also found other innovative uses for his ambulances. Apart from responding to medical emergencies in different parts of the town, whether Hindu or Muslim predominant, he used the ambulances as hearses to transport the dead and their relatives to crematoriums or graveyards so that funerals could take place with dignity. Due to the prevailing tension in the city, parents were reluctant to send their children, particularly girls, out to the local commerce college where examinations were being held. Dr B. pressed his vehicles into service. Hindu and Muslim students travelled together in the safety of the ambulances and were able to appear for their examinations.

There are two other fine examples from the district, one Haroobhai Karsanbhai[10] who protected the sole Muslim family living in Desai Pol. Mehmoodbhai Shaikh's family lived here for over seventy years, safe among 200 Hindu families. But 2002 was different. The agenda of hate threatened this lone family. Haroobhai convinced others to stay on the side of reason and peace.

Nainpur village in the Kheda district has a sizeable Muslim population. There lived among other residents, a BJP worker, Chamanbhai,[11] who worked proactively to dispel rumours of revenge attacks. He persuaded his Hindu peers to stay calm and not seek revenge for Godhra.

Was it fate that brought Ramanbhai Singh,[12] a farmer from Ghodasar village, to the rescue of other Muslims? When our team met Ramanbhai, his elderly mother told us she trusted Muslims of the village more than others! Hailing from a royal family with a sarpanch in their midst, the Singhs' forefathers came from Rajasthan and brought Muslims with them to work on their lands and in their houses. It is believed that the village did not have any Muslim residents before that. This relationship of total trust and loyalty continues. Singh was in the village by accident, having returned from Udaipur where he worked in a hotel. He was there to sell the cotton harvest from the family farms, but his presence may well have saved over 150 Muslim lives in the village.

Ahmedabad is barely forty-three kilometres from Godhra, an hour's driving distance. Widespread violence made Ramanbhai delay his return. Muslims in neighbouring villages were being targeted and the social climate in Ghodasar became tense. Ramanbhai Singh, however, could not imagine riots ever taking place in his village and assured the Muslim villagers that he would see to their safety. He made regular rounds of their colony and spent time with them to reassure them. On 1 March, the tension mounted around Ghodasar. A mob of around 200–300 persons collected at the bus station outside the village. This incident rattled the Muslims of the village. Despite Ramanbhai Singh's assurances, they felt increasingly insecure. He advised them to hide in the fields and told them that they were free to seek shelter in his house if necessary. Most of the villagers hid in the nearby fields but three families, a total of eighteen Muslims, took up his offer and sought refuge in his house. He brought them home at about 9 p.m.

The mob prowled through the village looking for Muslims. It went on a rampage when it could not locate any Muslims. When Singh stood firm, the mob tried to attack him. Some inner conviction made him grab the leader of the mob by the collar and tell him that if he had some personal scores to settle with him, he should do so without involving innocent people. This aggression was unexpected. The leader was disconcerted.

Without a leader to egg it on, the mob soon calmed down. Singh managed to get them to turn back. He walked them out of the village to the bus station. However, this tale does not have a happy ending.

A day later, as stories of killings and retaliation flew fast and hard, Ramanbhai felt that the mood was turning against the Muslims and that he would no longer be able to protect them. He called his mother and asked her to inform those hiding in the fields that they were no longer safe there and that they should leave for the nearest safe village. One Nizam Khan later told us that the Muslims were gathered around the well in the field when they received Ramanbhai Singh's message at about 2 a.m. on 3 March. Realizing that there was no other option, they started walking towards Jinjar, the nearest Muslim-majority village. However, about fourteen Muslims, mainly old people, who were unable to walk the distance over an uneven terrain, decided to remain in the fields, convinced that no one would ever harm them since they were so old and had no enemies. These people, about whom even Ramanbhai Singh did not know, became easy fodder for the mob the following day. The brutality of the killings of these old and innocent residents whose bodies had been mutilated and maimed beyond recognition remains ingrained on all those who witnessed the violence in Gujarat 2002 to this day. I was among the first to capture images and news of these gruesome deaths when I visited the district on 4 March.

As tension mounted in Ghodasar over a week, the Muslims at the Singh residence were spotted. The mob surrounded their home and for several hours it was a tense and intimidatory stand-off. Finally, the Singhs realized that their safety lay with the Muslims. Having been singled out for protecting the Muslims, alone they would have been vulnerable to attacks. With Muslims providing strength in numbers, they rode out the bitter storm but not before the lives of the fourteen Muslim in the fields had been sacrificed to hatred.

Centre of Violence

A police sub-inspector in Ahmedabad, an advocate in Ahmedabad, a teacher in Naroda Patiya, an RSS worker, and a social worker who rescued Muslims in the same city—each of them swam against the tide of hate and kept the flag of humanity flying. Sub-inspector Sahu[13] demonstrated what a lone individual who follows his conscience and does his duty can achieve. By his selfless commitment to ordinary citizens, irrespective of caste and community, he helped redeem every peace-loving Gujarati's faith in the policeman's uniform. This SI had always been on very good terms with the Muslims in his jurisdiction and enjoyed their trust and respect. Full of pithy stories and cultural titbits, he has an enviable lineage—his maternal grandfather was a famed Urdu poet!

In February–March 2002, he was posted as the Detection Staff at Shahpur in Ahmedabad. Calls for help started pouring in as soon as trouble started in Ahmedabad early in the morning on 28 February. Shahpur, with its mixed population, is a communally sensitive area. Two incidents that could have turned as horrific as Naroda Patiya or Gulberg Society were prevented by his stoic presence.

Thirty-two Muslim women were trapped on the third floor of a building that had been set on fire. Other men in uniform had not assured them of help, leading them to suspect Sahu's intentions too. However, he was firm, quick, and fearless with the mob that he controlled virtually single-handedly. Still, it took him forty minutes to convince the trapped women to trust him. He then risked life and limb by jumping into the raging fire and managed to save them.

In yet another incident, near Halim ki Khidaki, 100–150 Muslim families were stranded in a colony off the main road. A street, about ten metres long, linked the colony to the main road. The colony was also vulnerable from the rear. A crowd of about 5,000 people attacked the chali from the main road and another mob, 2,000 strong, attacked it from the rear. Sahu rushed to the spot. The police fired tear gas shells to keep the mob at bay. However, the mob would disperse from one side only to regroup and attack again from the other side. This went on all day. This heroic sub-inspector, with the help of his colleagues and two police vehicles, managed to prevent the mob from traversing the ten-metre stretch from the main road to the colony. The stranded families were finally rescued that evening and arrangements were made to take them to the SRP camp.

During the first four or five days of intense violence, sub-inspector Sahu went without sleep or rest. He couldn't go home or see his family. Yet he was content about a job well done.

The former RSS worker Jigneshbhai,[14] from Saraspur in Ahmedabad, was constantly on the move and defied his peers to help where he could. He regularly visited the civil hospital and checked on those who had been admitted there. Regardless of whether they were Hindus or Muslims, he arranged for their food and medicine. Wherever the victims were too poor, he asked his friend, Jayeshbhai, who runs a trust, to provide meals for the victims, which he paid for himself. He also arranged for their medicines. In fact, an organizer of the Shah Alam camp contacted this RSS social worker every time they had to send someone from the camp to the hospital. He then arranged for their meals and medicines. When we spoke to him, he confessed that as a young man, he participated in many communal riots as a member of the Jana Sangh. But older now, he knows better.

Though his locality was under brute attack on 28 February 2002, for Nazir Khan Pathan, a school teacher from Naroda Patiya, his Hindu students were his main concern. Since the SSC exams were approaching, his coaching class students were studying at his house on the morning of 28 February. At around 10 a.m.–11 a.m., as the mob started collecting outside Naroda Patiya, Nazirbhai's first concern was the safety of the Hindu children under his care. He feared that they would be mistaken for Muslim children and attacked. So, he took them to a lane near the SRP headquarters and told them to go back to their own homes. However, one girl, Bharati was very scared and refused to leave his house. At first, he assured her that she was welcome to stay and would be looked after as his own, but as things got worse, he decided that he should help her escape. He noticed one of his students, Raju, in the mob. Raju recognized Bharati. Nazirbhai handed her over to him, and thus managed to ensure that all the Hindu children got out safely and in time. His fellow community members were not so lucky.

Ishwarbhai Desai, an advocate at the metropolitan court in Ahmedabad was vice-president of the local Bar Association in 2002. He lived in Saijpur Bogha near Naroda Patiya and Chamanpura, the location of some of the worst massacres during the 2002 genocide. His colony had about 200 Muslim families, mostly poor, and about 500–700 Hindu families, largely from the Rabari community. After the disturbances began in Ahmedabad, the Muslims were scared. Ishwarbhai had a plot of land in the colony. The 200 families came there for refuge and help. For three days, these families stayed there and Ishwarbhai and his neighbours fed and protected the Muslims.

Eventually, news spread about this safe haven and families from Naroda Patiya, Chamanpura, and other disturbed areas also came there for shelter. They were also taken in and provided for by the residents of the society using their personal resources. In this way, about 500–600 people were sheltered there. A temporary but effective relief camp was run for displaced persons.

But then word spread that Muslims had collected there and large mobs came for them. Some of the mob leaders were personally known to Ishwarbhai. All of them had only one demand—that Ishwarbhai turn the Muslims out. But Ishwarbhai and his neighbours refused. They were adamant that they would not let anyone touch the Muslims who had sought refuge there. 'We have grown up together, our families have known each other for the last seventy to eighty years. How can we desert them now?' Ishwarbhai asked the Hindu mob leaders. Even as he tried talking to people in the mob and engaging them in dialogue, other colony residents were prepared to face and repulse the mobs if necessary. In the three days that the Muslims took shelter there, on about a dozen occasions, mobs grouped and regrouped, but Ishwarbhai and his neighbours remained firm.

Even after the Muslims had left for the camp, a mob came to loot Muslim property and set it on fire. Once again, Ishwarbhai and his neighbours intervened. They were determined that not a stone would be hurled at a Muslim house, not a nail would be pulled out. For ten more days, they were pestered by the mob but the violence slowly petered out. When the Muslim families returned two months later, they found their houses in exactly the same condition as they had left them. However, the mobs did damage the mosque behind the colony.

For his troubles, Ishwarbhai had to face questions and taunts from his friends and colleagues for months. But the Muslim neighbours whom he rescued remain firm friends. None of them have felt the need to move to a safer place.

There were of course rights activists who also stood firm and newspapers like the *Kutch Mitra*, *Gujarat Today*, *Indian Express*, and the *Times of India* whose courageous teams documented the horrors unleashed with relentless consistency. The report of the Editor's Guild, *Rights and Wrongs*[15] has documented these stray beacons of light even as it contains ream upon ream on how mainstream Gujarati papers danced to the proverbial piper's tune.

When we recorded testimonies of expert witnesses for the Concerned Citizens Tribunal's inquiry into the carnage,[16] some of the narratives detailed above multiplied—there were many more instances of lone voices saving neighbours or Hindu doctors being threatened for performing their duty. One particular testimony was that of Piyush Desai, chairman of the Wagh Bakri tea company, whom I later interviewed.[17] Wagh Bakri is a popular brand of tea in the state of Gujarat. For six months, this tea was distributed free of charge to relief camps in the city of Ahmedabad and many other parts of the state.

In July 2002, Piyushbhai told me, 'In the last eight to ten years, through various platforms, this poison of communal conflict and hatred by one community towards the other is being spread. There are groups—I do not wish to take any names—who make me feel ashamed to call myself a Hindu. When we go to the market in the morning, we hear stories of small incidents that depict this corrosion of the mind and heart.

'Young minds are being poisoned through education. It is a dangerous venom that is affecting the quality of everyday life. Four days back, on 12 July, I felt ashamed when the Lord Jagannath Yatra was taken out. Our Muslim brothers were asked to observe self-imposed curfew, shoot-at-sight orders were issued on the route of the procession. Do we even remember that the Muharram tazia procession that means something to them and is a tenet of their faith did not take place this year? What message are we sending by suppressing only one section?

'We need to ensure that those who are not noble of heart and mind, those who have no respect for the feelings of other communities, such leaders should not cross the corporator level let alone become MLAs. They should not go to parliament either, where national policy is framed.

'"Aren't you Hindu? Why do you want to help them? Are the Wagh Bakri owners Muslims?" I am ashamed when these questions are put to me every other day in Ahmedabad. Our Wagh Bakri brand was started with the help of a Muslim who gave us a loan of ₹10,000 over 150 years ago. We are indebted to him. How can we ever pay off this debt?' asked Piyushbhai.

In his testimony to the tribunal, he recounted how efforts from the business and trading community to ensure interest-free loans to Muslim businessmen destroyed by the violence in 2002 were actively disrupted by groups like the Vishva Hindu Parishad.[18]

'In the initial days, there was an unbearable level of hatred and suspicion,' he said. 'By early May, we tried to bring the trading community together across community lines, despite the fact that political elements threatened our attempts. I was disturbed then and remain concerned now about talks of economic non-cooperation among some Hindu traders who are not ready to supply to Muslim traders; they refuse to extend credit, cash etc. There are groups here—and I make bold to say this—who are even now pressuring traders not to sell goods and enforcing an economic boycott. People like us need to resist such efforts. We are trying to form a body on a cooperative basis to collect materials from both sides and ensure free flow without any disturbance,' said Piyush Desai.

Some measure of a people's apology came in the form of a quiet march on the streets of Naroda Patiya in 2016 when Dalits and Chharas—members of a nomadic tribe in Gujarat—mobilized by a committed young Dalit leadership took out a silent march during the Una agitation, with a banner prominently saying, 'We are sorry' to the Muslim minority there. The Una march was a welcome expression of Dalit–Muslim unity, especially when Dalits have been used by Hindutva forces to target Muslims.[19]

Mass targeted violence did not take place for the first or last time in Gujarat in 2002. It has seen periodic premeditated appearances especially since the early 1980s, when the behaviour of the Indian police and paramilitary forces displayed a partisan hue. Nellie in Assam (February 1983) and Delhi (October–November 1984) are brute markers of targeted anti-Muslim and anti-Sikh pogroms that have only increased in frequency since the mid-1980s.[20]

In those early weeks of February–March 2002, as I scoured the streets of Ahmedabad, Vadodara, Godhra, Satnagar, Pandharwada, Sanjeli, Randhikpur, and Anand in a frenzy to document the tragedy and also reflect both reality and hope, an echo of an anthropological-sociological 'truth' was told and retold to me. Elderly Muslims, young women and men in anguished conversations recounted the earthquake—in Gujarat's Kutch region, home to the desert and artisanship of beautiful hues and colours—that brought everything that is good and beautiful in the state to the fore. Even cities like Ahmedabad were affected. The relief efforts that spontaneously flowed reflected tremendous solidarity and fraternity between communities. Muslim relief efforts were mammoth and humbling. The two communities rubbed shoulders with each other and did what they could to ease the suffering and misery of those affected.[21]

Even then, while the state (and VHP/RSS) relief efforts tried to draw lines along caste and community, the people of Gujarat simply did not allow it.[22] This was a threat to the politics of the state in Gujarat, which had abandoned the constitutional path decades ago. This solid bond of unity and camaraderie threatened the edifice of the politics erected in this state. So, the truth retold to me in the early days of 2002 was that it was to break this forged bond that the fires of vengeance and violence were lit. They have never quite been completely extinguished though it has been over two decades.

The state has truly abandoned its role. The people of Gujarat, however, continue to give us lasting hope. As this tableau of tales shows.

7

VIOLENCE IN CHHATTISGARH
MANY PEACEMAKERS, NO PEACE

Sunil Kumar

The Bastar region of Chhattisgarh has witnessed the worst form of bureaucratic and social exploitation of tribal villagers. In addition to being subjected to forced labour, tribal communities, especially women, have historically been physically exploited. Government employees coming from outside Bastar used tribal women as sex slaves.

It's no wonder then, that this forest and mineral rich area presented fertile ground for the Communist Party of India (Maoist), or as its cadre is colloquially called, Naxal, to move in. Since no politician, from the Congress or BJP, had any credibility with the people, there was a huge sociopolitical vacuum in which the Maoists were able to easily mobilize the tribal population. All they had to do was keep the security forces at bay. Although the Congress and the BJP are in contrast with each other in political philosophies, their approach to the Naxal issue, whether from the state capital Raipur or national capital New Delhi, is identical.

Naxalism in Bastar is close to completing half a century. And for half of this period, Bastar was part of undivided Madhya Pradesh. It has been twenty-two years since Chhattisgarh was carved out of Madhya Pradesh as a separate state. Yet, Naxalism, now a little more under control, doesn't appear to be dying out anytime soon. Chhattisgarh inherited Maoist violence from undivided Madhya Pradesh, which was governed from Bhopal, more than a thousand kilometres away. The governance was always very diluted. This has been true of other Maoist-affected areas too, which are also far from their respective capitals; with the violence being more intense in the remote areas.

Sparks of Peace

Both Congress and BJP state governments have occasionally made peace offerings to Maoists as lip service. The first chief minister of the state, Congress party's Ajit Jogi spent most of his term fighting legal battles to prove his 'tribalness'.[1] Clearly, he could not find time to address the Naxal problem in tribal Bastar.

His government was unseated by the BJP, which ruled for the next fifteen years, helmed by chief minister Dr Raman Singh. Upon taking charge, Singh issued a couple of statements to the effect that if the Naxals desired peace, he was ready to go alone in the middle of the night to the jungle to talk with them.[2] But his words remained just that, despite an opening in 2012.

Alex Paul Menon, an IAS officer, was abducted from Raman Singh's district Sukma in Bastar in 2012.[3] Singh tried his best to get him released. Finally, a negotiation channel opened up. This led to the formation of a committee. An IAS officer of the Madhya Pradesh cadre, Nirmala Buch, was nominated by the state government to the committee, and the Naxals nominated Professor Haragopal from Hyderabad, who had earlier been part of a broader and high-level peace talk between Naxals and the government of Andhra Pradesh. The third member was former bureaucrat-turned-social activist Dr B. D. Sharma, who, though nominated by the Naxals, straddled both sides. The committee had a very limited agenda of securing Menon's release.[4] The Naxals demanded the release of tribals from Chhattisgarh jails who were facing charges of being ultras. The state government agreed to consider these cases and treat them sympathetically in the courts.

The committee secured the release of Menon, and also helped dozens of innocent tribals to get an early release. This was the most serious negotiation of any kind between the Naxals and the Chhattisgarh government. Though, of course, over the decades, several people did their bit to restore peace between the two sides.

One such Gandhian activist, Himanshu Kumar, had been working in the Dantewada district of Bastar for nearly two decades starting the late 1990s. His focus was rural development and empowerment of the tribals so that they were less vulnerable to violence from the Naxals as well as the state. Gradually, he also got involved in a legal battle of the tribals against atrocities committed by the security forces. Kumar had some access to the union home minister P. Chidambaram during the first term of Congress-led United Progress Alliance government (2004–09). He managed to convince Chidambaram to initiate peace talks with Naxals.[5]

Given the nature of his work and the fact that he had no engagement with the security forces (state police and central police), the Naxals did not distrust Himanshu Kumar. Like any other Gandhian, he had a clear socio-economic objective, but the security forces in the conflict zone of Bastar had always been suspicious of anyone who was not working in tandem with them. Sure enough, he had occasional disagreements with the state police because of their high-handedness towards the tribals, as well as what Kumar regarded as human rights violations by the police. This also came in the way of his peace initiative.

Despite all this, Kumar recalls that around 2010, he had convinced Chidambaram[6] to come to Bastar for a public hearing.

But Chidambaram did not make it to the hearing. Later, Kumar read Prime Minister Manmohan Singh's statement to *Indian Express* saying he had asked Chidambaram not to go to such a public hearing because it would hurt the morale of the security forces.

This was not only the end of Kumar's peace initiative, but also the beginning of the end of his work in Bastar. He was forced to leave Bastar in 2010. 'I had confirmed information that I would have been killed by the police had I stayed another day,' he says. 'Justice is essential for peace,' he says, and absence of justice has been the biggest roadblock to any peace process. In fact, it was his fight for justice for the tribals that eventually forced him to leave Bastar. More recently, Kumar was slapped with a fine of ₹5 lakh for filing a PIL about the atrocities committed against the tribals of Dantewada. Kumar has refused to pay the fine.[7]

Fire in the Forest

However, the fight for justice was not the only source of his problems. The most powerful Congress leader of Bastar, Mahendra Karma,[8] was hostile to him because Karma wanted a head-on confrontation with Naxals. To that purpose Karma collaborated with the BJP-ruled state government of Raman Singh to engineer a tribal movement against the Naxals called Salwa Judum,[9] colloquially translated as Peace March. It was designed and executed by the state police deployed in Bastar in collaboration with tribal leader Karma and with the blessings of Raman Singh. Thousands of unemployed tribal youth were mobilized and armed by the police. Even though the state government never owned up to creating this violent militia, calling it a spontaneous people's movement instead, it supported the organization all along.

In its brief lifespan of six years (2005–11), Salwa Judum was responsible for the worst bloodshed in Bastar. The ill-equipped and ill-trained Salwa Judum cadre were sitting ducks for the Naxals. In retaliation, the security forces went after the tribals who they thought were collaborating with the Naxals. In effect, the vulnerable tribal population was killed by both sides. Ironically, the Raman Singh government knew that this would happen.[10] I got the sense of this when Ramvichar Netam, then a minister in Raman Singh's cabinet, came to me for advice one evening in June 2005. Apparently, Singh had told Netam that he was to take over the home ministry as the state government's counter Maoist-operation in the form of Salwa Judum was to begin[11] in Bastar in a few days, and it could mean a large number of tribal killings. The home minister then was Brijmohan Agrawal, an upper-caste Baniya. Netam told me that Singh believed that a large number of tribal deaths, with an upper-caste home minister at the helm would not be well received by the tribal population, which will regard this as upper-caste cruelty and not counter-Maoist strategy. Hence, Singh wanted Netam to take charge as home minister to avoid the allegation of prejudice against tribals. Eventually, Netam, a tribal himself, accepted the challenge. Thereafter, he spent over three years issuing condolences for the killed innocent tribals and saluting endless dead bodies of security personnel.

Incidentally, Agarwal too met me a few days before he was removed. He was upset with chief minister's decision of replacing him. He corroborated Netam's comment on Raman Singh being conscious of large number of tribal deaths and Singh's desire to protect Agarwal's reputation. Agarwal, who was keen to continue as home minister, told me that he assured the chief minister that he was willing to face the consequences. But Singh had already made up his mind about Netam.[12]

In 2007, the Independent Citizen's Initiative Group comprising author-historian Ramachandra Guha, journalist-activist B. G. Verghese, and sociologist-activist Nandini Sundar among others, went on a fact-finding mission to Chhattisgarh. Their report, *War in the Heart of India*, observed that 'The creation and support of the Salwa Judum has divided entire villages and families.... A cycle of retribution and revenge has been set in motion, with the Salwa Judum targeting villagers believed to be sympathetic to the Maoists and the Maoists in turn killing those active in Salwa Judum.'[13]

Eventually, Sunder and Guha, along with retired IAS officer E. A. S. Sarma, Adivasi Mahasabha leader Manish Kunjam, and CPI activists Kartam Joga and Dudhi Joga filed a petition against Salwa Judum in 2007. Ironically, both political parties, the Congress at the centre and the BJP in the state, fought hard in the Supreme Court and outside to justify Salwa Judum. However, in 2011, the Supreme Court declared Salwa Judum illegal. It ordered the state government to take back all arms and ammunition from the tribals. It also ordered enquiries into all crimes allegedly committed by the militia.[14]

Like Kumar, Sundar also had to pay a price for her activism in support of the tribals. In 2016, a case of murder was filed against her and others by the Chhattisgarh police. The charges were eventually dropped in 2019, under the Congress government and the National Human Rights Commission ordered compensation.[15] In 2016, Sundar published a book, *The Burning Forest: India's War in Bastar*, in which she has narrated the peace efforts that were undertaken:

> Like their differing positions on violence, the government, Maoists, and the civil society activists, each have their own stand on dialogue. The government has never wanted peace

> talks, though in a democratic setup, it cannot fully afford to be seen as letting that possibility go.... The police sell the view that talks are merely a tactical line to give the Maoists breathing time, to regroup.... The Maoists, like the government, have not been keen on peace talks. In the past, peace talks have proved fatal for Maoists presence and organisation, not just in Andhra Pradesh and West Bengal, but also in Nepal.... While all activists claim they want peace talks, they provide a range of reasons for being sceptical, including the fact that talks will not address questions of land and forest rights or mining which are the real issues behind the Maoist struggle.[16]

Much has happened since her book came out, including the change of government in Chhattisgarh. In 2018, the Raman Singh government lost the election and the Congress came to power with Bhupesh Bhagel as chief minister. In an email interaction with me, Sundar says, 'I tried to meet Bhupesh Baghel after he got elected and became chief minister of Chhattisgarh. I wanted to suggest that he implements our rehabilitation plan for Bastar. I also conveyed all the notes we had prepared on the peace process. But he refused to give me an appointment. I submitted the same to T. S. Singh Deo (state health minister), he was kind enough to meet. I also met P. Chidambaram, who said he would pass on the letter. I tried to meet Rahul Gandhi but did not get an appointment.'

With regret, she says, 'The basic aim was to have a high-level monitoring committee, which would serve as a forum of truth and reconciliation, record losses, initiate criminal prosecution, and provide compensation.'[17] The government has never agreed to this.

Quest For Peace

Dr B. D. Sharma was a bureaucrat turned social activist who had worked in Bastar, in both capacities, for many years. His involvement in peace negotiations with the Naxals was limited to Menon's abduction (as we saw before) but he was a strong believer in tribal wisdom, and self-rule through gram sabhas in scheduled areas. Until he passed away in 2015, he worked for tribal empowerment.

His junior in service and a long-term admirer-cum-collaborator Sunil Kumar (incidentally, my namesake) remembers him very fondly. According to him, Sharma strongly felt that the weakening of traditional institutions of the tribals had led to external influences, and Naxalism was one such influence. A great votary of Panchayats Extension to Scheduled Areas (PESA) Act, 1996, [18] particularly by respecting the powers of gram sabhas, Sharma was convinced that restoring community rights to the tribal population as envisaged under PESA was the only just way of neutralizing violence. Kumar told me that Sharma had frequent run-ins with the governments, both in the state as well as the centre, on the question of respecting the constitutional rights guaranteed to gram sabhas in tribal areas.

'Sharma felt that the tribal way of life was being inundated with laws and institutions alien to these communities, leading to distrust, which in turn was being exploited by the extremists,' says Kumar, who was chief secretary of Chhattisgarh when Menon was abducted. He says, 'It was Sharma's presence in the committee that negotiated Menon's release which largely ensured that talks did not breakdown with the Maoists.'[19]

Another person who tried to bring about a rapprochement between the state and the Maoists was social activist Agnivesh. Although from Chhattisgarh, he had worked outside the state all his life and had access to all political parties. In early 2010, Agnivesh announced a peace march from the state capital Raipur to Dantewada in the Bastar region, along with a few Gandhians and peace activists. He suggested that there be a ceasefire between the Naxals and security forces during the march. The idea was that the march and the ceasefire would create the atmosphere in which peace talks could commence.[20]

Upon the completion of the march, Home Minister Chidambaram wrote to Agnivesh commending the peace march and the idea of talks. Among the points he made in his letter were:

- The CPI (Maoist) should announce that they will abjure violence. To start with, they could say that they will not indulge in any violent activities beginning a specific date.
- Once the announcement is made, the central government will consult the chief ministers of the affected states and prepare a response well before the specified date. The response will include an invitation to the CPI (Maoist) to hold talks.
- On the specified date, we would expect that the CPI (Maoist) will stop all violent activities. We would closely observe whether the CPI (Maoist) will maintain the position of 'no violence' for seventy-two hours. It goes without saying that, during the said period of seventy-two hours, the security forces will not conduct any operations against the CPI (Maoist).
- It is our hope that talks will begin during the period of seventy-two hours when there is 'no violence'.
- Once the talk begins, we would expect that the CPI (Maoist) will continue to maintain its position of 'no violence' until the talks are concluded.

This letter was leaked to the media. Thereafter, spokesperson of CPI (Maoist), 'Azad' Cherukuri Rajkumar, wrote to Swami Agnivesh.[21] And a window opened. Briefly. In August, when Azad was on his way from Andhra Pradesh to meet with Agnivesh he was killed in an encounter with the Andhra police. Killed along with him was freelance journalist Hem Chandra Pandey. Whether Pandey was picked up separately and killed or he was accompanying Azad remains mired in speculation.[22] Agnivesh blamed both the union home minister and the Andhra government for sabotaging peace.[23]

Undeterred, the following year, Agnivesh set off on another peace march. This time, he intended to visit three villages which were allegedly burnt down by the security forces in the course of the infamous Operation Green Hunt.[24] When he and his co-travellers were still 50 kilometres from the destroyed villages, a mob attacked his vehicle. His turban was knocked off, and he was beaten up severely. It was a matter of common belief in Bastar that the attack was orchestrated by the police, with Salwa Judum as the front to prevent them from reaching the villages it had destroyed.[25] Clearly, peace was not in the interest of all.

The bitter truth in Chhattisgarh has been that a very strong faction within the administration believes that peace can only prevail after the annihilation of the Maoists. I have had the opportunity to interview every director general of police in Chhattisgarh in the last twenty-one years, both formally and informally. I have spoken with directors general of a few central security forces as well. The universal view has been that negotiations should only take place once Naxals become very weak and willing to surrender. Vishwaranjan, who was the DGP for a long period in Chhattisgarh, and had led a strong action in Bastar, was never optimistic about any peace talk unless security forces very clearly had the upper hand.

To a large extent, this view has also been shared by the consecutive state governments, irrespective of their public posturing. Perhaps this is the reason that led to the perception that politicians and security forces have a vested interest in continuation of protracted violence as it brings in funding from the centre and from the state budget in various forms, including Security Related Expenditure (SRE). Of course, there's no evidence to prove this, but the perception endures. The only fact that fuels this feeling is that most of the tenders for infrastructure and capability building in conflict zones are never properly scrutinized.

Police State

Chhattisgarh became a separate state on 1 November 2000. Retired IPS officer Dinesh Nandan Sahay became its first governor. He was followed by Lieutenant General K. M. Seth (retd). The third governor was again an IPS officer, from the Intelligence Bureau, E. S. L. Narasimhan. Shekhar Dutt, an ex-short-service army officer who transitioned to the IAS, succeeded Narasimhan. Before coming to the Chhattisgarh Raj Bhavan, Dutt had also served as deputy national security advisor.

In the first fifteen years of the state's creation, irrespective of the government in Delhi, the governors were uniformed people, all of whom supported the state police's position on peace and talks with the Maoists. The fifth governor Balram Das Tandon was from the RSS. He was hostile to anything leftist, and talking to ultra-left Naxals would have been unthinkable.

These were the formative years of Chhattisgarh, and the early chief ministers—Ajit Jogi and Raman Singh—had exceptionally good relations with Raj Bhavan. As editor of *Daily Deshbandhu*, I had interviewed Ajit Jogi within twenty days of his taking oath. I asked him if he could think of a solution to the Naxal problem. His response was, 'When development takes place, the problem will get reduced.' According to him, 'It is a socio-economic problem, as well as a problem of law and order. The police is dealing with the law and order part of it, but more important is to consider it as a socio-economic problem.'

I have already alluded to his successor Raman Singh's fifteen-year tenure as chief minister during which he was content to let the police take the lead. When the Congress party won the state elections in 2018 and Bhupesh Baghel took over as the third chief minister, there was a glimmer of hope once again. During his campaign through 2018, Baghel, who was also the state party president, had committed that a policy would be prepared to solve the Naxal problem and that serious efforts would be made to initiate talks.

Perhaps that was why, in May 2022, the Maoists issued a statement saying that they were ready for talks. They had only two conditions: the release of their leaders from jail and withdrawal of security forces from conflict areas. Baghel's response to this overture was: 'Peace talks with Naxals can take place only if they express faith in the Constitution.' Expanding on this theme, he told journalists in an interaction that the Naxals have been pushed back and their influence has declined. 'If they want to talk, our doors are always open, but only on one condition—that they express faith in the constitution. If they do not believe in the Indian Constitution, I cannot talk to them,' he said.[26]

Like his predecessors, it seems Baghel was also being led by the police. Perhaps that also explains why he could not make time for Sundar, as mentioned earlier. It was clear that a pre-condition that Naxals profess faith in the Indian Constitution was not going to create any possibility of talks.

India has a long history of talking with disaffected people without any pre-conditions. But the rigidity in this instance gives credence to the perception that the government is interested in peace only on its terms. But as journalist and author Ashutosh Bharadwaj points out, this is a fallacious position. 'The governments, both the centre and the state, seem to believe that they can bring [about] peace only by security operations,' he says. 'This misplaced understanding of the conflict zone has prolonged the crisis. The government should immediately make an unconditional offer of negotiation to the Naxals. The Naxals may or may not want it, but it's the duty of the state to take all possible steps to bring a quick end to the conflict, with civil society leaders as the mediators.'[27]

Attack on Civil Society

In 2003, when the Ajit Jogi-led Chhattisgarh government was conceptualizing a rural health programme called Mitanin, it urged Dr Binayak Sen, a paediatrician who had been working among the state's tribals, to help structure it. Dr Sen had won several international awards for his work at the grassroots level. However, by 2007, the Raman Singh-led government deemed him a Maoist sympathizer and arrested him on charges of sedition.[28]

Flimsy evidence, such as Left literature and some correspondence with Maoists in his possession, was used by the district level trial court to pronounce a life sentence. The Chhattisgarh High Court upheld the sentence.[29] He finally got bail from the Supreme Court of India in 2011, even as his case continues to drag on in the high court. Thereafter, the union government invited him in a consultative capacity for the Twelfth Five Year Plan (2012–17).

In an interview to *FORCE* after his release, he spoke of the distrust between the state and civil society. He said, 'Similar processes of economic polarisation are recorded for the world economy as a whole as well as for specific national economies, including China and Russia. Given this situation, it is, of course, incumbent on all those who love peace and justice to do everything they can to "bridge this gap" and bring about a dialogue. Ultimately, it is only through dialogue that a solution is possible. Confrontation, including military confrontation, is simply incapable of yielding any acceptable solution. If enough people come to share this understanding and take up this cause as their own, then surely this "space" can be created.'

As for the future of peace in Chhattisgarh, he said, 'I am already involved in working with the People's Union for Civil Liberties, and the Right to Food and Right to Healthcare campaigns. I am also involved in working for peace. I plan to continue these engagements as far as I can.'[30]

Another person who was punished by the state for working to create this space is Sudha Bharadwaj. A practicing lawyer in Chhattisgarh High Court who frequently defended tribal people, Bharadwaj was also a trade unionist with the biggest trade union of Chhattisgarh, Chhattisgarh Mukti Morcha. Even though her work did not attract the ire of the Chhattisgarh government, she was arrested in 2018 under the Unlawful Activities Prevention Act in the Bhima Koregaon case of Maharashtra along with several academics, activists, and journalists. The charges against them ranged from plotting a caste war to planning the assassination of Prime Minister Narendra Modi.[31] However, the assassination conspiracy was dropped in the draft charges filed by NIA.[32] While the case continues, she was granted bail by a NIA Court in 2021 with serious bail conditions imposed by the court. Consequently, Bharadwaj now lives in Mumbai.

Sen and Bharadwaj could have been effective in mediating peace with the Maoists in Bastar provided the government didn't regard them as enemies.

The Many Faces of Peacemakers

'Peacemaking is a dynamic concept,' says Bharadwaj. 'Anyone who operates as an interlocutor in a conflict zone, or attempts to transcribe or report on the conflict, or makes the outside world aware about the conflict, or those who fight for the rights of the victims of the conflict, can be termed peacemakers. All of them may work in different fields with varying objectives, but they share a common objective to bring peace to the zone. Thus, journalists who report from Bastar and uncover various aspects of violence and the tragedy, activists and lawyers who undertake arduous struggles to ensure rights to the Adivasis are all peacemakers.'[33]

Bela Bhatia, a social activist and well-known lawyer fighting for tribal rights in Bastar, concurs. She says, 'In the special context of Bastar, peacemaking cannot have a limited and conventional definition. Fighting for justice for tribals is also a peace effort because without justice no peace can be established. And justice is not possible without respect for rights and freedoms that are available to us as citizens of India and as humans. Only when we consider all these together would we be able to address the diverse but interconnected set of problems that prevail in an area that has been a conflict zone for a long time.'[34]

Bela has been legally defending innocent tribals against charges of being Maoist. She also helps them get justice in cases of human rights violations by security forces. 'Bastar has become a battlefield where death has become old news,' she says. 'No one really cares except those who are suffering from violence.

In every war zone there is blood money to be made, and Bastar is no exception,' she says referring to the funds the region gets ostensibly for fighting Naxalism as well as for development work which gets siphoned off at various levels. 'These vested interests do not want peace.'

According to her, 'The Indian government should invite the Maoists for a political dialogue without laying any conditions. Declaration of a ceasefire would be the first step towards peace. Desire for peace has been expressed from time to time by government officials as well as members of civil society but no sustained and credible effort has been made so far from all sides.'

Recounting the Agnivesh initiative, she says, 'A few years ago, Swami Agnivesh had tried mediation, but that effort came to a grinding halt after the [killing] of Azad. If such underhand games are played while talking of peace how can trust be built? First and foremost, a sincerity of purpose by the government is required. But even as we are thinking about the way towards peace, the government is infringing upon the constitutional rights of Adivasis and an insurgent is being born. In such a situation how can peace be achieved?'

Despite her disillusionment, Bhatia is committed to the idea of pursuing peace. According to her, public servants with impeccable reputations and credible persons from civil society could form a committee to facilitate the negotiation between the government and the Maoists. However, senior leader of CPI(M) in Chhattisgarh, Sanjay Parate is disillusioned with the intervention of social activists and writers on the Naxal issue. He says, 'People like Arundhati Roy, Swami Agnivesh, and Mahashweta Devi have frequently intervened on the Naxal issue. This gave the Naxals a certain revolutionary romantic aura. Yet, these intellectuals often remain silent over the violence perpetrated by the Naxals. Even when they speak, they try very hard to justify the reasons behind the violence.'

Parate believes in the empowerment capacity of the Constitution through such Acts as PESA, Forest Act of India, as well as the Fifth Schedule which grants privileges and rights to the people. 'In reality, none of these are being enforced in the right spirit. The tribals are rotting in prisons or dying outside, but the governor of the state does not even alert the union government,' he rues. Once again, the idea of vested interests crops up. 'In this state thousands of crores are being spent in the name of handling Naxal violence. Who would like to kill the goose that lays the golden eggs?' he asks.

But not everyone is as pessimistic as Parate. Shubhranshu Choudhary, who works on a peace journalism project in central India and is also the convener of the New Peace Process—a loose group of individuals and organizations trying to break the silence on ongoing violence—believes that a window of opportunity still exists for a peaceful resolution of the Naxal problem.

'The security forces have done their work over the last several years and the Maoists have been weakened. Now it's time for a clean closure by accepting some of their pro-Adivasi demands,' he says. 'We in the New Peace Process are trying to push both sides to come to the table. The Maoist leadership is old. They haven't been able to create a second rung of political leadership among the Adivasis who are 99 per cent of the fighters now. Soon there won't be anyone left to talk, and a gang war will be more difficult to handle. There hasn't been a better time to solve this problem than the present moment. And there won't be one after a few years,' he says.

Choudhary says that India needs to learn from examples like Colombia and Nepal where Maoists gradually became part of the mainstream. And then there is a contrary viewpoint. Freelance journalist and author Alok Prakash Putul insists that, 'There is minimum possibility of a peace process. Maoists want to seize power, nothing short of this would be acceptable to them. They have been fighting for the last fifty years and they are still ready to fight a long battle. When they are weakened, they retreat. When they recoup their strength, they attack. This is a common tactic in guerrilla warfare all over the world.'

Putul says that the practical way forward would be to acknowledge the reasons for which Maoist ideology finds ground in certain areas and work towards removing those. No movement can sustain itself without ground support.

Many people, many voices. But the truism remains as Bela Bhatia says, 'Peace is possible if you want it.' The question is: do the tribals, Maoists, government, and civil society all want the same peace?

8

INSIDERS AND OUTSIDERS IN ASSAM
THE ANT OF ROWMARI

Teresa Rehman

Gasps rose from the constables and home guards at the Sidli thana in Assam's Chirang district as a Bolero car screeched to a halt inside the thana premises. Driver Ulupi Biswas stepped out of the car, and everyone gawked at the diminutive woman. She had brought members of her organization, the ant[1] (The Action Northeast Trust) for police training on gender laws. She looked like an ant, literally.

A senior policeman came out and gaped incredulously. 'She's so tiny. I don't believe that she drove the car,' he exclaimed. Grinning, Ulupi took out the car keys, started the car, and drove it around the thana compound again. The cops applauded. 'It felt very good,' Ulupi puffs up with pride. She is arguably the first professional female driver in the entire area.

Her journey as a driver started when her photographer husband died unexpectedly of cancer, leaving her to fend for herself and her son. She heard about the ant, made enquiries, and finally joined the organization in 2016 at the age of thirty-three. The story of the ant is set in a nondescript village called Rowmari in Bijni sub-division of Chirang, an administrative district in the Bodoland Territorial Region (BTR) in western Assam. This geographical patch of land on the edge of the

Indo-Bhutan border has witnessed several decades of insurgency and repeated rounds of ethnic conflict in 1996, 1998, and 2012 among different communities. In an area recuperating from conflict, the ant has been working persistently for peace and development in over 900 villages in the areas of education, child protection, women's empowerment through weaving, peace building, countering domestic violence, preserving traditional art and music, legal aid, and mental health.[2]

Sunil Kaul, founder member of the ant explains, 'In complex political emergencies like insurgency, violence gets normalized and often people get accultured to it. One can dare say that this tendency is higher in some tribal societies where defending by violence was acceptable against the "other" and treating wives as property too was acceptable until recently. Hence, the ant works with children to reduce the "other-ization" through an inclusive sport like Rainbow (Ultimate) Frisbee and gender sensitization at young ages.'

'It also identifies domestic violence as being at the root of building and perpetuating the culture of violence in societies, because the most socio-emotional learning of a human being happens within the first 1,000 days of life starting when the child is still in the womb (the 1,000 days end at two years of age when the child is still listening and not talking much!). The domestic violence projects work with village level groups of men, women, and youth who are conscientized to accept that domestic violence is not a domestic but a social issue and hence a response to it must happen at the village level itself, not waiting for the police etc. to intervene.'

A tiny rectangular signboard at the entrance of this 'anthill' gently reminds everyone: 'Peace Zone. No Arms Please'. The chirping of birds and the synchronized sound of the handlooms fills the air as one enters the serene precincts of the ant campus.

Ants of all hues scurry around and are involved in a hub of diverse activities with co-founder Jennifer Liang, popularly known as Jenny baideo, as the fulcrum. Candid and resourceful, Jennifer holds the organization together. She introduced local village women to new ideas. In 2016, it so happened that Ulupi heard Jennifer talking about hiring a female driver.

There were no takers. The idea stirred Ulupi. She turned to her mother-in-law, who cheered her on, 'If it makes you feel good, do it by all means.' She decided to take the plunge. She left her ten-year-old son with her mother-in-law and set off for Jaipur in Rajasthan to join Azad Foundation's 'Women with Wheels' programme that trains resource-poor women to become self-sustaining professional drivers.[3]

The training refashioned her life as she did many things for the first time—venturing out of home, travelling by train, taking a rigorous six-month course in driving, learning traffic rules, spoken English and even self-defence. Initially, she did not understand the Hindi accent of the instructors and was at a loss. On her return, she had to make a tough transition—from driving on Rajasthan's roads in a small car to the kuccha village roads in Rowmari in a big car.

In the beginning, the ant ran on bicycles. 'We never had a vehicle. But once we had it, we wanted to have female drivers. Ulupi is just 4 feet 10 inches tall. She volunteered to go for the training though she did not even ride a cycle before. When she sat in the Bolero for the first time, we had to give her two pillows to sit on as her legs would not reach the brakes and the accelerator,' recalls Jennifer.

Ulupi faced initial hitches when neighbours, including her brother-in-law, smirked at her. But her mother-in-law stood by her. After her son left for Navodaya Vidyalaya, a government residential school, she started living on the ant campus. She goes home on weekends, dividing her time between her mother and mother-in-law's house. Interestingly, she can drive for long hours and not feel sleepy. Whenever she feels tired, she takes a short walk, drinks water, and eats candies or chocolates to keep herself awake. She has never been teased or chased as often happens with female drivers. Astonished men ogle and laugh at her while women approach her to teach them driving. 'I feel good that I can inspire someone,' she smiles.

Small ant, Big Impact

The ant is both a visual and symbolic leitmotif in this anthill of hope where a few women and men have been working for the holistic development of communities around them. Jennifer Liang is a ubiquitous presence at the two-decade-old organization and like the resilient ant, believes that she is not too small to do anything. She and her husband Dr Sunil Kaul founded the ant in 2000. The ant is now a high-calibre and diverse team with six trustees having years of experience in the professional development sector. They have more than twenty postgraduates and professionals as full-time staff, 58 per cent tribals, 24 per cent minorities, and 42 per cent women as part of the young team. The name 'the ant' was also a spur of the moment decision.

While writing the trust deed in October 2000, Sunil thought of the name and Jennifer agreed immediately—in lower case. 'We prefer lower case to go against the grain of proper nouns in capital letters as they are about building a personality, ego, etc.,' explains Sunil. 'This lowercase insistence is one of the ways to remind ourselves to remain small like the ant—it may lift fifty times its weight, it may make up 25 per cent of the weight of all animals in the world, it may be more enduring than the big animals around it, but it goes about its work at the bottom of the pyramid, cleaning up the muck others create and does well with just that. I insist on writing the ant in lower case,' he says. The logo was designed by a communication designer from the National Institute of Design who stayed with the team for a few months. In return for learning how to weave, he made the present catchy logo with a thumb print as a base.

With a mission to work for the sustainable development of the rural and voiceless communities, the ant was carefully steered by Jennifer and Sunil with support from a noted Gandhian of the Sarvodaya movement, the late Ravindranath Upadhyay. A third-generation Indian Chinese from Kolkata, Jennifer has always been an action-oriented person with interest in adventure sports, trekking, and mountaineering. Her family moved to Bangalore in the early 1980s where her father started a noodle factory. Her training at the Tata Institute of Social Sciences (TISS), Mumbai, where she studied social work, inspired her to work in remote and inaccessible areas. After her graduation, Jennifer met Sanjoy Ghose, a rural development activist and founder of AVARD-NE at a conference. Sanjoy invited her to join his team as they were moving to Majuli in Assam. Thus began her sojourn in Assam in 1996. She met Sunil here who was part of the team. Sanjoy Ghose was abducted and later killed allegedly by the United Liberation Front of Assam (ULFA).[4] After the initial recoil, she and her husband wanted to come back to northeast India. 'Inside us, we felt that we needed to come back as we have some unfinished things to do. Whatever happened to Sanjoy was not right and we can't give in to violence like that,' she says.

Jennifer also felt more at home in this region. She would always stick out like a sore thumb whenever she went to work in villages in North India. 'I looked like a foreigner. Here, I felt I might blend in. In fact, when I reached Guwahati railway station, bus drivers started talking to me in Mizo and Meitei. It was comforting,' she says. Sunil had a northeast connection as well—he spent his childhood in Manipur as his father worked in All India Radio, Imphal. In fact, Sunil's first job as an army doctor entailed giving medical cover to the infantry and engineers regiments who were building a road in Tawang, Arunachal Pradesh.

Sipping her tea, Jennifer talks about the 'fear factor' in a matter-of-fact way. They knew what they were getting into. They were aware of the hazards though they tried to downplay it to their family. 'We even signed a declaration to each other that if something happens to either of us, we did not want others to negotiate,' she explains.

They decided to come back and work in lower Assam. There were no big towns, villages were impoverished, and the Bodo movement was at its peak. There was an all-pervasive fear. Most importantly, there was no presence of civil society. 'People had never heard of NGOs. We felt we would be starting from scratch,' recalls Jennifer. 'We wanted to move much deeper inside close to the Indo-Bhutan border. There was no connection, no roads. The train route was the only connectivity.' A TISS alumnus whose father was a farmer in a village near Rowmari helped them connect to resources on the ground. They moved to Rowmari and started working in multiple sectors.

Women on Motorcycles

Jennifer believes that challenging gender norms is vital within an organization. She has been inspiring village women to do audacious things like ride a motorcycle, drive a car, and even run the accounts department. Apart from setting up a bicycle bank, organizing cycle rallies, workshops to ride bicycles, and all-women kabbadi and frisbee tournaments, Jennifer places great importance on riding the motorcycle. The motorcycle denotes a masculine power and privilege. There are few women on motorcycles, even in cities.

'Any other vehicle is unstable on these roads. We had to get motorcycles and get women to ride them,' she says. 'Unless women are mobile, they cannot rise in leadership and manage a big team. In civil society organizations, we often find women in the lower rungs as very good field workers and mobilizers—wherever their feet or their bicycle takes them. However, the responsibility of team leader and middle and upper management is often taken over by the men. This is because women are less mobile,' she adds. Jennifer set an example by riding a motorcycle on the bad village roads and even pushing across streams with her three-year-old daughter perched on the tank. 'My daughter would wonder why people were staring at us. I used to tell her that they have probably never seen a woman riding before,' she adds. Her daughter had her initial education in a Bodo-medium school. She is proficient in the Bodo language and is connected to the people around her.

As I am chatting with Jennifer, a woman roars in on her motorcycle. She is thirty-five-year-old Hasina Khatun. Jennifer pats her back and says, 'Hasina came to us as an enthusiastic young child. She was just a student of class nine when she joined our children's group.' Hasina is upbeat as she narrates her stint in the children's group. The children's group initiated after-school learning sessions, ultimate Frisbee, and sports for development sessions.[5] 'We had weekly meetings, made greeting cards with natural colours made from vegetables and fruits, and sold them in the villages. We also earned some money,' she recalls.

Hasina, a dewy-eyed young girl who only knew the way

to her school and the village market made an unusual choice. Tied to a conservative family setting where girls were married off early, Hasina was keen to move away from her hardscrabble life. What has made a tiny legend of this happy-go-lucky young woman is her honesty to herself. It so happened that her sister-in-law was a health worker who was trained by the ant and Hasina used to accompany her as a baby-sitter. Hasina used to watch the ant team moving around in bicycles in the midst of her frugal existence. After her class ten exams, she convinced her family to let her join the ant as a field worker. At the age of nineteen, she was the first girl from her community to venture out like this—travelling to different villages with the team, forming self-help groups (SHG), giving lectures, and conducting training. Hasina did not pay heed to what people gossiped about her. 'I loved meeting people and learning new things. I got energy from my work. As I work on issues of domestic violence, I was accused of spoiling these women. I taught them the laws and urged them to speak for their rights,' she says.

The team at ant pushed Hasina from walking to cycling to riding the motorcycle. They encouraged her to chart her own journey. Jennifer introduced her to the motorcycle. She would ride and make Hasina sit behind her. Then she asked Hasina to ride the motorcycle in and around the office. One day, she rode pillion and made Hasina ride on a bad village road. Hasina managed to ride, and there was a collective whoop of joy among her colleagues. Now, she and her motorcycle are inseparable. Hasina is a popular field worker as she knows a smattering of the local languages—Bodo, Bengali, and Nepali. She holds Jennifer and Sunil in high esteem. 'Both could have led comfortable lives in the city. But they chose to live and work with the poorest of the poor. I want to be like them,' says this plucky young woman.

Hasina's life has been quite eventful since she joined ant. She recalls an incident during the 2012 conflict between the Bodos and Bengali Muslims. She was newly married and had gone for a training session that had ended at around 10 p.m. 'I called my husband and a cousin and was cycling home with them. It was a stretch of three to four kilometres. I had to cross a Bodo village. The road was full of villagers with machetes. They stopped me. When I shouted that I am Hasina, they recognized me and urged me to hurry up. I reached home safe,' she narrates. Clad in a salwar kameez, she carefully ties her daughter Sarjina to herself while riding the motorcycle with a cloth gifted by Jennifer. She has big dreams for her daughter. She wants her to be brave, educated, and work for the betterment of society.

In order to make riding motorcycles easier for women, the ant had even got fashion designers to design clothes that looked like traditional attire but were actually adapted. 'It's very difficult to get women in a dokhona, sari, or mekhela sador to ride a motorcycle. We had to do until the communities accept whatever attire they wear,' Jennifer explains. She points out to another 'woman on a motorcycle'—Noni Bhagat. Noni is a thirty-four-year-old Adivasi woman from a neighbouring village. She started working with the ant since July 2009 when she was a student of class twelve. She had enrolled for a college degree but dropped out. She thought she would complete her graduation and get a coveted government job. She also aspired to join the army, but failed to clear the test.

Noni's farmer father was left in the lurch after the River Ai eroded their land. She was the third of nine siblings. Her father started working as a daily wage labourer while her mother sold local vegetables to make ends meet. She joined the ant as a village organizer at the age of twenty-one. She started liking her work on different projects for children, youth, and adolescent girls. This shy and reticent girl realized that she enjoyed travelling and meeting people. The major breakthrough came when she started riding a motorcycle. She used to accompany a member of staff on his motorcycle for field visits. She used to observe him while he rode the motorcycle. Once, after an event, she had to take some items from the venue to the office. She told him, 'Give me the keys. I will ride the motorcycle.' He refused but Noni was adamant. She argued, 'If you do not give me the keys, I will throw the motorcycle in the drain.' The staff member told everyone in jest, 'I am giving her the keys, but nobody should teach her.' To everyone's astonishment, Noni started the bike, drove straight to the office, and stopped it. She did not change gears. She did nothing. She just switched on and stopped the bike on reaching the office.

She chuckled as she narrates her funny 'motorcycle incidents'. She prefers wearing pants and a shirt when she is riding the motorcycle. Once, a man stopped her and asked for a ride. When she lifted her helmet's visor, he yelled, 'Oh God, it's a girl.' Noni offered him a ride, but the man refused outright! Noni narrates another amusing incident when a prospective groom came to see her.

'My father called me and said that there were some guests waiting for me. I rushed home in my usual attire. The groom's family was shocked to see me alighting from the motorcycle. They felt that I would be a dangerous girl. They left in a huff,' she laughs. She narrates an encounter with security personnel on the eve of Republic Day. It was dark and she was coming back alone from a training session. The army was patrolling and frisking people at several checkpoints. A group of army personnel stopped her and asked for her identity card. They asked her to open her helmet and flashed the torchlight on her face. They exclaimed, 'Oh, it's a girl. Where did you go at this hour?' She told them about the ant, and they let her go.

'We are treated with respect by the authorities, traffic police, and the government officials. They know we stand for the truth,' she asserts.

Conflict to Cooperation

Social divide creates unpredictable tensions and quiet, unseen tragedies lie in the layers of every conversation. Conflict finds its way into the lives of all people. But the touch of the ant has always been gentle and nurturing. It has been a cocoon for women from different communities who engage with each other and work together in harmony.

'There are many things that I cannot share with my own family, but I can open up with the ant family,' says Noni. In the 2012 Bodo–Muslim conflict, they went to do relief work on behalf of their organization. Noni and Hasina took boxes of medicine to the Muslim community in their relief camps. 'I did not feel unsafe. We just went to help people. Nobody questioned my presence,' says Noni. In December 2012, she was in a Bodo village. 'I was not scared as our staff was there. I did not face any problem. Working for the community makes me feel good. It's both easy and tough,' she says. The shy Noni has now metamorphosed into a poised and articulate woman.

Guilt, rage, hatred, suspicion, brutalization of survivors—Jennifer reminds us that the legacy of violence is more dangerous than violence itself. For the first few years, the ant kept the number of members at the bare minimum while its work kept growing. In fact, the team was obsessed with sustainability. They started a project and quickly tried to make it sustainable and make it run on its own.

'We were obsessed with the idea that if something happens to us, it should not fail. We did not know what would happen to us tomorrow. We told ourselves that we would take one day at a time. We were so obsessed, our team had to tell us off,' she says. They instilled strong ethics in the team. Financially, they wanted to be above board. Being in a conflict-torn place, they had to face monetary demands and threats from various militant groups, but they managed to negotiate and steer away from trouble. They got by with Hindi and a smattering of Assamese and Bodo to work with the communities around them. They also carefully stayed away from media coverage for the first few years. They knew that they needed time and patience to win the trust of the people.

There was a logic at play when Jennifer and Sunil decided to hand over the accounts department to women. They felt that a woman will understand their needs and the system. They managed to form an all-women finance and accounts team led by thirty-nine-year-old Bhaswati Roy Choudhury, a qualified company secretary. This overturned the stereotype that women cannot handle finances. Bhaswati lives in Bongaigaon and travels regularly to her office in Chirang. She is happy to lead a six-women finance team—cashier, accounts assistant, and an accountant. Bhaswati is comfortable with numbers. Everyone in her team is a commerce graduate and has knowledge of accounts. 'I handle the finances. I like the corruption-free environment here. Often NGOs are accused of misappropriation of funds. I have adapted well in the age of plastic money and online transactions,' she explains.

Over the years, the ant has become more about explorations, discoveries, shared journeys, and a collective search for alternatives. Jennifer, however, has one regret. She feels that they should have focused more on building people-led community institutions instead of being project-oriented. Now, the couple feels that they should transition out of leadership. As founder members, they did not want to hang on. 'It is not our organization. It is a public institution that we built with public money. Even if our daughter takes a sheet of chart paper from the office, she has to pay for it. There are no privileges.' The couple tried some experiments to transition from 2016 onwards. Now, they have both stepped down and are playing a much more supportive role to create a more resilient team.

It was an emotionally difficult decision, but they left the campus and moved to Guwahati. 'Sunil still remains on the board. If both of us are on the board, there is an over concentration of power,' explains Jennifer. Sunil has always been a full-time volunteer. He never took money for his work at the ant. Jennifer used to get a stipend and that's how they managed. She is sometimes invited to attend board meetings. 'I don't have any voting rights. We keep governance and personal life separate. We want them to grow on their own. I think the message is very clear to our team,' she says.

The ant is seen as impartial and inclusive. They work with many communities though some communities are more receptive. Within the organization, Jennifer finds the presence of forty-four-year-old Damayanti Brahma very comforting. Damayanti speaks in a slow halting voice. Every now and then, she stops and asks, 'Can you understand my bhanga-singa (broken) Assamese?' She has a strong Bodo accent as well. As a field facilitator for the ant, Damayanti has seen more of the world than many of her contemporaries. This is also because she is different. She is keen to absorb new things. As a child, she had a multi-cultural upbringing as her village had a mixed population of Bodos and Bengali Muslims. Her childhood home was in an idyllic village in Assam's Kokrajhar district. She and her friend Morjina used to roll up clothes, tie them with thread, and create their own dolls. Her friend Mariam would cook in their self-made tiny kitchen with old, unused utensils. They used to walk to the school together and visit the weekly markets to buy fancy trinkets and cosmetics.

Education was a slow process for her as she had to dropout for a number of years because of the agitation and conflict in Bodoland. By the time she was in class ten, she was already eighteen and married off. Her husband had to take care of his joint family and so Damayanti started working with the ant as the secretary of a self-help group in 2011. 'We needed some extra income. I had joined as a field facilitator,' she says. When her husband suddenly died twelve years after marriage, leaving her with two young kids in 2012, she found succour in the ant. She is happiest when she is on the field, working with villagers. She works on various issues like organizing self-help groups for women, counselling on domestic violence, and holding meetings with the elders and members of the Bengali Muslim community.

Working with a different community in a rural area has its challenges. Damayanti built rapport with them by conducting home visits and trainings. In order to win their trust, she also helps them in other sundry tasks like their children's school admissions, filling up of forms, and writing petitions. 'Initially, they were suspicious of my intentions. They would not attend meetings if their community leaders stopped them. I have now forged ties with their leaders, panchayat members, political activists, and self-help groups. I have developed a good rapport with them,' she says.

Her phone number is like a local helpline for survivors of domestic violence. They trust her with their problems as going to the police may cost them money and undue harassment. Damayanti understands that family matters are delicate and calls for a measured response. She cannot afford to be impulsive when dealing with such issues. Reconciling the couple is her first priority. She uses multiple ways to approach the problem and solve it amicably. Domestic violence against women is an accepted phenomenon in most societies. A survey by the ant revealed that 24 per cent women get beaten daily, 38 per cent once in two weeks, and 56 per cent reported physical violence from their husbands. These shocking figures laid the foundation for the ant's Project Avahan (Against Violence at Home-Act Now) in May 2017 that sought to reduce the incidence of domestic violence through legal services, emotional and counselling support, and secured shelter and livelihood support to survivors.

'I am a simple person. But I am important for some people. People seek my help and I try my best to help them. When I die, I want to be remembered as a lady who worked for the people,' Damayanti says, pointing to her grey hair. Her steadfast friend is Sahiba who helps her in making posters for campaigns and rallies as well as writing songs. Sometimes, she even handles the cash book and takes down minutes of the meetings. They share their joys and sorrows and family problems with each other. Another close aide is Hasina, now considered an old-timer in the ant.

'Hasina is a don. She is brave, rides the motorcycle, and can handle tough situations,' smiles Damayanti. During the 2012 riots, she had faced several problems. Her friends from the other end called to tell her that there were rumours that their houses would be burnt. She tried her best to reassure them and asked them to stay indoors. She kept the communication open. She told them that the damage was mutual, and they have to coexist as human beings. Any kind of conflict requires immediate relief. She had devised an innovative way to get relief materials to those affected. She tied all the materials together and walked half the distance and they walked half the distance to collect it from her.

Riding a bicycle in a dokhona, Damayanti is now a popular figure. Some call her didi, some call her baideo. 'They are curious about my dokhona. Sometimes, I have to open it and show how it's worn,' she giggles. Festivals are also occasions to build and renew ties. She visits the Muslim communities on Eid. She eats sweets, sewiyan, and pulao with them. Strangely enough, Damayanti faces ostracism in her own village for her work. She is not allowed to enter the big temple in her village. Some households, even her relatives, do not allow her to enter their kitchen because she has been working with the Adivasi and Muslim communities who have different food habits. Damayanti is unruffled and tries to reason with them. She explains that her religion is not about rituals. 'My religion is humanity. I pray at home. I have a small temple at home. I will not leave my job. Instead, I will try to change the mindset of the people,' she says calmly. She is a much-travelled woman now. Thanks to her training, staff annual meetings, and exposure trips, she's been to Delhi, Kolkata, Kaziranga, Mumbai, Lucknow, Darjeeling, Shillong, Jorhat, and cities in Odisha and Sikkim. She feels that she can think differently because the ant has opened her mind. 'Otherwise, I would have been held captive by my own walls and my thoughts. Now, I meet a lot of people and learn and see new things from them,' she smiles.

Jennifer calls the ant 'a work in progress'. She feels that there is a need for a lot more ants across Assam and the Northeast. They want people with the same spirit, passion, honesty, and also with a certain amount of competency. In a bid to strengthen, incubate, and provide mentoring support to fledging and committed NGOs, they started the Institute of Development Action (IDeA). They shifted their focus to help incubate small organizations with limited funding support—looking for technical assistance, serving a remote location or a marginalized group, or having an innovative concept—with a small grant which ranges between a period of three to five years.

'We wanted something in the spirit of smallness and humility, but knowing that ants can do things that defy their size, work in groups, take up challenges that are beyond their size and weight. There is a grudging respect from our detractors who feel that we can't do anything financially or morally wrong. That is important for us,' says Jennifer.

A true humanist, Jennifer writes 'humanity' in the religion column whenever she is asked to fill a form. She has been honoured with the first Niwano Peace Prize Visionary Award by Japan's Niwano Peace Foundation for her efforts to 'alleviate poverty through her conviction of non-violence, wisdom, and strength of action'.

With an indefatigable spirit, Jennifer has been able to create a tight net of loyalty, sisterhood, and love in an uncharted, unfamiliar, and volatile territory. She had to deal with situations where the trauma was embedded deep for many years. In prolonged conflicts, after a certain point, ethnicity stops making a difference. These life sketches draw out the tiny changes and deep interventions the ant has been able to make in these women's lives in the midst of physical violence, multiple levels of vulnerabilities, and the psychological debris of a post-conflict society. Knowing them, trusting them, and changing their lives forever, for the better.

9

JAMMU AND KASHMIR 2004–19
NO PEACE WITHOUT JUSTICE

Ghazala Wahab

She was fair, as Kashmiri women tend to be, but not beautiful in the popular sense. Maybe the harsh lines on her face, a consequence of difficult life experiences, had taken a toll. I knew I had seen her before. Maybe spoken with her too. But that late afternoon in Srinagar's now closed Coffea Arabica, I stared at her in frustration. I couldn't place her. She was engaged in animated conversation with another woman, speaking as much with her eyes and hands. There was a semblance of hijab, a casually worn dupatta over her head that added an old-fashioned allure to her appearance. *Where had I met her before?*

As I watched, she grinned at her interlocutor. It was no ordinary grin. Her mouth opened wide, revealing a set of perfect teeth. Her eyes lit up. One of her hands reached up to steady her dupatta. Suddenly she was beautiful. And I recognized her. She was one of the ground staffers with the now defunct Kingfisher Airlines at Srinagar airport. She had checked me in several times, dressed in a red pantsuit with a natty scarf at her neck, wearing ruby lipstick. Those days, I frequently flew Kingfisher in and out of Srinagar. At the relatively small airport with few flights, we had come to recognize each other's names and faces. Often at the check-in counter she would look at me and say, 'Oh, it's you again.'

At the airport she always looked beautiful. And glamorous. Because she was smiling all the time, I told myself, sitting at a distance from her in Coffea Arabica. She was dressed in a lightly embroidered pale-coloured salwar suit. Her lips were bare. But her smile was still dazzling. I had an uncontrollable urge to walk over to her table and say hello.

'Oh, it's you again,' she said, her smile receding.

I smiled as widely as I could. 'What a pleasant surprise to find you here.'

'Yes,' she said, with much less enthusiasm.

'May I sit with you two for some time,' I asked, as I pulled up a chair next to her companion.

The companion instinctively pushed her chair away with some alarm. 'Actually, we were just leaving.'

By this time, I had already seated myself. 'We never got a chance to chat before,' I said to both of them. 'I am a journalist, and I write a lot about Kashmir.'

The Kingfisher lady, let's call her Parveen, pretended to relax, but I could tell that she was caught between her job-trained patience and experience-induced anxiety.

'How are you?' she asked.

It was late spring in 2008. The days were pleasantly cold, and the evenings colder. The tulips were in full bloom. And the locals were out in the streets to soak in the sun after the immobilizing winter, referred to as chillai kalan in Kashmir. Chillai kalan, which means the season when nothing grows because of the frigidity of the soil, refers to an almost month-long period between December and January when the winter is at its most unforgiving. Kashmiris hunker down in their homes during this time, venturing out only when absolutely necessary.

'This is a lovely place,' I said, hoping to bring some warmth to the table where a chill had set in. 'I am so happy that Srinagar now has a place where one can casually meet people.'

'There are other places too,' said Parveen. 'But this is the best.' Her companion nodded in agreement.

'Sitting here feels like everything is normal in Kashmir,' I said. 'That there is no conflict.'

'Yes,' she replied.

Kashmir had been going through an exceptionally long period of near peace since 2004. Both the state and the central government were talking about resolution. The Line of Control (LoC) with Pakistan was calm. The streets were thronging with locals and tourists. Almost all airlines, state-owned and private, were operating at least one flight a day in and out of Srinagar's new airport, ambitiously called Srinagar International Airport on the basis of a solitary weekly flight to the Gulf and in the hope of more in the future. Entrepreneurs were scouring the length and breadth of the state, sniffing out investment opportunities.

Coffea Arabica was one such opportunity which enjoyed the early bird advantage. It was among the first few places where people with resources could hang out, instead of deferring such an outing to when they visited Chandigarh or Delhi. It helped that it served delicious non-Kashmiri food along with an array of hot and cold beverages, introducing the aspirational local youth to an international experience, which was also close to their emotional landscape. So, while it served a range of Middle Eastern fast food, such as shawarma and shish taouk, it also offered an assortment of comfort items like kathi rolls and grilled sandwiches. The wall art traced the origins of coffee—from Ethiopia to Yemen and to the rest of the world. The mostly Islamic history of coffee was both reassuring and gratifying.

'What does this normalcy mean to young people like her?' I wanted to know.

'This is a big step forward because it has opened up new

employment opportunities for people like us,' Parveen said. 'Absence of employment opportunities has been the biggest problem for educated youth in Kashmir. Since there is no industry here, the largest employer is the government. Everyone wants a government job because there is respect and stability in it. There are also other benefits. But everyone can't get a government job.'

By now her companion, let's call her Sameena, was at ease too. She added, 'Even though normalcy has not returned, militancy has come down. This has encouraged a lot of people to start their businesses here. Tourism is increasing. So, there are jobs for educated youth like us.'

The decrease in militancy and public violence, however, opened the space up for violence of another kind—moral vigilantism. A quasi-dormant religious proselytizing organization, Dukhtaran-e-Millat (daughters of faith, DeM), founded in 1987 by Asiya Andrabi, a graduate in biochemistry, had become powerful in the middle years of the decade of 2000.[1] The fully veiled women cadre of DeM started accosting young women in public places, forcing them to cover themselves up. In some instances, women who resisted were roughed up and their faces painted black. Some cybercafes complained of vandalism by over-excited DeM women.[2]

However, notwithstanding government action against Andrabi, fear of humiliation by the DeM cadre forced many women to restrict their movements and circumscribe their appearance. Like most conservative Muslim organizations, DeM also approved of only certain kinds of education and employment for women.[3] Working in private airlines with a job profile that required public interaction was certainly not among the approved careers for women.

Parveen rewarded me her full smile, suggesting it was a

question she liked. 'When militancy started, everyone suffered. Women suffered even more. So many mothers lost their sons, sisters lost their brothers, wives became widows, and so many women became half-widows. Their husbands disappeared. Nobody knows if they are alive or dead. These women couldn't marry again. They had no money. They had to work. But when they went out to work, people questioned their character. Women were also scared that something bad would happen to them, so they started wearing a veil so that nobody would recognize them in public.'

When militancy reduced, the fear reduced too. And opportunities opened up for people like Parveen who aspired to a career beyond the traditional options. 'I go to work in salwar-kameez with my head covered,' she said, instinctively reaching for her dupatta. 'Then I change into my uniform. It is important for me to do my job. But at the same time, I don't want anybody to harass me or abuse my family.'

Pursuing a career was not just a personal requirement for Parveen and her friend. It was also an act of subversion against everyone who was trying to define what Kashmir was, what it ought to be, and portraying Islam as a synonym for oppressed women.

'Over the last fifteen years, so many different narratives have been created about Kashmir. Even well-wishers of the Kashmiri people look at statistics about the number of dead and disappeared people. They don't realize that every dead or disappeared person leaves behind at least four to five women—mother, sisters, wife, daughters—whose lives are irrevocably changed,' Parveen said. She was not smiling, and the hard lines on her face seemed to have hardened even more; there was such emotion on her face that it was difficult to look at her. It was even more difficult to look away.

'When a woman goes out to work,' Sameena chipped in, 'she is not only pursuing a career, she is also showing other women that it is possible to step out of the house, no matter how difficult the situation is, and earn a livelihood...ensure that your parents can get good medical treatment and your children can get decent education which can help them break out of this cycle of violence.'

'And change the narrative about women in Kashmir?' I asked.

Parveen smiled. 'Maybe, but honestly, I don't think about that too much.'

'Of course, you have your own issues to take care of.'

'Narratives are built deliberately,' Sameena, who I learnt was a part-time teacher enrolled in a PhD programme in Kashmir University, said.

'The army has one narrative, the government has another narrative, the militants also have a narrative, the separatists also have a narrative,' she continued. 'These are narratives of their convenience. Where is the space for women's narrative here?'

'What is the Kashmiri women's narrative?' I asked.

'Women don't want conflict,' they said, almost in unison.

'But we cannot forget that there is a conflict,' Sameena said. 'That thousands of Kashmiri men have been killed, made to disappear. That Kashmiri women have been raped and forced into sex trade[4] by members of the security forces. And no one is punished. So, we don't want conflict. We want normalcy. But we also want justice.'

'Isn't injustice being meted out by the separatists? By organizations like DeM, which are forcing women to behave in a certain way?'

'There are many organizations in Kashmir,' said Sameena. 'Nobody knows if they are genuine or not, or if they are promoting the agenda of another organization. We don't know who gives them the money to do what they do.'

Interrupting her, Parveen added, 'DeM is not a violent organization. It just wants to impose an Islamic way of life. I think it is alright for now. Perhaps, once normalcy returns, DeM will become less consequential.'

None of us had any idea that afternoon, that in just a few weeks, DeM would be made irrelevant by an even deadlier force—the wrath of the youth who would soak the streets with their blood, starting a new spiral of violence not seen in Kashmir before. And that the hope of the spring would disappear like a wisp of smoke.

Small Window, Big Hope

In Kashmir, the words normalcy and normal means different things. Normalcy implies resolution of the political problem, which, depending on who one speaks with, could mean any of the following—azadi (freedom), merger with Pakistan, or conversion of the LoC into the international border. Normal means the absence of violence and its consequences—curfew or bandh—on a particular day or week. Basically, normal means that people can go about their everyday lives without interruption.

In the five years leading up to the spring of 2008, it seemed that normal would eventually slip into normalcy. Everyone was a peacemaker. The November 2003 ceasefire on the LoC and the beginning of the peace process between India and Pakistan had dangled the promise of a resolution and lasting peace—in Kashmirspeak, normalcy. Politicians from India, Pakistan, and Kashmir were engaged both officially and non-officially in conversations on three axes: India–Pakistan, India–Kashmir, and Kashmir–Pakistan.

Most importantly, this was a bipartisan initiative and there was continuity on the Indian side. The call for peace was given by Prime Minister Atal Bihari Vajpayee, who headed the Bharatiya Janata Party (BJP)-led National Democratic Alliance (NDA) government, during his visit to Kashmir in 2003. Pakistan President Pervez Musharraf had responded by announcing a ceasefire on the LoC in November 2003. When the Congress-led United Progressive Alliance (UPA) government came to power with Manmohan Singh as prime minister in 2004, the peace process was taken forward. While publicly, Prime Minister Singh was personally engaged in conversation with an array of Kashmiri stakeholders, away from the media glare, his representative, diplomat Satinder Kumar Lambah, was holding backchannel discussions with his counterpart Tariq Aziz.[5]

This discussion was based on an old formula first propounded by the US-based think tank, Kashmir Study Group (KSG), founded by a Kashmiri businessman M. Farooq Kathwari.[6] This formula envisaged creating regional councils in all the five regions of Kashmir—Jammu, the Valley, and Ladakh in India; Pakistan-occupied Kashmir and Gilgit-Baltistan in Pakistan. The councils were to govern themselves and coordinate with each other as well as with India and Pakistan on larger issues. In this way, the borders would become irrelevant over a period of time. Gradually, it implied porous borders in Kashmir with freedom of movement for Kashmiris; 'self-governance' within each region of Kashmir; phased demilitarization of all regions; and, finally, a 'joint supervisory mechanism', with representatives from India, Pakistan, and all parts of Kashmir, to oversee the plan's implementation.

Select Kashmiris were in the know of these discussions, even though the peace and resolution talks were not in the public realm. In an interview to me in 2005, then chairperson of the All

Parties Hurriyat Conference (a conglomerate of non-mainstream Kashmiri separatist organizations), Mirwaiz Umar Farooq, said, 'We feel that a solution will come out of this process. We are open to everything, except two things that are not acceptable to us at all: conversion of the ceasefire line into a permanent border and the current status quo. We are ready to consider some kind of a federal system where all the five regions of Kashmir form a super or a supra-council. All these things can be worked out, provided we sit down to talk sincerely.'[7]

Meanwhile, to create a conducive environment within the Valley, mainstream Kashmiri politicians, including Chief Minister Mufti Mohammed Sayeed who came to power in 2002 in an alliance with the Congress party, presented the Government of India with three confidence-building measures: release of Kashmiris arrested under the draconian Public Safety Act (PSA), revocation of the Armed Forces (Special Powers) Act (AFSPA), and withdrawal of troops from civilian areas. The Manmohan Singh government also appeared amenable to these ideas. Within months of assuming office, Singh visited Kashmir and announced the withdrawal of troops in November 2004.

Eventually, some troops did withdraw; but in reality, these were the troops that had been inducted in haste during the Kargil conflict of 1999. This feel-good measure was followed up with the commencement of the Srinagar–Muzaffarabad bus service (April 2005), opening of a few meeting points along the LoC for the reunion of divided families on either side, and the beginning of the Round Table Conferences (RTC) between Delhi and the Kashmiri people. After the second RTC on 25 May 2006, Prime Minister Singh announced the creation of five working groups.

The first working group was to focus on confidence-building measures within the state and also issues such as the rehabilitation of those affected by militant violence in the state. The second group was to work out mechanisms for strengthening trans-LoC relations by introducing trade as well as free movement of people. The third's focus was on economic development, creation of jobs for the youth (thereby trying to draw them into the mainstream), and restoring inter-regional economic balance within the state. The fourth group's responsibility was to draw up principles of good governance by making the state administration more responsive, accountable, and transparent. This was to be implemented at the state level with the central government's oversight. Some of the ways of doing this was to be through the Right to Information Act and Panchayati Raj Act. While the Right to Information Act was passed in 2004, the Panchayati Raj Act was passed in 2011. The fifth, and the most important working group, was to find ways to strengthen centre–state relations. It was to look into reversing the gradual dilution of the special status that J&K enjoyed within the Indian Constitution and see how best the aspirations of the people from the three regions of the state could be met. Basically it would explore the parameters for autonomy.

The prime minister also invited Kashmiris to give their suggestions to the fifth working group on lasting peace in the state. The all-pervasive optimism among the people in those years showed how drastically the daily situation would change if the Kashmir issue was resolved. The streets of Kashmir were filled with local people, convinced that a resolution and peace were round the corner. A semblance of nightlife also returned, as people remained on the streets after dusk—either just hanging around to enjoy the time of day or walking to visit friends or restaurants for dinner.

Even visitors like me felt confident about walking back a couple of kilometres to the hotel after dinner. On one such walk I had a mild scare when a pack of street dogs decided to accompany me. I was later advised by a local to be careful with the dogs. 'Everyday there is a case of dog bite in some part of Srinagar,' he said rather vehemently. 'And the government does nothing.'

After this conversation, I started noticing news reports about dog bites in the inside pages of the local newspapers. When people start complaining about the violence unleashed by canines rather than humans, you know that things are as normal as they could be in a place with unresolved political problems.

The year 2007 began with even more heightened hopes. Talking to local journalists in Srinagar in April 2007, Mirwaiz Umar Farooq said that India–Pakistan governments will announce the resolution by September 2007. He alluded to diplomats working on finalizing a visit by Manmohan Singh to Pakistan in late 2007, where the broad contours of the resolution were to be announced.[8]

And then, everything started to unravel just as quickly. A localized protest by lawyers in Pakistan, which started in March 2007,[9] grew in momentum and engulfed several cities and eventually destabilized Musharraf, who had to resign in early 2008. Singh's Pakistan visit was deferred for a better time, which never came. In Kashmir, the ineptitude of the first-time chief minister Ghulam Nabi Azad led to mass outpouring of anger in the summer of 2008, just a few weeks after my meeting with Parveen and Sameena.

On 26 May 2008, the Azad-led state government transferred 100 acres of land to the Shri Amarnath Shrine Board (SASB) which organizes the annual Amarnath pilgrimage in the Valley. In a state with a delicate religious balance, where the Muslim majority lives with the memories of oppression it suffered in the past at the hands of the Hindu minority, and the latter fears a complete erosion of their religious and cultural heritage, an action like this was bound to be viewed with suspicion. Azad failed to understand the need for sensitivity.

Consequently, articles started appearing in local newspapers about the ecological and environmental implications of the transfer of land. Until then, the media had not picked up the issue of demographical changes in the state. Hence, it was still possible to address the issue in a non-sectarian manner. As the state government issued neither clarifications nor engaged with the civil society to quell their concerns, Kashmiri analysts started wondering in the media if the transfer was permanent or for the duration of the pilgrimage. Once the principal secretary to Governor Lieutenant General S. K. Sinha (Retd) and the chief executive officer of the SASB Arun Kumar announced that the transfer was permanent in nature, the Valley-based media accused the state government of being complicit in effecting demographical change.

Not just the state bureaucracy, even the chief minister was slow to respond to the insecurity of the people. Protests erupted in the cities, which were sought to be quelled by force—first tepid and then brute. This had three long-term consequences.

One, all the anticipation of a resolution was washed away by the blood spilt on the streets. It was back to the people of Kashmir versus the state of India. This discredited those moderate separatist politicians, such as Mirwaiz Umar Farooq, who had openly identified with the peace process, ceding space to hardliners like Syed Ali Shah Geelani. By the end of the summer, forty-six civilians armed with stones had been killed in retaliatory firing by the security forces.[10]

In an interview to *FORCE*, president of the National Conference, Omar Abdullah, said, 'The illusion of this peace process with Pakistan being irreversible has been shattered... there has been a series of mistakes and misjudgements...in not keeping the moderate faction of Hurriyat engaged in dialogue....'[11]

Two, the protests against the transfer of land in the Valley were matched by protests in favour of it in the Jammu region of the state, bringing the delicate religious balance into sharp relief. Worse, supported by Hindu right-wing organizations, protestors in Jammu imposed a land blockade on National Highway 1A, the only road connecting Kashmir to the rest of India, preventing not only essential commodities from reaching the Valley but also stopping the truckers carrying harvested apples from the Valley into the plains of India.

According to a Srinagar-based senior police official, 'It is a misnomer that tourism is the biggest industry in Kashmir. It is horticulture. The entire economy of the Valley depends on its fruit produce. The harvest begins in August. Thousands of trucks have to come in from the plains to transport apples, pears, and walnuts back. The fruit-growers' anxiety was only natural. Most of them take heavy loans through the year for this crop. If they are not able to send their produce to the markets in the plains they would be ruined.'[12]

'Even in the worst days of militancy, nobody ever blockaded the Kashmir Valley,' said Abdullah. 'Though people were talking about severing the political link, there was this very strong economic link.'[13] Forced by the road closure, the separatists, under the umbrella of the Apple Growers Association, organized a 'Chalo Muzaffarabad' march which stopped short of Baramullah after army intervention.

The deep cleave between Jammu and Kashmir was widened by the discriminatory retaliatory action by the security forces, including the state police, on protestors in the Valley and in Jammu. In September 2008, a senior paramilitary officer told me, 'It was a mistake to allow the law and order situation to deteriorate so much in Jammu. Just because the arsonists are carrying the Indian flag does not mean that we allow them to destroy government property. This has sent the wrong message to the people in Kashmir who think that we were soft on the protestors in Jammu and harder on Kashmiris.'[14]

However, a counter view was offered by the inspector general of police in Kashmir, who said that while there has been a disproportionate use of force in certain instances in Kashmir, police reaction is often calibrated by the nature of the protest. 'If you are carrying a Pakistani flag and shouting anti-India slogans, a policeman is bound to react differently than when you are carrying an Indian flag and shouting anti-government slogans,' he said.[15] The consequence of this cleavage was seen in the 2014 state elections when Mufti's People's Democratic Party (PDP) got the maximum numbers of seats in Kashmir and BJP in Jammu.[16]

Three, both the people and the separatists found a new form of resistance—stone-throwing. For the next two years, each summer was swallowed by mass protests in the Valley with 2010 being the worst year in recent times in terms of civilian deaths. Mehbooba Mufti admitted to 101 killed in police firing[17], but the locals claim the figure was higher. However, even after 2010, Kashmiri people, including women and children frequently came out into the streets to vent their anger as a form of collective catharsis. The Valley has not been the same since. From striving for normalcy, the government was back to seeking as many normal days as possible.

The small window that promised a lot of hope was eventually sealed on 5 August 2019, when the Indian government revoked Articles 370 and 35(A), removing all doubts. Furthermore, the state was converted into two union territories of Jammu-Kashmir and Ladakh. The message was clear—Kashmir matters. Kashmiris don't.

The Conscience Keepers

The revocation of the Constitutional Acts of Article 370 and 35A that bestowed special status on the state of Jammu and Kashmir by way of notional autonomy was not only aimed at complete integration with the rest of the nation but also to recast the narrative about the Valley. Normal was redefined as normalcy. No matter what the ground situation was, the Government of India declared that normalcy was finally restored in the restive Kashmir Valley. Anyone who challenged this was deemed anti-national.[18]

On 31 December 2019, Khurram Parvez, chairperson of the Asian Federation Against Involuntary Disappearances (AFAD) and Programme Coordinator of Jammu Kashmir Coalition of Civil Society (JKCCS), released the *Annual Review of Human Rights Situation in Indian Administered Jammu and Kashmir*.[19] Since internet services had been suspended in the Kashmir Valley after the revocation, Parvez came to Jammu to release the report. He sent a copy to me as well.

While the report focussed on the entire year, chronicling the death of '80 civilians (including 12 women), 159 militants, and 129 armed forces' personnel, chapter four of the report was focussed entirely on the aftermath of the revocation of Article 370.

According to the report, 'While the government of India has refused to acknowledge any civilian killing, the documented cases of killings by JKCCS and APDP (Association of Parents of Disappeared Persons) post 5 August at the hands of state forces state otherwise. JKCCS and APDP have been able to document at least six killings at the hands of the Indian armed forces following the abrogation of the Article 370 on 5 August.'[20]

However, more damning than the number of deaths was Parvez's exposé of the government's claim of normalcy. The report chronicled in great detail how this normalcy had been achieved. 'Soon after the abrogation of Article 370...as the entire Kashmir Valley was put under a military and communication lockdown, allegations of torture by armed forces, night raids, and harassment in several rural districts emerged. JKCCS and APDP was able to gather information concerning the torture of 14 individuals, mostly youth, on the night of 5 August in Pulwama district of South Kashmir...JKCCS and APDP has documented another twenty-four additional cases of torture from Gulshanabad, Gung Bugh, Tengpora, Firdosabad, Boatmen's Colony, Mansoor Colony, Shanpora, Habak in Srinagar District.'

Moreover, 'According to the government, since 5 August, 5,161 people had been detained and about 609 persons are presently under detention.' This figure included Kashmiri politicians—both mainstream and separatist. Even former chief ministers were not spared. 'However, reports from the field suggest that a much higher number of people were detained and there are reports of ongoing detentions.... Some people reported that they were required to report and remain at the local police stations from 9 a.m. to 9 p.m....'

The report went on to describe the torture and detention of people by name, district, as well as the prisons when the detenu were kept in places as diverse as 'Agra, Bareilly, Jodhpur, Jaggad, Prayagraj (formerly Allahabad), Tihar, and Lucknow.' In many cases, they were first tortured publicly and then sent to detention to ensure that the local people got the message.

When I received the PDF of the report on WhatsApp, I became worried for Parvez's safety. Parvez had earlier been arrested in 2016 under the PSA, after he was stopped from attending the thirty-third session of the United Nations Human Rights Council in Switzerland. He had eventually been released after seventy-two days.

I messaged him at night asking about his well-being and urging him to lie low lest he came in harm's way again. He replied, '...the surveillance against us has been very...intimidating but nobody approached us this time.'

Both of us knew that it was only a matter of time before a 'free' Parvez, one of the most prominent and globally recognized Kashmiri human rights activists and the recipient of the Reebok Human Rights Award in 2006, became too much for the government. Just as both of us knew that he would not lie low. In an interview to a Kashmiri YouTube channel on 2 November 2020, he said that though the human rights situation in Kashmir has been bad for the last thirty years, since the revocation of Article 370, 'The government has used its heavy military might to enforce silence in Jammu and Kashmir.... The government has criminalized all opinions contrary to the government position.'[21]

Eventually, he was arrested on 22 November 2021 under the anti-terror Unlawful Activities Prevention Act (UAPA) and remains incarcerated since then. In November 2022, the Office of the High Commissioner UN Human Rights (OHCHR) demanded his immediate release. The OHCHR press statement read, 'We are dismayed at the continued deprivation of liberty of Mr Parvez, in what is increasingly proving to be an act of retaliation against a human rights defender for his tireless work documenting and reporting serious human rights violations, including enforced disappearances and unlawful killings in Indian-administered Jammu and Kashmir.'[22] Also in 2022, *Time* magazine featured him as one of the 100 most influential people in the world.[23]

I first became aware of the breadth of Parvez's work in 2009. Like all peacemakers during the promising window of 2004–07, Parvez was also engaged in fashioning a peaceful and just future for the Kashmiri people after the expected political resolution, which at that time seemed within reach. But he was different from other peacemakers. He came from a privileged background, growing up in the most elite neighbourhood of Srinagar, Gupkar Road, and attending one of the best missionary schools in the city. And yet, despite speaking the King's English without the Kashmiri inflection, he remained rooted to the land of his birth. He chose to finish his education in Kashmir—with a Master's in journalism from Kashmir University in 2004—instead of going to mainland India or abroad like most of his peers.

The reason for this was as much personal as communitarian. In 1990, when he was only thirteen, his grandfather was shot dead in the Gawkadal massacre[24] in Srinagar. In a video posted on the account 'Free Khurram Campaign 2021' on Twitter,[25] Parvez says that he was filled with rage after his grandfather's killing. But over time he decided to channel his rage and desire for revenge into working for the benefit of the Kashmiri people. Six years later, when he was nineteen, he started a helpline for Kashmiri teenagers affected by continuous violence. By 1999, he had started volunteering for the Association of Parents of Disappeared Persons (APDP), which was founded by Parveena Ahanger in 1994 after her son was picked up by the National Security Guards (NSG) and never returned.

In 2000, while still studying, he joined hands with another kindred soul and his namesake, Parvez Imroz, a veteran human rights lawyer, to amalgamate disparate non-governmental organizations in the Kashmir Valley, including the APDP, Public Commission on Human Rights, and International Peoples' Tribunal on Human Rights and Justice in Indian-administered Kashmir to form JKCCS. While Imroz became its president, Parvez, barely twenty-three, became its executive programme coordinator—a hands-on, on the ground job.

When the assembly elections of 2002 were announced,

JKCCS formed several independent monitoring teams to record if the polling was free and fair. Parvez steered the monitoring teams. Free and fair elections reinforced the faith in democracy and justice. During the 2004 general elections, he along with his colleague Asiya Jeelani drove to the militancy-infested Lolab region of north Kashmir to record the polling. On the way, the vehicle drove over a landmine. Jeelani and the driver were killed on the spot. Parvez lost one of his legs—it was amputated above the knee.[26]

'He overcame the trauma very fast,' recounted a person close to him who does not want to be identified for security reasons. 'He said, "I have only lost a leg, not life. There is a reason why this has happened. I have to work harder."' Thereafter, campaigning for a global ban on landmines was added to his already burgeoning portfolio.

Eventually, Parvez got a prosthetic leg and, until 2008, walked with the aid of a stick, after which he became comfortable with the new leg. Yet, he was out on the streets in 2005, when as part of JKCCS, he organized a public event called People's Vision which was attended by the likes of Omar Abdullah as well as moderate separatist leadership. A year later, he organized the second edition of the interaction. The idea was to get Kashmiri leadership of different persuasions on one platform so that they could deliberate upon ideas for the future. After all, these were those halcyon years when peace seemed imminent.

The following year, JKCCS held an inter-region and inter-religion dialogue between Kashmiri Muslims and the Kashmiri Hindus who had been forced to leave the Valley in the 1990s. The idea was to look beyond the mistrust of the past and seek a common future together.

In August 2009, I visited the JKCCS office. Instead of Parvez, I met his mentor Imroz. Imroz rightly assessed that as a journalist for a magazine on national security and defence,[27] I brought a different mindset to the human rights issue in Kashmir. Hence, instead of giving me statistics, he told me about his clients, whose lawsuits he represented pro bono. While I was interested in his views on the future of Kashmir after the collapse of the India–Pakistan dialogue, Imroz gestured to me to listen to the stories of the people sitting in his office. Some had come with fresh complaints and some for update on their cases.[28] The only comment he made that uncomfortable afternoon was while escorting me out of his office. 'Whenever the Kashmir issue is resolved and whichever way it is resolved, there can be no peace without justice,' he said. Those words have stayed with me.

Imroz is a recipient of several international awards for human rights, including the 11th Ludovic-Trarieux International Human Rights Prize by Human Rights Institute of The Bar of Bordeaux, France, and the European Bar Human Rights Institute (IDHAE) in 2006. In 2017, he was awarded the Thorolf Rafto Memorial Prize for Human Rights along with Parveena Ahanger of the APDP.

I eventually met Parvez at Ahanger's residence in October 2011. He facilitated my meeting with her. While Ahanger was, understandably, angry and bitter, both of which made her a difficult and recriminatory interlocutor, Parvez was calm, warm, and sophisticated. His English was impeccable and his perspective pragmatic. Like Imroz, his focus was the future—both of Kashmir and Kashmiris.

As he told American journalist David Barsamian in a radio interview, 'We do not want our state to be an oppressor, because it would be a nightmare for us if we replace Indian rule with a bad Kashmir rule. We don't want that to happen. That's why we are striving hard to promote the values of international humanitarian law and the values of non-violence, truth, justice, and democracy. And we are hopeful that Kashmir will be better than many other existing nations in the world.'[29]

When the peace process was ongoing, it was easy for everyone to ride the peacemaking bandwagon. After all, what seems imminent is easier to embrace. However, when the future becomes an obstacle course lined with concertina wires, inspiring people to not give up and keep the faith takes courage and belief of extraordinary order. It is the resilience of this faith and courage which unnerves those who are seeking to rewrite the narrative of Kashmir by imposing a blanket of silence over the people.

By staying the course, people like Parvez, Imroz, and Ahanger have poked holes in that blanket, through which voices that challenge the new narrative are squeaking out. While Parvez is still in a jail in Delhi, Imroz and Ahanger continue to open their offices in Srinagar whenever possible, even if fewer people visit now. By doing so, they are holding onto the promise of justice—because as Imroz said many years ago, there can be no peace without justice.

10

MUZAFFARNAGAR RIOTS 2013
SLIDING TOWARDS VIOLENCE

Shivam Mogha

Melding together the sensibilities of a village with the aspirations of the city, Muzaffarnagar, my hometown, is representative of many small towns of Uttar Pradesh where modernity has arrived, but only in the form of technology, not 'thinking'. So, smart phones and high-speed internet coexist with deeply entrenched archaic mores driving religious and caste hierarchies. Local politics is also shaped by this; hence it is violently competitive and segregated. While growing up in the late 1990s in Muzaffarnagar, 'Us vs Them' for me was not a mere slogan or internalized fear. It was a living reality. We saw it every day. We enforced it every day.

Consequently, curfews were commonplace. I remember at least two curfews very well, and one vaguely. I had no idea that a curfew was a mark of abnormality. I took pride in the fact that I had experienced more curfews than my cousins from the neighbouring Saharanpur district. In fact, negotiating life during a curfew used to be a bragging point in my interactions with them.

I was born in a Dalit lower middle-class family. Since my father kept poor health and I was the eldest child, I started part-time work when I was eleven. I distributed newspapers before going to the local government school. In the evenings, I worked as a helper in a roadside eatery. We lived in the part of the town reserved for Dalits, which, as is the case in most small towns of Uttar Pradesh, was close to Muslim localities. Given these surroundings, my exposure to Hindutva was organic. It was all around us.

The Rashtriya Swayamsevak Sangh (RSS) had been making an outreach towards the Scheduled Castes and Scheduled Tribes for decades; roping them in, both as 'Hindu' statistics and foot soldiers against Muslims. For the people of my community, the temptation of Hindutva was not new. It promised some measure of power and prominence within the larger community. I remember my father being upset when Atal Bihari Vajpayee lost the election in 2004. I was upset too, and fearful as well. Having grown up on the rhetoric that the Muslim population was growing at a phenomenal rate, I feared that with the BJP out of power, our neighbouring Muslim localities would overpower us.

Despite living together since Independence, the relations between the two communities could be gauged by the fact that Eid, the biggest Muslim festival, was not a holiday for us, but a day of reckoning. We used to wake up early to stand in the street and watch the Muslims go to the eidgah, located in the main market, for namaz. We lined up to watch the Muslims in pure hatred, and to guesstimate their population as well as the demographics. The eye contact between 'us and them' was full of loathing.

However, my feelings changed when I spotted Bilal Ansari. He studied in a government school largely attended by Hindu students. He too did part-time work in the same newspaper distribution agency where I worked. Unlike other Muslim boys, he hung around with me and other Hindu boys. From my perspective, he was a 'good' Muslim. As if to validate my assumption of him, he subsequently enrolled in a LLB programme in Dayanand Anglo Vaidik (DAV) College. He was my friend despite being a Muslim and living in a different segregated locality than ours.

City as an Enabler

The religious- and caste-segregated localities in small towns are both a source of insularity and insecurity. When you live only among your own, the community determines your day-to-day life, even taking decisions on your behalf. To ensure that one remains committed to the community, it is important that one is always fearful, seeking security in numbers. This process requires not just an opponent, but a constant conflict with that opponent, so that the community members stick together.

The Muzaffarnagar of my childhood was similarly laid out, with localities determined by religion and caste, which in turn determined the trade people plied. And within these religious- and caste-based categories were sub-categories, which were a consequence of a sharp hierarchy within. For example, the manual scavengers lived in areas earmarked exclusively for them in the outermost periphery of the city. Interestingly, low-caste Muslims and non-caste 'Hindus' (Dalits) lived in overlapping neighbourhoods, with people frequently running into each other trying to access basic amenities that the town offered; and yet enforcing a distance between themselves.

This set-up was a tinderbox, ready to catch fire at the slightest provocation. Consequently, there was an everyday communalism which kept the tensions on simmer. I remember that I grew up having a sense of belonging to my community because we believed that we wouldn't be safe if we didn't become part of the group and abide by the rules set by our elders. Slowly, the paranoia took on a different form in our area as we established a fraternity based on the same social category and the same religion and constructed a common enemy: 'the Muslim'.

As a kid, the biggest adventure for me was to walk hundred metres till the square, where the town road intersected with the national highway going to Dehradun. The square was the hub of activities, with several jhatka[1] meat shops and alcohol vendors. The halal[2] meat shops run by Muslims were a few metres off the main road inside the by-lanes. I later learnt that this was not a coincidence. One of the family elders told me that the Muslim butchers were also from our community, whose traditional trade was animal slaughter. Even after they converted to Islam a few centuries ago, they continued with their caste-based trade but were pushed into the by-lanes for both economic and social reasons. Their conversion and practice of the new faith was one of the causes of religious tension, common ancestry notwithstanding.

The RSS and I

I started noticing the RSS's penetration in my locality sometime after the BJP lost the general elections in 2004. There was increased activity in my mohalla with more people joining the shakha (local unit). Our ward member in the local municipality also started going to the shakha wearing what I thought was the DAV College uniform. I always aspired to join the DAV College run by the Arya Samaj, but my parents would not allow it. I did not know then that the RSS uniform was similar to DAV College's, hence I confused the two.

This similarity of the uniform was not a coincidence. There was considerable 'RSS-ization' of the Arya Samaj. This was one of the reasons it failed to stand up against the totalitarian religious version of the RSS. Interestingly, many in my community resented the RSS activities in our mohalla because it took the children away from the odd jobs they did to supplement their family incomes. Since I was one of these children, my mother discouraged me from joining the RSS as it would eat into the time I could spend working. However, in spite of my mother's objections, I joined the shakha.

My early attraction to the shakha was because of its involvement in sports activities, conveniently scheduled in the evenings. Gradually, my involvement deepened, and I eventually became the mukhya shikshak (prime teacher) of the newly constituted Eklavya Shakha. This shakha was meant for adolescents like me, while adults went to the Ganesh Shakha, slightly far from our locality. We were given a flag, a pole to hold it, and a booklet of nationalist songs. Bilal was not allowed into the shakha, and unlike me, did not insist on joining.

From 'Namaste Sada Vatsale Matrabhoomi' to 'Janni Janm Bhoomi Swarg Se Mahan Hain', we were taught most of the slogans. My association with the RSS continued for one and half years. The organization shaped my early political thinking. I followed that framework for the next few years until the 'identity-based' politics of the Bahujan Samaj Party and Samajwadi Party began to gain traction in the region, and I became conscious of my identity. I realized how local Baniyas, the traditional trading community (Vaishya) according to the Hindu varna system, dominated the RSS. There were a few praant sanyojaks (regional organizers) from the eastern part of Uttar Pradesh who came to the city to study in the medical college and stayed in the organization's office. Their caste accorded them primacy within the organization.

Despite the RSS's huge influence on my early thinking, my association was short-lived. My father was diagnosed with tuberculosis. Being the eldest son, I had to take on greater financial responsibilities. Between my education and multiple jobs, I could not spare the time for the shakha. However, another reason was the growing awareness of my Dalit identity. I learnt about Ambedkarism, and that gradually replaced the RSS's poisonous ideas in my mind. However, the real test of my evolution happened during the Muzaffarnagar riots of 2013.

Communalism and Competition

Much has been written about the communal problem of western Uttar Pradesh. Experts say that the root of communal violence has been economic rivalry, which stems from the nature of the land and the landowning pattern. For instance, in the Muzaffarnagar-Shamli region, a sizable number of Muslims own land. They are also active in rural politics, which puts them in direct clash with Jat Hindus.

In the Kairana-Shamli region, the rivalry is between Gurjars (pastoralists) of both communities. Since they share common ethnicity and ancestry, even a small localized argument often flares up into a dispute, assuming religious overtones and leading to violence. The arguments usually pertain to local politics, as the focus is becoming the zila panchayat adhyaksh (head of the district governing body). The clout of the Muslims in Muzaffarnagar can also be judged by the fact that the district returned many Muslim members of Parliament until 2014. Even during the 2013 riots, the constituency was represented by a Muslim, Kadir Rana of the BSP.

The politics in Muzaffarnagar is dominated by the idea of agrarian populism, which impacts all aspects of life, including the social hierarchy. Hence, it is important to understand the influence of the kisani (farming) politics in the region. This is especially pertinent for the upper doab of western Uttar Pradesh, a region historically pivoted towards the importance of kisani ideas. Chaudhary Charan Singh, who rose to briefly become the prime minister (1979-80), came from this area and even capitalized on kisani electorally. He left the Congress in the late 1960s and founded his own parties, first the Bhartiya Kisan Dal, and thereafter the Dalit Mazdoor Kisan Party. Cashing in on his heritage, his son Ajit Singh founded the Rashtriya Lok Dal (RLD) that has a sizeable presence among a section of farmers of the area.

Given the influence of rural politics on society, khaps, which are clan-based power groups, have a very strong presence in the region. These are supplemented by the activism of the Bharatiya Kisan Union. The BKU was founded by Mahendra Singh Tikait of Muzaffarnagar with the village Sisauli as its headquarters. Tikait eventually spearheaded the national level farmer movement in 1980s. He was considered one of the most rigid voices of radical farmers' politics in India, drawing his influence from agrarian populism. He pioneered a unique method of protest, including against World Trade Organization (WTO) meetings in Delhi, which involved blocking the highways and capturing the toll plazas.[3] This, as well as his ability to connect with the local farmers in their language, is not only still remembered, but emulated by other protestors.

BKU had substantial participation from Muslim farmers. To maintain the non-sectarian nature of the organization, Tikait ensured that both 'Har Har Mahadev' and 'Allah Hu Akbar' were chanted at BKU meetings. He always spoke against communalism among the farmers, urging them to unite as farmers. His active involvement in stopping the riots of Meerut in the late 1980s is worth remembering. He personally visited every village and held inter-community panchayats (meetings of village elders) to impress upon them the importance of Hindu–Muslim unity.[4] What's more, he did not let violence spread to the villages of Muzaffarnagar. He led one of the biggest marches against the state government when a young Muslim woman, Naema, from Muzaffarnagar was found raped and killed. The pinnacle of the protest was when he mobilized not only Muslim but Hindu farmers too.

Slide Towards Violence

The 2013 Muzaffarnagar riots were an aberration, but perhaps not a shocking one given the carefully nurtured polarization of the town over the years. Like most riots, this one also had a build-up and many versions. A Muslim boy Shahnawaz Qureshi was killed by two Hindu brothers, Sachin Singh and Gaurav Singh. Thereafter, the Singh brothers were killed by a Muslim mob.[5]

The killings had two retrospective versions. The Hindu version ascribed the killings to the harassment of the Singh brothers' female cousin by Shahnawaz. The Muslim version said that the killings were a consequence of an accident involving the boys and their bikes. According to this second version, the suspicion and mistrust between the communities caused a small incident to blow up into a riot.[6] Clearly, the versions don't matter. The deaths do. And three deaths led to many more. Incidentally, there was a suitable warning period before the bloodbath began.

The first sign of violence emerged on 21 August 2013, when a Hindu–Muslim mob clashed. There were no fatalities, though many were injured. The state police arrested fourteen people for rioting but didn't bother with brokering a truce between the communities and quashing the rumours. Tension continued to simmer. On 27 August, another clash took place. Once again there were no fatalities. But this clash had another consequence—the consolidation of Hindu groups with Hindutva politicians and lumpen elements—all of which culminated in the mahapanchayat (grand meeting of several village governing bodies) on 7 September 2013[7]. By this time, Tikait had withdrawn from active politics, and his sons were swayed by the lucrativeness of Hindutva politics.

On that day, one of the close associates of Tikait, Ghulam Mohammad Jaula left BKU. He formed his own Rashtriya Kisan Mazdoor Sabha. That was the end of Hindu-Muslim farmer bhaichara (brotherhood).

The mahapanchayat called by the Bharatiya Kisan Union was attended by politicians from the BJP and the RLD. Jats from the neighbouring states of Uttarakhand and Haryana also attended. Incendiary speeches against Muslims were made at the gathering, which was a show of power and closing of ranks. Some participants of the mahapanchayat waylaid the family of one Insar Vakeel on the way to the meeting. Apparently, Vakeel was taken to the meeting as a 'prize catch' and killed there when he tried to escape.[8]

It was clear that the day would not end peacefully.

Those days, I worked as an office boy in a real estate firm at Vasundhara Residency. Sanjeev Balyan, who won the parliamentary seat from Muzaffarnagar in 2014 on the BJP ticket after defeating BSP's Kadir Rana, had a stake in the firm. Balyan's victory was the fruit of his labour of the previous years he had spent cleaving apart the two communities in Muzaffarnagar.

Vasundhara Residency was run by some Jat youths, who had profited from selling their village land. They had managed to convince the Muzaffarnagar Development Authority to convert the agricultural land into a residential one so that a housing complex could be built there. One of the USPs of the complex was that 'no Muslims' or 'Valmikis' (Dalits) were allowed there.

On 7 September 2013, I accompanied other members of my firm to the mahapanchayat. The firm made all the arrangements. We were told that this was the day for show of strength. Jats from neighbouring districts of Haryana were brought to the mahapanchayat in tractor-trolleys. The speeches made at the mahapanchayat shook me to my core. I was scared, not only for myself but for what the speeches and sloganeering portended for the place I regarded as home. Since I had gone with my colleagues from the firm and under Balyan's benediction, I returned safely. Not everyone was that lucky.

Two incidents took place after the mahapanchayat. In one, a Muslim mob clashed with the returning Hindus. In the ensuing violence six people were killed, including journalist Rajesh Verma and police photographer Israr.[9] In another incident, the returning Hindus were ambushed by a heavily armed Muslim mob near Jauli canal. In a reprising of the Hashimpura massacre of 1987, in which the Provincial Armed Constabulary had rounded up forty-five Muslim men, killed them, and thrown the bodies in the Hindon canal,[10] armed Muslims attacked the unsuspecting, and lightly armed, Hindus. While rumours spread widely about the number of dead, the police eventually fished out six bodies from the Jauli canal.[11] According to the police, the Muslim mobs had collected as the news of Vakeel's murder spread. After the Jauli canal incident, Hindu mobs gathered and went on a rampage. The cycle of violence had commenced.

In the following days, the police became scarce. And every political leader aligned with their own community, adding fuel to the fire. Two weeks later, when the government released the statistics, the total dead after a fortnight of madness stood at sixty-two: forty-two Muslims and twenty Hindus.[12]

Restoring Bhaichara

Even though the villages of Muzaffarnagar and Shamli districts continued to burn, the curfew in the city was lifted after three days. Since I had attended the mahapanchayat, I couldn't hold back from stepping out and seeing for myself the consequences of hatred. It was not difficult to find the relief camps set up by the state government. I had no objective in mind, except to bear witness to what humans were capable of doing to other humans. What I saw there was enough to make one lose one's faith in humanity. Yet, I was determined not to forget what I was witnessing. The record-keeping was all in my head; the impact in my heart.

Eventually, word reached my superiors in the real estate firm, who objected to my visiting the relief camps for Muslims. I mustered courage and quit my job. This freed me from everything. Over the next few days, Delhi-based journalists, and even small NGOs started approaching me to become their guide to the camps. I realized that many NGOs were not allowed to cross the Muzaffarnagar boundary. The administration was vetting those who were to be allowed in. And just as there was a communal streak among the police, many journalists were also afflicted by this prejudice. They wanted to write only certain kinds of stories. This motivated me to write a couple of ground reports about the survivors' accounts and problems faced by them in the camps, especially with the winter approaching. These were published in *Jansatta*.

Then a team from Jamia Millia Islamia, comprising students and teachers, reached out to me. I joined them in their rehabilitation work and in recording the testimonies of the survivors. These accounts were horrifying. Equally horrifying was the persistent communal sentiment. People with a Delhi number plate on their cars wanting to visit the villages were eyed with suspicion. The vehicles were frequently stopped and questions were asked about their destination and motive. I too faced this situation when I was accompanying a journalist from a Delhi-based Hindi magazine. We were allowed in by the local villagers once it was discovered that the journalist had a right-wing inclination.

Once I accompanied a team of Dalit activists and writers from Delhi to the Dalit camps. Listening to the survivors was tough because most of them were poor and marginalized daily wage labourers, only slightly different from people like me. But since the Muslim casualties were much higher, the larger chunk of the relief and rehabilitation effort was expended towards them. This was exploited by the Vishva Hindu Parishad and other local Hindu outfits, which were carrying out relief work only in the Dalit camps. Interestingly, there were hardly any upper-caste Hindu relief camps. The victims were largely Muslims, followed by Dalits.

Though some philanthropists from Delhi and Meerut gave funds directly to the NGOs for relief work, given the history and the nature of the township, there were no local organizations. One NGO that carried out substantive relief work was Rehana Adib's Astitwa Samajik Sanstha from Saharanpur. She even took some members of the civil society from Muzaffarnagar to the relief camps in a bid to build solidarity and understanding, but even civil society was divided on communal lines. Other organizations which carried out commendable work were Action Aid India, Oxfam India, Human Rights Law Network, Muzaffarnagar Welfare Association, and Rihai Manch from Lucknow. Rihai Manch provided legal support to the victims and continued to follow up on their court cases.

The only ray of hope in those gloomy days was the commitment of some people towards Hindu–Muslim brotherhood despite widespread communal hatred. There were many reports about people coming together to help each other during this difficult time, communities providing shelter and support to the displaced, and volunteers fearlessly moving from camp to camp distributing food, water, and other essential supplies, irrespective of religion and caste.

However, the biggest impact was from a few village elders from the affected areas who came together to promote peace and communal harmony. These elders played an important role in diffusing tension and bringing the two communities together, even if sporadically. The efforts of these elders led to the formation of peace committees managed by the district administration. These committees were tasked with promoting peace and reconciliation in the affected areas. They organized peace meetings and held dialogues between different communities across villages to rebuild trust.

One such initiative led to the formation of Aman Ekta Manch, which acted as a reconciliatory balm over raw wounds. Comprising members from both communities, the manch not only called for peace but also underscored the importance of accountability and justice. This reassured the victims that they were not expected to simply forgive and forget, but that they would be supported in their quest for justice. This helped reinforce their shaken faith in the 'system'.

One of the most celebrated examples was of the eighty-year-old Haji Abdul Rashid from Lisadh village and his friend, seventy-five-year-old Satbir Singh from Shahpur village. Rashid's house was burnt down during the riots. He and his family were forced to take refuge in a relief camp. Singh, who had known Rashid for decades, went to the relief camp to visit him and offer his support. The two men then decided to join hands. They began by organizing a meeting between elders from both communities, which was attended by more than 200 people. At the meeting, they spoke about the importance of living together in harmony and resolving conflicts peacefully. They also formed a peace committee, made up of elders from both communities.

Politically, the biggest consequence of the violence was the turnaround of the RLD, which has been trying to rebuild its core constituency of Hindu–Muslim farmers since the Muzaffarnagar riots. When politicians seek stakes in peace, it usually prevails. The RLD revived the slogan of 'Bhaichara Zindabad' after 2014,[13] and fought the 2022 state assembly election on the 'bhaichara' plank.[14]

In the assembly by-elections in December 2022, RLD's Madan Bhaiya managed to wrest the Khatauli seat in the Muzaffarnagar district from the BJP. The BJP candidate Vikram Saini was disqualified from contesting the election because of his involvement in the riots. Consequently, his wife, Rajkumari, was fielded by the party. She lost to 'Bhaichara Zindabad'.

On 28 January 2023, M. S. Tikait's son Rakesh Tikait, the national spokesperson for BKU, had the proverbial homecoming to his father's turf. He made an emotional appeal for unity among farmers irrespective of religion at another mahapanchayat. Gulam Mohhamad Jaula, who had walked out in 2013, came back to attend the mahapanchayat. And once again, chants of 'Har Har Mahadev' and 'Allah Hu Akbar' reverberated through the meeting.

It would be naive to regard this as the turning of the tide. But even these small steps to reclaim a shared heritage are reason for hope. Perhaps these steps will eventually build a momentum, and individual peacemakers will start a movement against hate.

11

DELHI VIOLENCE, FEBRUARY 2020
THE DOCTOR WHO BORE WITNESS

Natasha Badhwar and Oishika Neogi

'When I opened my eyes in the hospital, it was to the sound of pain and suffering. Everywhere I looked, there were injured people. There was so much blood. I had no idea where I was or how I reached there.'

Shokat Ali, an AC technician in his mid-forties, is sitting on a ledge outside the door of his one-room home in Gali No. 3 in Babunagar, a congested working-class neighbourhood in northeast Delhi. It has been raining since late last night and there are puddles around us reflecting the clear sky. Shokat is recalling the scene around him on the terrace of Al Hind Hospital where he was in the middle of the night between 25 and 26 February 2020. As he speaks, his hand moves over his right thigh, where the scars are still fresh.

'It was all a blur. I was in immense pain. But I did not know yet that I had a bullet in my right leg. All I remembered was that I had stepped out in the evening in response to the news that a relative had died and I should come to their home. We usually take our dead back to our village for burial.' Shokat recalls that he knew that the area was not safe anymore, but he felt compelled to respond to the news of a death in the family. Within minutes, Shokat realized that he himself was in danger.

He could hear gunshots and the cacophony of mobs nearby. In the three decades that he has lived here, nothing had prepared him for this moment of abject terror.

Shokat has no memory of being shot. He remembers sudden, blinding pain. He took a step forward and fell on his face. The next time he opened his eyes, he was one of the many injured people on the terrace of Dr Mohammad Ahtasham Anwar's fifteen-bed private hospital in New Mustafabad. It would be a year before Shokat would walk again.

'I don't think I can ever forget those dark nights,' forty-two-year-old Dr Anwar recalled at a people's tribunal in New Delhi's Constitution Club, organized a few weeks after the violence. 'Victims who were being brought to us had wounds deliberately inflicted in ways that their chances of survival would be diminished. There were some things I witnessed that I cannot shake off. One man was torn apart from between his legs. [The] mobs had been merciless and brutal. Hate and anger are different from pure evil. This was evil.'

In the last week of February 2020, New Delhi's north-eastern areas had been the site of egregious communal violence where victims had been beaten, tortured, and left dead on pavements and in drains. Those targeted were attacked on the streets and ambushed in their homes and shops with sticks, rods, guns, knives, and crude bombs. Chants of 'Jai Shree Ram' echoed in neighbourhoods as mosques were desecrated and saffron flags hoisted atop minarets.

According to a list titled 'Dead bodies Accounted For' compiled by the Delhi Police on 21 March 2020, fifty-three people had died.[1] Thirteen of them were Hindu, and forty Muslim. 'The figures on deaths quoted for each day are limited to what was known on that day and may not represent the actual death toll for the given day,' noted *Uncertain Justice,* a citizens' committee report on the northeast Delhi violence in 2020[2]. Published in October 2022, the report was a result of evidence collected by a team of former judges and civil servants, led by Justice Madan B. Lokur, a former judge of the Supreme Court of India.

'I'm not willing to call these riots. They were not riots,' said author and political activist Arundhati Roy at an event organized at the Press Club of India to mark two years of the violence in northeast Delhi. 'This was a pre-planned massacre.'[3]

The morbid spectacle unfolded within a few kilometres of the offices of India's central government; it was a massacre that was broadcast live by many of the perpetrators on Facebook pages and WhatsApp broadcast channels. Videos that went viral on social media show the presence of heavily armoured police and paramilitary deployment, standing by passively as the violence escalates. 25 February was the day with the highest fatalities in the worst communal violence that New Delhi had witnessed in over thirty years since the pogrom targeting Sikhs in 1984.

Victims recognized many of the perpetrators of violence as long-time neighbours and acquaintances. Others reported that their streets had been taken over by armed outsiders—rioters who had been mobilized and transported to wreak violence in this area. Thousands of residents were rendered refugees as they fled their homes in the bitter cold, leaving behind their animals, possessions, and means of livelihood, knowing that if they ever returned, they would find only debris and carcasses.

In the first twenty-four hours of the violence—preceding 25 February—the Delhi Police Control Room received over 4,200 calls seeking rescue and refuge. According to their own data, the Delhi Police Control Room received over 13,200 calls between 23 and 26 February on their emergency numbers: 112 and 100.[4]

The View from Al Hind Hospital

'I remember running up to the third floor to tell Bhai that the violence is escalating and it might be safer for us to shut the hospital till peace is restored,' says Mohammad Shiraj bin Ikram, a pharmaceutical graduate and the younger brother of Dr Anwar. 'But Bhai refused instantly. He made it clear that we are a hospital and we cannot pull down our shutters. As a doctor he will not refuse treatment to anybody who needs it.'

The azure blue board printed with the name of Al Hind Hospital is visible from a distance. The three-storey building—the third floor being the residence of Dr Anwar's family—is the most prominent address in the row. The lanes around it are narrow; in usual times, they ebb and flow with the rhythm of the day. Due to the lack of open spaces nearby, groups of children compete with street vendors and regular traffic as they play in the evening.

It had just been a day since Dr Anwar had returned from his hometown in Champaran. The atmosphere was charged, but nothing prepared him for the deluge of frantic calls and the constant stream of injured people that started to come in, confirming that the area was under siege. The small waiting area of the hospital was stained with blood and resounding with the screams of the injured. They had injuries that the doctor had never imagined seeing.

'We tried every possible way to summon help. We received no response on the 102 state ambulance number or the national emergency number 112,' says Dr Anwar. 'These numbers are made to be used in times of emergencies and disasters. But we realized that this is not true. Ambulance drivers blatantly refused to come inside Mustafabad when we called them. The station house officer (SHO) would either not pick up our calls, or the phone number would be busy. It is hard to express the helplessness, desperation, and pain we endured.'

As victims languished without access to any state or medical intervention, Shokat became one of the hundreds of people who were rushed to Al Hind Hospital. This is how he found himself gaining consciousness among other victims on its terrace on 25 February. Many others had bullet injuries like him. 'Is this what hell looks like?' he thought to himself.

As the violence continued to be unleashed in the barricaded streets of northeast Delhi, Dr Anwar's small team and basic medical facilities became the hub of rescue efforts. Volunteers and staff repurposed old mattresses and spare tarpaulin sheets as beds for the wounded, creating partitions between them out of curtains. Neighbours contributed what they could, and overnight, the space was converted into a 24x7 emergency ward.

Despite the mayhem, uncertainty, and threat to personal safety, Dr Anwar's Al Hind Hospital refused to pull down its shutters.

The Build-up to the Violence

The violence in northeast Delhi in February 2020 is an ominous marker of the sharp rift in the sociopolitical dynamics of contemporary India. It would be naive to assume that this violence was in any way sudden.

'Polarization between communities, particularly anti-Muslim hate, was deliberately fuelled in the months preceding the violence,' the citizens' committee report states.[5]

'Violence is never an isolated, one-time event that ends instantly. Violence is a result of a systematic process in play over the years. It then gives rise to various other processes that eventually spiral beyond human control,' said Professor

Apoorvanand at the press conference to mark two years of the mayhem in northeast Delhi.[6]

In an election rally in Bongaon, West Bengal, on 1 May 2019, minister of home affairs Amit Shah had announced, 'According to the Citizenship (Amendment) Act (CAA) we are going to implement, we shall give citizenship to every Hindu, Buddhist, Sikh, Christian and Jain who have settled in this country.'[7] After leaving out Muslims from the list of people who would get Indian citizenship, he framed a rhetorical question. 'You tell me—shouldn't the infiltrators be eradicated from the country? From Kashmir to Kanyakumari, and Assam to Gujarat, the Bharatiya Janata Party (BJP) government shall eradicate each and every infiltrator in this country. They are the termites in India.'[8]

For months, India's Muslim community had been grappling with deep fears of loss of citizenship, stemming from the combined effect of the CAA, passed in December 2019, and the threat of exclusion in the National Register of Citizens (NRC).

By mid-December 2019, as nationwide protests erupted against the law, Delhi emerged as the epicentre of the anti-CAA movement. Students of Jamia Millia Islamia University and Aligarh Muslim University were among the earliest protestors, and Shaheen Bagh was the first of many locations where women-led sit-ins were organized—not only against the new laws, but also to protest against the police violence unleashed on students in university campuses. Shaheen Bagh became an inspiration and a model for democratic agitation. In northeast Delhi, Seelampur, Chand Bagh, Khajuri Khas, and Jaffrabad were prominent locations of sit-in protests.

Across the country, anti-CAA protest sites were vibrant spaces where people across economic, social, and religious backgrounds mingled in solidarity. Children played freely, volunteers organized art camps, roadside libraries sprung up, and civil society donors arranged daily community meals for all. Visitors and protesters mingled through the nights. On stage, poetry was recited, patriotic songs sung, and the Indian Constitution was celebrated every day. It was an unprecedented, one-of-a-kind people's resistance. Collectively, the idea of India, of belonging and owning an Indian identity, became everyday public conversation.

'We were protesting peacefully from 15 December 2019 to 24 February 2020. Suddenly, on 23 February, a third party comes and asks us to stop protesting,' Nadeem Khan, activist and founding member of United Against Hate—a collective of human rights' defenders in Delhi—recalled when he spoke at the same forum as Arundhati Roy and Apoorvanand.

As the 2020 Delhi assembly elections drew close in January, ruling party leaders of the BJP propagated a divisive narrative, vilifying the anti-CAA protests as anti-national and violent. In public speeches at election rallies, belligerent slogans were amplified, most prominently by party leaders such as Kapil Mishra, a former member of legislative assembly (MLA), and Anurag Thakur, who went on to become a minister in the ruling party's cabinet in July 2021. Many widely viewed television news channels amplified anti-Muslim rhetoric and unsubstantiated conspiracy theories about the protests. Ignoring the constitutional guarantee to the right to assemble, they called for the forcible shutdown of protest sites.

In an election campaign rally, Thakur, who was a member of parliament from the BJP, thundered, 'Desh ke gaddaron ko, goli maaro saalon ko'—Shoot the traitors of the country.[9]

The violence in northeast Delhi was triggered within a few hours of one such public ultimatum. Accompanied by the then-deputy commissioner of police (northeast Delhi) Ved Prakash Surya, Kapil Mishra gathered his supporters at Maujpur Chowk, near the Jaffrabad protest site on the afternoon of 23 February. 'We will be peaceful till [Donald] Trump leaves. After that, we will not listen to even you if the roads are not cleared. We will have to take matters into our own hands,' Mishra declared, addressing the police.[10]

Less than an hour later, stone-pelting and clashes between pro-CAA and anti-CAA protestors broke out in the area, spreading to newer areas as the rumours of widespread rioting spread.[11]

Section 144 of the Criminal Procedure Code (CrPC), prohibiting the assembly of four or more people in an area, was imposed the next day along with the deployment of Central Reserve Police Force (CRPF), Rapid Action Force (RAF), Delhi Police, and paramilitary personnel across the district of northeast Delhi.

None of this would have any impact in controlling the lawlessness and savagery that was unleashed on the streets across neighbourhoods with a significant Muslim population—Karawal Nagar, Chand Bagh, Babarpur, Jaffrabad, Seelampur, Maujpur, Khajuri Khas, Gokulpuri, Kardampuri, Shiv Vihar, Bhajanpura, Brijpuri, and Mustafabad.

The Shutters That Never Shut

'When we saw the injuries of victims of the communal violence, we were compelled to consider the fact that they were inflicted by trained and organized groups,' says Dr Anwar in a moment of candour. 'I have a basic and fundamental duty as a doctor. Asking a patient their name, religion, caste, or even money frightens them. They no longer feel safe. The responsibility of a doctor is to keep all of that aside, and just try to save the patient's life. Hence, we let go of all these formalities at our hospital during the days and nights of violence. We just wanted to save them;

we just wanted to give them hope.'

Dr Anwar's voice changes every time he recalls the ordeal of the community during the violence. He speaks with conviction but is unable to hide his own trauma. He frames his sentences as questions as he strives to make sense of our collective experiences. 'I kept thinking how the people who did this to innocents were part of our very society. They were sons and brothers of so many like us.'

After two decades of working in government hospitals, Dr Anwar had set up his private practice as a basic, affordable medical facility in Mustafabad in 2019. Less than a year later, on the evening of 25 February 2020, two people were brought in who were declared dead on arrival. Patients with grievous injuries were brought in. Some had been stabbed multiple times, others had embedded shrapnel and bullet wounds. Some came in with their eyes and parts of their faces melted with acid, others with limbs fractured by steel rods.

Desperate for an ambulance and additional resources to cater to the emergencies, Dr Anwar put out appeals on social media, hoping for amplification and help. He sent messages to civil society groups in a bid to reach anyone who could figure out a way to get the state administration to respond.

'Hospital has more than fifty people. It is a small hospital. It is short of supplies and arrangements. Three journo inside waiting for rescue,' reads one of the messages from Dr Anwar that was circulated widely across WhatsApp groups in the city.

'People were pulling at me from all directions. They were crying and pleading to me to help their loved ones. Those patients could have easily been my near and dear ones. And I felt helpless. I tried reassuring them, but I knew that they needed more. My patients needed more,' recalls Dr Anwar.

Twenty-eight-year-old Imran Saifi, a welder from Brijpuri,

was shot in his scrotum when he was caught in the violence on his way to get milk for his family. Unable to take him to a bigger hospital because all the exit points of the area had been sealed, his father brought him to Al Hind Hospital. 'My treatment there began around midnight. I needed emergency reconstruction surgery and Dr Anwar's intervention saved my life,' Saifi recalls. 'Eighty-five stitches is no joke and Al Hind didn't charge me any money for it. His focus was to transfer me to a bigger hospital for better treatment.'

The Delhi High Court Intervenes

One of the most astounding parts about the violence unleashed in Delhi was that despite its wide visibility—literally live-streaming on social media platforms—it had been allowed to escalate as if all the powers who could intervene had become wilfully deaf, mute, and blind.

'The response of the Government of India, namely the Ministry of Home Affairs (MHA), was wholly inadequate. Despite having command over both the Delhi Police and the central paramilitary forces, the MHA failed to take effective steps to stem the spread of communal violence. Repeated assurances on 24 and 25 February from police top brass and government officials that the situation was under control did not match the visibility of violence on the ground,' the Citizens' Committee report noted.[12]

The efforts of civil society members to aid victims trapped and injured amidst the chaos were thwarted as well. Vehicles were not allowed to pass the police barricades bordering the affected district. According to police personnel on duty, they did not have permission to let anyone in—including ambulances. Over forty-eight hours into the violence, thousands trapped inside northeast Delhi were not allowed access to medical care or evacuation.

The first rays of intervention broke through the darkness when advocate Suroor Mander and the team from Karwan e Mohabbat—a civil society campaign against hate crimes—filed a writ petition on behalf of filmmaker and civil society activist Rahul Roy at the Delhi High Court late in the evening of 25 February. A few hours later, a special midnight hearing was held in front of a bench comprising Justice S. Muralidhar and Justice A. J. Bhambhani, at the latter's residence. The purpose of the appeal was to allow and facilitate the safe entry of ambulances to rescue those who were grievously injured and others who were trapped in arson affected areas.

'We started getting calls from Al Hind Hospital in Mustafabad at 5 p.m. on 25 February evening saying they were in urgent need of ambulances and they did not have the capacity to deal with the kind of injuries that people were coming in with. By 9 p.m., they called saying they had more than twenty-five people in a critical condition and two dead bodies,' Mander recalls about the events leading up to the hearing that would change the trajectory of the heinous rampage that had engulfed northeast Delhi.

In the presence of the joint commissioner of police (northeast Delhi), deputy commissioner of police, police legal liaison, and advocate Sanjay Ghose, they convened at the residence of Justice S. Muralidhar at 12:30 a.m. on 26 February 2020. Mander called Dr Anwar at Al Hind Hospital and put him on speakerphone for the judges to hear his testimony as a witness trapped in the violence. Surrounded by the injured and helpless beyond his own individual capacity as a doctor, he relayed the gravity of the situation from Mustafabad over the phone.

'...One of us [Justice S. Muralidhar] received a call from an advocate, Suroor Mander, explaining the dire circumstances under which certain grievously wounded victims of the riots taking place in the northeastern district of Delhi were unable to be transferred from the Al Hind Hospital in New Mustafabad, a fairly small hospital which lacks the facilities for treating seriously wounded persons, for treatment at the GTB Hospital in Dilshad Gardens. She prayed for urgent orders for safe passage of the ambulances, both to the Al Hind Hospital and from the said hospital for the injured victims,' the court's order read.[13]

The court's order distinctly notes Dr Anwar's heartfelt and truthful testimony. The justices took cognisance of the fact that the facility had two dead bodies, as well as around twenty-two injured patients that the doctor had been trying to seek police assistance for since 4 p.m. on 25 February, without any success.

At 1.42 a.m. that Wednesday morning, the emergency court passed an order. Ambulances were to be let inside Mustafabad, and to Al Hind Hospital. The Delhi Police was to ensure safe passage and the secure evacuation of all injured patients to bigger state hospitals immediately.[14]

After over forty-eight hours of unceasing mayhem and intractable despair, Dr Anwar stopped to rest. 'I think the first time Bhai saw the ambulance finally arrive, he froze,' Shiraj recalls. A key member of Dr Anwar's paramedical team, Shiraj had been by his side throughout. 'We knew that some of the patients leaving through the door of his hospital may not survive—be it because of the delayed treatment...or the sheer criticality of their injuries.' The brothers also anticipated that many of them may never recover fully and would be disabled for life. Yet the relief was tangible. Help had finally arrived. They were no longer alone and isolated—trying to douse a fire that threatened to overwhelm them.

'Despite everything, I'd like to acknowledge and thank the members of the judiciary who allowed a special midnight hearing and ordered ambulances to reach victims in northeast Delhi. If not for that unprecedented hearing, the entirety of Mustafabad would be in ashes today,' says Dr Anwar.

Evacuations of patients in heavily-guarded ambulances to government facilities such as the Guru Teg Bahadur Hospital in Shahdara and Lok Nayak Jayaprakash Narayan Hospital near Delhi Gate started and continued till the next day.

Medical Bias and Negligence

'It is only after they utilized all the resources they had at their disposal that they decided to transfer me to a bigger government facility in an ambulance at approximately 6 a.m. that morning. Dr Anwar wanted better treatment for me,' says Saifi, who was in so much pain despite first aid, that he relies on his father's version of events on the morning after he was shot.

Neither the parent nor Dr Anwar knew that Saifi's worst ordeal was yet to come. Like many other victims who were evacuated from the violence-gripped area, Saifi was brought to the emergency ward of one of Delhi's largest government hospitals. Paramedics put him on a glucose drip, and it was a while before a doctor attended to him.

'The doctor asked my name when he arrived. I told him I was Imran Saifi. Instead of attending to my grievous wounds, he stepped back. In the emergency ward, Muslims were being accused of being rioters. They told me I was a stone-pelter; that I was responsible for the violence; that I was a jihadi. My father begged them to help me. But they didn't. The glucose drip was removed from my arm. I was asked to leave,' he says.

Despite being equipped to admit and treat him, the hospital turned Saifi out. 'Unable to move, I sat on a pavement outside the hospital. That is where I met Gufraan Bhai,' Saifi recalls. It was much later that Saifi would learn that Gufraan was one of the volunteers of Karwan e Mohabbat and among the first responders to reach the victims.

For the next month and a half, he stayed at a shelter home for the homeless near Yamuna Pushta in north Delhi. He received medical treatment there among other sick, homeless persons.

Accounts similar to Saifi's echo in the narrow alleys of northeast Delhi. While some injured victims were merely bandaged and asked to leave the emergency wards, many others received only abuse. They were blamed for their own condition and were asked if this was the azadi (freedom) they wanted. Besides state apathy and the complicity of the police, medical bias and negligence was another layer of injustice heaped on survivors of the violence.

Allegations and Conspiracies

Two years later, by February 2022, the Delhi Police had registered 758 cases of rioting, arson and violence. Chargesheets have been filed in only 52 per cent of the cases.[15] Dr Anwar is named in two of them.

The first accusation is that he was one of the organizers of an anti-CAA/NRC protest that incited people to take to the streets. Two days after Dr Anwar engineered the successful evacuation of the most critical patients from his hospital to bigger and better facilities, his name was typed into a First Information Report (FIR) filed in a police station approximately 3 kilometres away from Al Hind Hospital. This was FIR 39/20 at the Gokulpuri Police Station—informally known as the Dilbar Negi case.

On 26 February 2020, Negi, a twenty-year-old waiter at Anil Sweet Shop in Shiv Vihar, was found dead in a godown. His body was charred, and his lower limbs severed. According to the FIR, the twelve men accused of the murder of Negi were allegedly incited at an anti-CAA/ NRC protest site, specifically the one near Farooqia Masjid—less than a kilometre away from Al Hind Hospital. The masjid was one of the most prominent places burnt down during the violence on the night of 23 February. Dr Anwar has been named as one of the organizers of the protest. Accusing him of being a conspirator, the FIR states:

> On the outside, this protest site had pictures of BR Ambedkar, Shaheed Bhagat Singh, Mahatma Gandhi and the Tricolor was waved. However, one particular community was incited against the central government.... Those who participated in this protest, who were incited, on the night of 23.02.2020 took part in the violence following which the FIR was registered at police station Dayalpur. The organisers of the protest which took place at Farooqia Masjid are 1. Arshad Pradhan 2. Dr Anwar, owner of Al-Hind hospital. The above mentioned persons could not be interrogated; they will be questioned later and we will accordingly investigate. The violence which took place on February 23-24 was not an isolated incident.

The chargesheet does not address a fundamental gap in facts. Dr Anwar was not in Delhi on the day he is alleged to have organized the protest. He left for Champaran in Bihar on 19 February to attend the last rites of his deceased aunt. He returned on the evening of 23 February. Within hours he had converted his private hospital in into a day-and-night emergency ward that attended to nearly 600 patients through the next few days of incessant violence.

Three months later, on 2 June, Dr Anwar was named in another chargesheet—FIR 50/20, the Tahir Hussain case. A former Aam Aadmi Party (AAP) councillor, Hussain, had been charged for instigating violence and for the murder of Ankit Sharma, an

Intelligence Bureau staffer, on 25 February 2020. According to the chargesheet, Hussain was in touch with Dr Anwar in his capacity as the co-organizer of the protests held near Farooqia Masjid.

The doctor—who has been publicly vocal about the state and central administration's lack of action to curb the violence—was baffled by the charges. As a prominent person in the neighbourhood, Dr Anwar was well-known to the residents as well as the area's local police.

A month after the chargesheet naming Dr Anwar was filed at the Karkardooma District Court, civil society members released a statement condemning the allegations as blatantly false and communally motivated. Signed by public health professionals, bureaucrats, lawyers, academics, and women's rights' activists, this statement was endorsed by groups such as the Jan Swasthya Abhiyan, All India Drug Action Network, Medico Friend Circle, People's Union for Civil Liberties, and Right to Food Campaign. An excerpt from the statement reads:

> We would like to assert that Dr Anwar as a medical professional, followed the code of medical ethics, and treated every person who was injured in the riots and who approached his hospital with empathy and diligence. His prompt action to help injured people during the riots was praised by many persons, including the Hon'ble High Court of Delhi, and reports on the violence that recorded the role of Al Hind hospital and its owner, Dr Anwar in helping victims of the violence, irrespective of their religion or caste or class.

The Importance of Being Dr Anwar

'Despite the fact that my injuries were documented as a medico-legal case (MLC), I was told by the authorities that the bullet wounds were not grave enough for a compensation of more than ₹20,000,' Shokat Ali recalls. This despite the fact that according to the Delhi government's assistance scheme for the help of riot victims, victims falling under the category of 'serious injuries' were to be awarded ₹2 lakh.[16] 'I could not walk for about a year. I was unable to work as an AC technician. I had no resources for medical treatment in that state. Throughout the entire time, Al Hind Hospital did not charge me at all.'

'What can be more unjust than the hounding of the man who saved so many lives,' says Saifi, his voice low and laced with pain. 'I would have died without Dr Anwar's intervention; so many more of us would have died with nowhere to go, without him.' Saifi smiles as he recalls his last interaction with Dr Anwar. The doctor assured him that even though his medications would continue, he was going to be okay. 'You are not alone, he said to me. We are tied together.'

These words of Dr Anwar resonate in many homes across the violence-affected areas of northeast Delhi. He did everything to save the injured when they were first rushed to him. When the nationwide Covid-19 lockdown was imposed less than three weeks after the violence, he ensured that Al Hind Hospital remained open for riot victims, and he continues to reassure them two-and-a-half years after the violence.

For the rest of us, he has a few questions. 'It is important for us to ask who those rioters were. What were their affiliations? Where were they trained? How were the riots planned? We ought to think about such things. Are we, as a society, not responsible for everything they're doing? Perhaps, along the way, we stopped working on ourselves—on our society.'

12

BHARAT JODO YATRA 2022–23
RETURN OF HOPE

Ramani Atkuri

'Do you think it will change anything?' asked the receptionist of the tiny hotel we had checked into in Jaipur when my friend and I told him we were returning from the Bharat Jodo Yatra (Unite India March). I smiled at him. 'I'm not sure, but one has to try.'

His question was like other questions that I had been asked earlier: What good will the Bharat Jodo Yatra do? What will it achieve? Will your walking make a difference? Will you get into trouble for walking with a political party?

Others were cynical: nothing will change.

I had walked with the yatra twice—in Karnataka in October 2022, and again in Rajasthan in December. Now, three months after the conclusion of the yatra, I look back on my experience and try to answer the question the young receptionist in Jaipur asked me.

The Bharat Jodo Yatra was a walk across the length of the country, starting from Kanyakumari on 7 September 2022 and ending in Srinagar in Kashmir on 30 January 2023. The route covered over 4,000 kilometres. A hundred and fifty people were chosen to walk the entire length after a rigorous selection process, most (though not all) from the Congress party. They were the Bharat yatris. In each state, pradesh yatris were chosen (these slots had to be applied for as well) to walk through the state with the bharat yatris.

Why was I even interested in the yatra? For several years now, I have been feeling dejected about the state of the country. The hate and bigotry, the shrinking of personal freedoms, the fear that the slightest criticism can attract severe punishment—all this was making me wonder whether things would ever change for the better. Discussions with friends about what would be an effective way to counter this, or at least to register protest against the prevailing atmosphere in the country, did not lead to definite solutions. There was also some apprehension of being arrested or jailed if one is too outspoken and critical. Concerned citizens went to court, but many of the cases are yet to come up for hearing. As a public health physician, it has also been frustrating to see the increasing levels of hunger among the rural and urban poor, worsened by the scarcity of jobs and galloping inflation. Illnesses are much more severe in malnourished people. But this does not seem to be a priority for anyone.

I was angry and felt helpless. What was one to do? How could I say—I don't agree with what is happening in the country?

Then came news of the Bharat Jodo Yatra. The idea of walking the length of the country to unite people was daring and audacious, and while I knew I would not be doing the entire length, I wanted to participate. The yatra sought to acknowledge the rampant unemployment and inflation, the politics of hate and division, and the over-centralization of the political system. Though primarily organized by the Congress, everyone was welcome to join. The yatra, as its name suggests, aimed to unite the country—a country that is currently fractured by hate, bigotry, and majoritarianism. The announcement of such a yatra, therefore, gave me some hope, something to hold on to. I read up all I could about it, following the various news items that appeared in print (very few) and online news portals.

The yatra was a place where I could walk to protest, to show my unhappiness at the state of affairs in the country, where I could stand in support with others who were taking a stand. I wanted to walk for the idea of an inclusive India, with the freedoms guaranteed to us in our constitution.

I first joined the yatra in Tumkur district in Karnataka along with five friends.

Testing Ground

'Why are you going to Tumkur?' asked the young woman seated next to me in the crowded train from Bangalore. 'Do you live there?'

'No,' I answered, 'I am going to join the Bharat Jodo Yatra.' She looked blank.

'What is that?' she asked.

I explained as she listened, bemused.

'So, you are going all the way just to walk?' was her final question before she replaced her earphones and resumed listening to music. The headlines about the Bharat Jodo Yatra in the newspapers seemed to have passed her by.

We were a mixed group. A journalist (and self-confessed election junkie), a writer, a technocrat-activist, a health policy expert, and two public health physicians.

We walked down from the station to the Tumkur Club where one among our group had managed to get us reservations. The building was old, with spacious rooms and beautifully carved furniture. Over dinner we couldn't stop discussing plans for the next day when we would join the yatra.

The yatra passed through numerous towns and villages. In

rural Tumkur, the yatra started at Kibannahalli (KB) Cross on 9 October. We got there after an hour's travel in pre-dawn darkness and waited a kilometre down the road from where the yatra was to begin. I was full of anticipation and excitement, unsure of what the day would bring. Large banners and bunting had been put up all along the route, with pictures of prominent Congress leaders as well as of Dr B. R. Ambedkar. There was a feeling of anticipation in the air even that early in the morning, with some villagers waiting at different points along the road for the yatra to pass by.

We had put in a request for a chance to present our health policy brief to Rahul Gandhi and were told to wait at the spot we were at till the main convoy caught up with us. Then we would be allowed into the security ring to walk alongside him. Therefore we waited as some yatris passed us, all of whom greeted us with warm smiles. A smartly dressed band went past, beating out a marching rhythm. The media vans came by, and right behind them, within a U-shaped ring formed by the police holding up a thick rope, were Rahul Gandhi and the several people walking beside him.

The media van brought a whole body of people accompanying the yatra—men, mostly young and middle-aged, who were walking and jogging alongside but kept outside the rope. 'Rahul anna!' they shouted and waited for an acknowledgement, which they promptly got. The tide of humanity advanced faster than we expected and we were elbowed out of the way by the surge of people. Before we realized what was happening, we were left in the wake of the convoy along with the trail of yatris who followed at a slower pace. The crowds, the shouts, the slogans, and the buzz of energy advanced further down the road.

We had missed our chance to present our brief since the coordinator inside the ring could not see us in the crowd and hoped that we would get another opportunity, which we did, the following day.

Getting ahead of the convoy meant we had to do some brisk walking, faster than the pace of the convoy, and even occasional jogging. When we managed to get a kilometre ahead, we slowed to a steady pace and walked with the other yatris amid slogans of 'Bharat Jodo' and 'Inquilab Zindabad'—long live the revolution.

I could now look around me and absorb what was going on. While stalls at regular intervals provided bottles of water and bananas, what I longed for was a cup of tea. We finally spotted a teashop, already thronged by yatris, and were lucky to get a cup of tea each. The shop owner ran out of milk soon after. He did not anticipate such crowds, he said, and had not purchased enough milk. It was the same story all along the route that day, and often we were unlucky. Who knew so many people would participate?—they asked. The teashop owners on the next day's route were better prepared.

I was pleasantly surprised to see the number of ordinary people like me who had joined the yatra. Many, like our group, had come from Bangalore for a day or longer, to show their solidarity with the causes the yatra stood for.

Jamina Khatum, a social worker fighting for better wages for bidi workers, agreed with the issues Gandhi had been raising through this yatra, especially the issue of hate and divisiveness in our country today. She is not a Congress supporter, she told me, but she strongly believed that the wage stagnation and runaway inflation in India was hurting the working class.

I also met a young man in his thirties, standing on the side of the road with his wife and child. I asked him why he was there. He had brought his family from forty kilometres away on a motorcycle to see the yatra.

'I do not want my daughter to grow up in a country like the

one we live in today,' he said. 'I wanted her to see that many people are walking for peace. So even though she is only three years old, I have brought her with me to witness this.'

Listening to him, I felt reassured that there were many in the younger generation too who believed in the idea of India, an India not defined by hatred and divisions between people, an India that belongs to every citizen equally.

Another couple—both professionals in Bangalore—drove down to join the yatra on Saturday and then returned on Sunday to show their support for this initiative to unite the country.

Rahul Rajbhar is a Congress worker from Varanasi and one of the Bharat yatris. It was difficult the first week or so, he confessed, but then you get used to this new way of life—a very early start in the morning, a late morning break, a walk again in the afternoon, and sessions in the evening with the other Bharat yatris. He saw the majoritarianism and religious divide in the country today as a real threat to the idea of India. One must fight against it, he said, but one must be ready for the long haul. 'The Constitution of India is worth fighting for,' he told me. Rajbhar works with Denotified Tribes to secure their rights.

Another Bharat yatri was Chandy Oommen, who walked most of the distance barefoot. We came across him time and again, in Karnataka and Rajasthan. He would hobble a bit if the gravel or stones on the path hurt his bare feet, but gamely completed each day's walk. I don't think I could have managed that.

Apart from the yatris, there were crowds of people lining the road whenever we passed through a village or hamlet: children dressed up in their best, some holding flowers to give to the yatris, and adults standing with folded hands. When we smiled at them, they would smile back, and a wave to the people standing on the terraces of their house never went unanswered.

The women would smile a little more tentatively. The people lining the roadsides were from all communities, jostling for a better look at the yatra. And we passed innumerable mobile phones held high, recording a few seconds of our progress along the day's walk. It was plain that the Congress party still had a lot of support and goodwill in Karnataka. The crowds were far more than either the party or political observers had expected.

It was carnivalesque too. The bands, dances, performances, and painting displays along the way were a delight to witness.

The organization of the yatra, too, was impressive. The Bharat yatris (not all from the Congress party) stayed at night in modified containers mounted on truck-beds. A vast camp would come up every evening when the containers would park at night, which would be dismantled as soon as the yatris started walking in the morning and moved to the next evening's camp site. Apart from this, large tents were put up—one for the Bharat yatris, a second for civil society yatris, and a third for people who had come for a few hours. Those too were dismantled and moved every day. Billboards in English and in the local language were taken down as soon as the yatra had passed by and taken ahead in trucks to be put up along the next day's route. Food was provided for everyone who walked. And a green truck would follow, picking up the waste left behind. The yatra was a meticulously planned and executed feat in logistics.

On the walk I met Dr Vanitha, a gynaecologist who quit her government job three years ago to join the Mahila Congress. She was a pradesh yatri, walking with the yatra in Karnataka. She said the walk gave her a chance to talk to a cross section of people across the state, which she could not have done otherwise. She was not provided accommodation (the containers were provided only for the Bharat yatris) but stayed each night in the house of someone in the village where the yatra halted in the evening. As

I passed by her later that morning, I found her surrounded by a group of village women who were complaining loudly about the price of cooking gas and how it left little money for provisions and vegetables. The women had been waiting on the roadside watching the yatra go by, and when Dr Vanitha stopped to speak to them, their grievances came pouring out.

The mid-morning halt was usually for four or five hours—a time for the yatris to rest before starting the evening walk. We stopped in a tent set up for civil society members, which consisted of forest rights activists, those campaigning against manual scavenging, and transgender rights activists that day. Everyone felt that they were up against a state that did not care for the rights of the marginalized, be they Adivasis, or the poor, or transgender: that the struggle against displacement, for land rights, for dignity, was getting more difficult by the day. All of them felt strongly that the country was headed in the wrong direction, that the targeting of minorities, and the clamping down on freedoms was a recipe for disaster. They were here to both show solidarity with the yatra and to advocate for their specific cause.

Gandhi himself was constantly surrounded by people—his security personnel, other party members, and members of the public who were allowed to walk alongside him for fifteen to twenty minutes at a stretch. All of them had issues they wanted to bring to his attention. Every twenty minutes or so, a new group would be brought alongside, and the previous people sent out of the security ring. All this was done seamlessly while walking at a brisk pace, ensuring no one tripped and fell. And with each group Rahul Gandhi would engage in all seriousness. We walked alongside him to talk about the right to health, the crisis of hunger and malnutrition in our country, and about social security. He asked for an explanation if there was something he did not understand and also quizzed us about what each of our suggestions would cost to implement. It cannot be easy switching between subjects: we had followed a group of transgender people who had submitted a memorandum to Rahul Gandhi about the problems they were facing. Yet, he was fully engaged in discussing the issues we raised.

Although we were walking together and walking through crowds of people in towns and villages, there were stretches when one was quite alone or maybe with just a couple of others nearby. In the vast stretches of India's countryside, with hamlets far apart, one is alone with one's thoughts and the road stretches endlessly ahead. What did it take for the yatris walking the length of the country to keep going day after day for 150 days? The conviction that this walk would inspire communal harmony and political change.

The Irresistibility of Hope

I went back to the yatra in December when it was in Rajasthan.

What drew me back? I knew what to expect, what the walk entailed—the hunt for a hotel in an obscure little town; waking up very early in the morning; following the Google coordinates we reached the starting point of the day's yatra when it was still dark; and long days of walking about twenty-four kilometres every day.

I knew that Rajasthan in December would be very cold, but there was the indefinable something—the strength in standing up to hate and protesting the assault on our freedoms. The message of peace and harmony, the easy-going and approachable leaders, and indeed the very inclusive and diverse nature of the yatra—was balm to the soul.

There were several civil society yatris who were walking

the length of the country. Their walk was tougher in a sense: no containers to live in; porta-toilets in varying states of cleanliness provided by the local administration; and no proper bathing place: women requested villagers for use of their bathing rooms while men bathed near the borewells. Yet, they persisted in walking day after day. Their banner, 'Hum Sab Bharat Jodo Yatra ke Saath'—all of us are with the Bharat Jodo Yatra—included in it people's movements, people's organizations, citizen groups, writers, and artists. The size of this group swelled and ebbed with people joining for a day, a few weeks, or even a few hours. A senior member of this group was Yogendra Yadav, who was recognized everywhere he went, and was constantly requested for selfies.

There was plenty of sloganeering, ranging from 'Nafrat Chodo, Bharat Jodo' (Let go of hate, unite the country) to 'Jaati-Dharm ka Bandhan Todo, Bharat Jodo Bharat Jodo' (Break the bonds of caste and religion, and unite India). Initially, I felt self-conscious raising such slogans, but later I started to enjoy the shouting and encouraged others to shout too. The same with walking at the head of the group, holding the banner—I initially felt awkward, and then it became a matter of course.

The crowds in Rajasthan were as big as those in Karnataka. We joined the yatra when it was passing through Dausa district, on the ninety-eighth day of the walk. Dausa was the constituency of Congress MLA Sachin Pilot's father, the late Rajesh Pilot. Sachin Pilot is a hero here, and in Dausa there were large numbers of youth on the roads, telling anyone willing to listen that though Ashok Gehlot was good, it was time to give the younger Pilot a chance to prove his mettle.

Stopping for tea just beyond Kaliasote in Rajasthan, I met a middle-aged couple from West Bengal. They were in Rajasthan for a holiday and had heard that the yatra would be passing through the state. So they hired a taxi to drive four hours to join the yatra.

'All these hate speeches and attacks on people are not good, so we are here.' The woman had walked for three hours by that time and was not sure whether she could complete the day's walk with her arthritic knees. She decided to walk slowly with frequent breaks, so I went on ahead.

I met several Bharat yatris for a second time in Rajasthan, having met them in Karnataka earlier. They greeted me like an old friend. They confessed that it was not easy to stay on the road for months, that they missed their families. But they felt that the statement they were making by walking across the country—that the country needs to be united again was important and worth the effort. Experiencing the diversity of each region they walked through the different languages, foods, customs, and culture was uniquely enriching, and something to treasure. Avani Bansal of the Congress party was emphatic that the party needed to take a clear ideological stand on issues that matter, like rights of minorities and women's rights and not waver from it, even if it meant some electoral losses in the short term.

What I found particularly encouraging was the number of young adults who were walking in the yatra. Individual men and women had decided to put their lives on hold, each with their own reasons.

Mohit Pahadiya is a twenty-six-year-old Youth Congress member from Bharatpur. He was walking the Rajasthan leg of the yatra. He had been busy helping migrants get home to Uttar Pradesh and Bihar during the lockdown and arranging rations for them. He wants to fight the communal disharmony and caste-based violence raging through India. He was also hoping to imbibe the Gandhian principles of tolerance and patience along the walk.

Also walking was a young woman from Calcutta. In her thirties, she had resigned from her job as a manager in an MSME when she was not given leave to join the yatra. As a citizen, she felt it was her duty to join the cause for which the yatra was being undertaken. 'I can get a job again,' she told me, 'but not this opportunity to walk in the yatra.' So, she travelled from Calcutta to Rajasthan to join the yatra. She eventually walked the entire distance to Srinagar.

Twenty-six-year-old Renuka Malviya is from Ujjain in Madhya Pradesh and works as a lawyer for Dalit causes. She helps Dalit women file FIRs in cases of caste atrocities as well as domestic violence. She joined the Bharat Jodo Yatra because of the oppression Dalits continue to face in India. She hoped to find strength in the work of other civil rights activists and meet people she could turn to for help in the future for her work. She joined the yatra in Madhya Pradesh in November, intending to walk for two days. She ended up walking till Srinagar.

Neelotpal, a law student in Jaipur, walked with the yatra for two weeks. Already attracted to Gandhian principles, the idea of the Bharat Jodo Yatra appealed to him as he felt it was a different kind of political agitation. There was no hierarchy of the leaders, with some traveling by motor vehicles and others by foot. He also liked that pertinent issues were being raised without personal attacks on anyone. For him, there was also an element of coming out of one's comfort zone—of sacrificing one's comfort for a cause. Staying in the cold tent at night and waking up early in the winter chill was not easy for him. He walked for two weeks with a group of civil society yatris.

'Just being with the group on the yatra has taught me a lot,' he said. 'One of the most exciting aspects of the yatra was getting to meet so many people who work selflessly.' He was particularly inspired by Yogendra Yadav. 'I have learnt so much by just walking with him.' Taking part in the yatra for two weeks meant he had to miss his examinations in December, but he did not seem perturbed. He planned to use the next few months to undergo training in Gandhian philosophy at the Jaipur Peace Foundation.

Although different celebrities joined the yatra at many points (Raghuram Rajan and Anand Patwardhan during the two days my friend and I were in Rajasthan), there were many others who joined the yatra and lent it strength—the many unknown walkers from towns and villages, young and old. These were the silent ones who subscribed to an alternate worldview, one based on amity and peaceful coexistence, and came to register their support. And by their silent presence for a few hours or a day, they stood up to be counted. Almost all civil society groups and many political parties joined the yatra at different places. Obviously, there is a yearning for a change. The yatra energized the Congress workers and senior leaders. For Congress supporters it was encouraging to see the great response. And for sympathizers of the party, or those not happy with the current dispensation, the Congress was once again a possible option to anchor an opposition. Whether the Congress party can build on this support and goodwill remains to be seen.

The five-month long yatra brought together the young and the old, the urban and rural, the rich and the poor, to express their desire for peace and unity in our country. The warmth and affection shown to us by people in various towns and villages through which we walked was comforting, reassuring, and humbling. The Bharat Jodo Yatra had started with the tagline, 'Saath hamare kaun chalega?'—who will walk with us? It invited everyone to join in, and in its peaceful and all-inclusive character, it provided a safe space for all. And I think its very nature brought people out on to the streets to join it—people who would not otherwise have dreamt of taking a political stand publicly. And in doing so, the yatra transformed everyone who was part of it.

A group of people walking together for a common cause generates great energy. There is comfort and strength in numbers, and change seems possible. What struck me about the yatra was that it was welcoming and non-threatening, and there was no hostility or anger in the places we walked or the things we discussed. It accepted everyone who joined, no questions asked. There were no speeches, no diktats, apart from one planned at the end of each day's walk. The mood was uniformly upbeat and cheerful. The entire body of the yatra, made up of hundreds and sometimes thousands of people, generated positivity and hope. All of us walked as concerned citizens, and the walk made us feel connected to each other and to our country. It reinforced my belief that peace, amity, and fraternity are worth striving for.

To some extent, it removed the fear that many of us have of standing up and speaking out. It showed us that we were not alone. Most of all, it gave everyone hope.

And that is often the beginning of change.

NOTES ON THE CONTRIBUTORS

GHAZALA WAHAB: A journalist and author. Weaving in personal encounters, Wahab has written on the struggle of human rights activists in Kashmir who have been seeking peace through justice. She is the author of *Born A Muslim: Some Truths About Islam in India* (2021) and co-author of *Dragon On our Doorstep: Managing China Through Military Power* (with Pravin Sawhney, 2017). She is the editor of *FORCE*, a monthly magazine on national security and defence.

JYOTI PUNWANI: A Mumbai-based freelance journalist, Punwani specializes in exploring relationships between majority and minority communities, processes of communalization, as well as the treatment of minorities by the state. She has written extensively on riots in Mumbai; and that is the subject she addresses here: testimonies of ordinary people who went beyond their ordinariness to challenge violence and restore peace during the 1992–92 riots. Along with a colleague, she published copies of the report of the B. N. Srikrishna Commission of Inquiry into the 1992–93 Bombay riots and brought out a booklet called *Witnesses Speak*, based on witness testimonies before the commission. She is also author of a booklet called *Dateline Godhra*, based on detailed reportage on the burning of the S-6 coach of the *Sabarmati Express* on 27 February 2002.

NANDITA HAKSAR: A human rights lawyer, activist, and author, Haksar has evolved India's first human rights courses. She has been involved both in the women's movement as well as the human rights movement since the 1970s. As part of her human rights work, she has been involved in the Naga Peace Process, which she chronicles here in her essay. She is the author of several books, including *Framing Geelani, Hanging Afzal: Patriotism in the Time of Terror* (2009); *Rogue Agent: How India's Military Intelligence Betrayed the Burmese Resistance* (2010); *The Judgement That Never Came: Army Rule in North East India* (with Sebastian Hongray, 2011); and *Kuknalim, Naga Armed Resistance: Testimonies of Leaders, Pastors, Healers and Soldiers* (2019) and *Across The Chicken's Neck* (2013), among others. Her books have been translated into several languages, including Burmese, Tamil, and Tangkhul.

NATASHA BADHWAR: A writer and filmmaker, Badhwar is a professor in the Media Studies Department at Ashoka University. She has led the media team for the human rights campaign, Karwan e Mohabbat since 2018. She is the author of *My Daughters' Mum* (2017) and *Immortal for a Moment* (2018), as well as co-author *Reconciliation: Karwan e Mohabbat's Journey of Solidarity Through a Wounded India* (with Harsh Mander and John Dayal, 2018) and *When The Mask Came Off–Lockdown 2020: A People's History of Cruelty and Compassion* (with Harsh Mander and Anirban Bhattacharya, 2020)

OISHIKA NEOGI: She is a human rights researcher and independent journalist with a focus on identity politics and hate crimes. Badhwar and Neogi have collaborated on an essay on human commitment, courage, and endurance during the Delhi violence of February 2020.

RAHUL BEDI: A journalist for forty-four years, Bedi began his career with the *Indian Express* in 1979. In 1984, when anti-Sikh violence broke out in Delhi and other parts of North India, he was deputed to cover it as a reporter. However, he went beyond his brief—bearing witness, he sought to intervene where possible, and this is what he chronicles in a moving essay here. In the late 1980s, he was posted in London with the now-lapsed India Abroad News Service, after attending the University of Oxford as a Reuters Fellow. Since the early 1990s, he has worked as the New Delhi correspondent for *Jane's Defence Weekly*, UK, the *Daily Telegraph*, *London Times* and *Irish Times*, Dublin, in addition to contributing to overseas newspapers, journals, and radio stations like the BBC.

RAJMOHAN GANDHI: Gandhi is a biographer, historian, and research professor at the Center for South Asian and Middle Eastern Studies, University of Illinois at Urbana-Champaign, US. He is the author of several books including *Why Gandhi Still Matters: An Appraisal of the Mahatma's Legacy* (2017), *Ghaffar Khan: Nonviolent Badshah of the Pakhtuns* (2004), and *Modern South India: A History from the 17th Century to Our Times* (2018). His most recent book is *India after 1947: Reflections & Recollections* (2022). He writes on the last few years of his grandfather Mahatma Gandhi's life when, putting his body on the line, Gandhi restored peace in the communally-inflamed Bihar and Bengal.

RAMANI ATKURI: Ramani Atkuri is a practitioner of community medicine who has spent over three decades working with different non-governmental organizations in central India. Committed to community service, she has provided primary healthcare in the tribal and rural areas of Odisha, Chhattisgarh, and Madhya Pradesh.

SHIVAM MOGHA: A research scholar at Jawaharlal Nehru University's Centre for the Study of Social Systems, Mogha comes from Muzaffarnagar in western Uttar Pradesh. He grew up enforcing communal polarization in his area along with others, and witnessed the consequences of it in the form of the riots in 2013. Thereafter, he became part of relief and rehabilitation programmes, even at the cost of personal safety. He recounts this very personal journey in his essay. He also co-edits *Trolley Times*, a newsletter that emerged from and documented the farmers' movement on Delhi borders.

SUNIL KUMAR: A Chhattisgarh-based journalist since 1976, Kumar is an opinion writer, columnist, and YouTuber. He has been reporting and commenting on left-wing extremism for several decades. He brings this reportage to his essay, chronicling multiple aborted efforts to bring peace among the tribals, Maoists, and the state.

TEESTA SETALVAD: A journalist, activist, and educationist, Setalvad, as secretary for Citizens for Justice & Peace, has led a campaign for justice and reparation for the survivors of the Gujarat 2002 violence. In an act of retaliation, she was incarcerated and jailed in the Sabarmati Women's Jail for these efforts in 2002. She still faces nine criminal cases, all initiated by the state. Her essay documents people who stood up against the tide of the violence of 2002 in different parts of Gujarat to uphold the values of humanity and historic co-existence.

TERESA REHMAN: An award-winning journalist and author based in northeast India, Rehman covers gender. That is what her essay, in the backdrop of the Bodo–Muslim conflict of Assam, reflects. A recipient of the WASH Media Awards 2009–10, Teresa also won the Ramnath Goenka Excellence in Journalism Award for two consecutive years: 2008–09 and 2009–10. She is also the recipient of Laadli Media Award for Gender Sensitivity 2011, Sanskriti Award 2009 for Excellence in Journalism, and the Seventh Sarojini Naidu Prize 2007 for Best Reporting on Panchayati Raj by the Hunger Project. She is the author of *The Mothers of Manipur* (2017) and *Bulletproof* (2019).

UTTAM SENGUPTA: A career journalist, Sengupta has reported for and edited several publications, including *Outlook, India Today,* the *Telegraph, Times of India,* and *Tribune* etc. His essay, set in Bihar, records how the state broke out of the terrible memories of Jamshedpur (now part of Jharkhand) and Bhagalpur to maintain peace during the late 1980s to early 1990s, when other parts of the country were witnessing frequent violence in the wake of the Babri Masjid demolition campaign.

ENDNOTES

Introduction

1 Neera Chandhoke, *The Violence in Our Bones: Mapping the Deadly Fault Lines Within Indian Society*, New Delhi: Aleph Book Company, 2021, p. xxi.

2 Ghazala Wahab, *Born a Muslim: Some Truths About Islam in India*, New Delhi: Aleph Book Company, 2021, pp. 67–71.

3 Asghar Ali Engineer, *Communal Riots After Independence: A Comprehensive Account*, New Delhi: Shipra Publications, 2004. Also see: Megha Kumar, *Communalism and Sexual Violence: Ahmedabad Since 1969*, New Delhi: Tulika Books, 2017; Sudha Pai and Sajjan Kumar, *Everyday Communalism: Riots in Contemporary Uttar Pradesh*, New Delhi: Oxford University Press, 2018.

4 Wahab, *Born a Muslim*, pp. 213–18.

5 Special Correspondent, 'If the government wants, any riot can stop: Harsh Mander', *Telegraph*, 2 March 2020.

6 'No riot can last for more than 24 hours unless the state wants it to continue', *Sabrang*, 11 February 1995.

7 Ibid.

8 Engineer, *Communal Riots After Independence*, p. 40 and pp. 128–29.

9 Mukesh Ranjan, 'Communal violence cases up 41% in 3 years: NCRB', *Tribune*, 27 July 2017, quoted in Wahab, *Born a Muslim*, p. 271.

10 Pravin Sawhney and Ghazala Wahab, 'State of the Union: Internal security remains a big challenge', *FORCE*, September 2014.

11 Rifat Fareed, 'The forgotten massacre that ignited the Kashmir dispute', *Al Jazeera*, 6 November 2017.

12 Christopher Snedden, *Kashmir: The Unwritten History*, New Delhi: HarperCollins India, pp. 41–47.

13 Pravin Sawhney and Ghazala Wahab, *Dragon on Our Doorstep: Managing China Through Military Power*, New Delhi: Aleph Book Company, 2017, p. 13.

14 Admiral Arun Prakash, 'Who Cries for India?', *FORCE*, September 2008.
15 Manash Firaq Bhattacharjee, *Nehru and the Spirit of India*, New Delhi: Penguin Random House India, 2022, p. 9.
16 Ibid, p. 12.
17 Arun Prakash, 'Who Cries for India?', *LiveFist*, 4 September 2008.
18 '1931 martyrs' graveyard in Srinagar sealed off,' *Mid-Day*, 14 July 2021.
19 Nandita Haksar and Sebastian M. Hongray, *Kuknalim, Naga Armed Resistance: Testimonies of Leaders, Pastors, Healers and Soldiers*, New Delhi: Speaking Tiger, 2019, pp. 12–15.
20 Harish Chandola, *The Naga Story: First Armed Struggle in India*, New Delhi: Chicken Neck Publishers, 2013, p. 10.
21 Bhattacharjee, *Nehru and the Spirit of India*, p. 119.
22 Chandola, *The Naga Story*, p. 1.
23 Ibid.
24 Ibid.
25 Ibid., p. 16.
26 Bertil Lintner, *Great Game East: India, China and the Struggle for Asia's Most Volatile Frontier*, New Delhi: HarperCollins India, 2012, pp. 5–6.
27 Sawhney and Wahab, *Dragon on Our Doorstep*, p. 361.
28 Haksar and Hongray, *Kuknalim, Naga Armed Resistance*, p. 11.
29 Hansda Sowvendra Shekhar, *The Adivasi Will Not Dance*, New Delhi: Speaking Tiger, 2015, p. 169–70.
30 John Vidal, 'Are we here just for your amusement?', *Guardian*, 25 July 2009.
31 Ghazala Wahab, 'No End in Sight', *FORCE*, June 2017.
32 Ibid.
33 Akhil Gupta, 'Revolution in Telengana 1946–1951 (Part One)', *Comparative Studies of South Asia, Africa and the Middle East*, 1 May 1984
34 Wahab, *Born A Muslim*, p. 224.
35 Pravin Sawhney and Ghazala Wahab, 'For the People: Giving people their due, will shrink Naxal-breeding grounds', *FORCE*, October 2005.
36 Ibid.
37 Ibid.
38 Scheduled Tribes And Other Traditional Forest Dwellers (Recognition Of Forest Rights) Act, 2006, available at: https://tribal.nic.in/FRA.aspx#:~:text=The%20Act%20encompasses%20Rights%20of,Pastoral%20

community%2C%20access%20to%20biodiversity%2C. Last accessed on 13 April 2023.

39 Acts, Rules & Policies, Department of Land Resources, available at: <https://dolr.gov.in/en/acts-rules-policiesacts/acts>. Last accessed on 13 April 2023.

40 Devesh Kumar, 'India among the "unhappiest" people in the world, reveals World Happiness Index', *Live Mint*, 20 March 2023.

Chapter 1: Before and after the Partition: Four Years in Gandhi's Life

1 *Collected Works of Mahatma Gandhi* (*CWMG*), accessible at the Gandhi Heritage Portal, Vol. 90, p. 471.

2 Sitanshu Das, *Subhas: A Political Biography*, New Delhi: Rupa Publications, 2000, pp. 574–75

3 *Hindustan Times*, 2 July 1945.

4 Letter of 12 August 1945 in M. K. Gandhi, *Letters to Sardar Patel*, Ahmedabad: Navajivan, Ahmedabad, 1957, p. 172.

5 Manu Gandhi, *Ekla Chalo Re*, Ahmedabad: Navajivan, 1957, pp. 91–92.

6 N. K. Bose, *My Days with Gandhi*, Calcutta: Nishana, 1953, p. 8, and N. K. Bose, *Lectures on Gandhism*, Ahmedabad: Navajivan, 1971, p. 65.

7 Bose, *Lectures on Gandhism*, p. 106.

8 D. G. Tendulkar, *Mahatma* (eight volumes), New Delhi: Publications Divisions, Ministry of Information and Broadcasting, Government of India, Vol. 7, 1969, p. 382.

9 Pyarelal, *Mahatma Gandhi: The Last Phase* (two volumes), Ahmedabad: Navajivan, Vol. 1, 1956, p. 515

10 Interviews by author in April and November 2000.

11 Tendulkar, *Mahatma*, Vol. 7, p. 383.

12 Pyarelal, *Last Phase*, Vol. 1, p. 641.

13 Ibid., p. 669.

14 Ibid., p. 624.

15 Ibid., p. 622.

16 *CWMG*, Vol. 87, pp. 118–19.

17 Ibid., p. 46.

18 Pyarelal, *Last Phase*, Vol. 1, p. 666.

19 Ibid., p. 661.

20 Ibid., pp. 641–42.

21 N. Mansergh and E. W. R. Lumby (eds.), *The Transfer of Power* (ten volumes), London: Her Majesty's Stationery Office, London, 1970–83, Vol. 10, p. 84.
22 Ibid., Vol. 10, p. 84.
23 Ibid., Vol. 10, p. 86.
24 Ibid., Vol. 10, p. 104.
25 *CWMG*, Vol. 87, p. 254.
26 Ibid., pp. 264–65.
27 *CWMG*, Vol. 89, p. 20.
28 Ibid., p. 28.
29 Ibid., p. 31.
30 Ibid., pp. 42–43.
31 Ibid., pp. 48–49.
32 Ibid., p. 127.
33 Ibid., p. 131.
34 Ibid., pp. 133–34.
35 Letter to Gandhi on 27 August 1947 quoted in G. M. Nandurkar (ed.), *Bapu, Sardar ane Mahadevbhai,* Ahmedabad, p. 348.
36 *CWMG*, Vol. 89, p. 134.
37 Amiya Chakravarty quoted in Gene Sharp, *Gandhi Wields the Weapon of Moral Power,* Ahmedabad: Navajivan, 1960, pp. 259–60.
38 *CWMG*, Vol. 89, p. 151.
39 *The Statesman,* Calcutta, 6 September 1947.
40 *CWMG*, Vol.89, p. 166.
41 *CWMG*, Vol. 89, pp. 168–70.
42 Brij Krishna, *Gandhiji ki Dilli Diary,* Delhi, 1970, Vol. 3, p. 382
43 Ibid., p. 287. Also letter of 27 October 1948 from Nehru to Patel in Durga Das (ed.), *Sardar Patel's Correspondence,* Ahmedabad: Navajivan, Vol. 7, p. 672.
44 *CWMG*, Vol. 89, pp. 194–95.
45 Ibid, pp. 174–75.
46 *CWMG*, Vol. 90, p. 98.
47 Ibid., p. 61.
48 Ibid., p. 43.
49 Ibid., p. 42.
50 Ibid., p. 425.
51 Ibid., p. 451.
52 Ibid., pp. 472–73.

Chapter 2: The Indo-Naga Peace Process: Conflict and Conversation

1 Bertil Lintner, *Great Game East: India, China and the Struggle for Asia's Most Volatile Frontier*, New Delhi: HarperCollins India, 2012, pp. 5–6.

2 According to the Armed Forces (Special Powers) Act, 1958, if, in relation to any state or union territory to which this act extends, the governor of that state or the administrator of that union territory or the central government, in either case, is of the opinion that the whole or any part of such state or union territory, as the case may be, is in such a disturbed or dangerous condition that the use of armed forces in aid of the civil power is necessary, the governor of that state or the administrator of that union territory or the central government, as the case may be, may declare the whole or such part of such state or union territory to be a disturbed area.

3 The Tribal Affairs Ministry removed all reference to 'Naga tribes' from the Scheduled Tribes list of Arunachal Pradesh in 2018, replacing it with the names of individual tribes (which claim to be Naga): Nocte, Tangsa, Tutsa, and Wancho.

4 The Armed Forces (Special Powers) Act, 1958, available on the Ministry of Home Affairs website, <https://www.mha.gov.in/sites/default/files/armed_forces_special_powers_act1958.pdf>.

5 Rinku Khumukcham, 'Human Rights Issues in Manipur and Participation of Tangkhul Women-3', *Imphal Times*, 22 September 2018.

6 Iboyaima Laithangbam, Blast from the past: Flashbacks on Namthilok & Oinam bloodbaths, *E-Pao.net*, 5 June 2015; *Getting Away With Murder: 50 Years of the Armed Forces (Special Powers) Act*, Human Rights Watch, 2008, available at: <https://archive.hrw.org/legacy/backgrounder/2008/india0808/>. Last accessed on 11 May 2023.

7 Rinku Khumukcham, 'Human Rights Issues In Manipur And Participation Of Tangkhul Women-3', *Imphal Times*, 22 September 2016.

8 Ibid.

9 Nandita Haksar, 'First person: When a Kashmiri met a Naga at JNU', *Scroll.in*, 29 February 2016.

10 More recently, Eastern Nagaland Peoples' Organisation, a pressure group representing the state's backward, hilly regions, has been demanding the creation of a separate state of 'Frontier Nagaland' comprising six backward districts of the state which were previously under the North East Frontier Agency or Arunachal Pradesh.

11 See V. K. Nuh, *Nagaland Church and Politics*, Nagaland: V. Nuh and Bro., 1986, p. 143. The Naga homeland is far bigger than the present state of Nagaland. The underground was demanding the integration of Naga-inhabited areas in Arunachal Pradesh, Manipur, Assam, and Nagaland state. The government calls this demand the demand for Greater Nagaland. But for the Nagas, it is the integration of all Naga inhabited areas which are contiguous.

12 D. P. Sinha, 'Nagaland: The Beginning of Insurgency – II', *Indian Defence Review*, 10 May 2011.

13 'India/Nagas (1947-present)', Political Science Department, University of Central Arkansas.

14 H. S. Panag, 'The turning point in Naga insurgency', *Times of India*, 15 September 2018.

15 Siddhartha Sarma, 'From Shillong to Delhi, Muivah came full circle as he signed Naga peace accord', *Times of India*, 9 August 2015.

16 Nandita Haksar, 'Justice Denied: Case Dairy of a Human Rights Lawyer', *Mainstream Weekly*, Vol. 57, No. 29, 6 July 2019.

17 Nandita Haksar, 'Human rights has been weaponised to justify wars. Liberals must recognise this and re-think strategy', *Scroll.in*, 10 December 2021; also see: Jessica Whyte, T*he Morals of the Market: Human Rights and the Rise of Neo-Liberalism*, London: Verso Books, 2019, for historical and political context.

18 Nandita Haksar, 'Irom Sharmila's Struggle Against Military Repression: A Critique', *Antyajaa Journal of Women and Social Change*, Vol. 1, No. 2, 23 February 2017.

19 Chronology of peace talks with NSCN-IM, available at: https://www.satp.org/satporgtp/countries/india/states/nagaland/data_sheets/Chronologytalknscnk.html.

20 The NSCN runs a parallel government in Naga-inhabited areas, with a government, courts, and laws. It collects taxes from its people and has an administrative set-up.

21 Operation Bluebird was launched by the Indian security forces led by the Assam Rifles to recover the arms and ammunition looted by the NSCN-IM in July 1987. This counter-insurgency operation covered more than thirty villages in Senapati district, home of the Poumai Nagas. The security forces committed large-scale human rights violations. I left my Supreme Court practice and stayed in Imphal and Guwahati from 1988 to 1991.

22 Nandita Haksar, 'First person: When Naga leader Isak Chishi Swu cooked me some soup, *Scroll.in*, 1 July 2016.
23 'Profile: National Socialist Council of Nagaland - Isak-Muivah (NSCN-IM)', *South Asia Terrorism Portal.*
24 Chandan Nandy, 'Muivah Arrest Bursts Bangkok Bubble', *The Telegraph*, 1 February 2000; Nandita Haksar, 'First person: When Naga leader Isak Chishi Swu cooked me some soup', *Scroll.in*, 1 July 2016.
25 Sudeep Chakravarti, 'Naga Peace and Deals Within the Rebel Structure', *LiveMint*, 7 December 2017.
26 PTI, 'Grinder Muivah had been discharged after hijack charges', *India Today*, 7 April 2016.
27 'Curfew imposed after Manipur clashes', *CNN*, 18 June 2001.
28 I spoke at length about this in the following interview: Newsclick Team, 'Shadow of Kashmir Over Nagaland Peace Talks?', *Newsclick*, 1 November 2019.
29 Nandita Haksar, 'Why the Indo-Naga Peace Process is Dead', *Newsclick*, 27 August 2020.

Chapter 3: The Anti-Sikh Pogrom of 1984: Three Days of Horror

1 'India: No Justice for 1984 Anti-Sikh Bloodshed', *Human Rights Watch*, 29 October 2014.
2 Justice Nanavati Commission of Inquiry, February 2005, available at: <https://www.mha.gov.in/sites/default/files/2022-08/Nanavati-I_eng_3%5B1%5D.pdf>. Last accessed on 17 April 2023.
3 Deeksha Bhardwaj, '4 commissions, 9 committees & 2 SITs—the long road to justice for 1984 Sikh killings', *The Print*, 16 November 2018.
4 'Delhi Police officials were complicit in 1984 anti-Sikh riots: Cobrapost sting', *India Today*, 22 April 2014.
5 The Wire Analysis, '1984: Thirty-Five Years On, Sikh Survivors of India's Deadliest Massacre Await Justice', *The Wire*, 31 October 2019.
6 'Delhi Riots – 1984 Eyewitness Accounts', *All About Sikhs*, available at: https://www.allaboutsikhs.com/sikh-history/1984-pogrom/delhi-riots-1984-eyewitness-accounts/. Last accessed on 11 May 2023.
7 'India: No Justice for 1984 Anti-Sikh Bloodshed', *Human Rights Watch.*
8 Adrija Roychowdhury, 'In tinderbox Trilokpuri, residents cling to peace', *Hindustan Times*, 2 March 2020.

9 'Delhi Police officials were complicit in 1984 anti-Sikh riots: Cobrapost sting', *India Today*.

10 Pav Singh, 'Exposing the powerful and influential men behind 1984 anti-Sikh pogroms', *DailyO*, 19 January 2018.

11 PTI, '1984 riots: Witness alleges Delhi police helped rioters' *Times of India*, 15 November 2010.

12 I subsequently filed an official complaint against H. C. Jatav, IPS, additional commissioner of police, Delhi; Nikhil Kumar, IPS, additional commissioner of police, Delhi, and Mr Seva Das, IPS, deputy commissioner of police (DCP), East District for negligence of duty. This complaint is in public domain and can be accessed here: <https://www.carnage84.com/affidavits/mishra/promi/rahul-kuldip.htm>. Last accessed on 11 May 2023.

13 Ibid.

14 Ibid.

15 Express News Service, ''His age won't help him': Delhi HC on cop charged with abdication and misconduct during 1984 anti-Sikh riots', *Indian Express*, 13 September 2022.

16 'Gavai refutes allegation of calling army late during '84 riots', *Zee News*, 29 August 2004.

17 'The Indian police officer who saved Sikhs during the 1984 riots', *BBC News*, 1 November 2017.

18 Ibid.

19 Ibid.

20 Erwin Fernandes, 'Sajjan Kumar's Conviction: Even Symbolic Justice Matters, Says HS Phoolka', *BQ Prime*, 17 December 2018.

21 Ibid.

22 'Who are the Guilty?', People's Union For Democratic Rights and People's Union For Civil Liberties, November 1984, available at: http://www.sacw.net/aii/WhoaretheGuilty.html. Last accessed on 11 May 2023.

23 Arnab Goswami, 'Debate: Congress Honours 1984 Riots Accused Tytler As Victims Await Justice', *Republic World*, 10 November 2022.

24 Ibid.

25 'Who are the Guilty?', People's Union For Democratic Rights and People's Union For Civil Liberties.

26 Hartosh Singh Bal, 'Sins of Commission: How nine official inquiries obscured the truth of the 1984 anti-Sikh violence' *The Caravan*, 1 October 2014.

27 Kuldip Nayar, 'Operation Blue Star: How Congress invented a saint', *India Today*, 6 June 2018.
28 PTI, 'Prime Minister apologises for 1984 anti-Sikh riots', *Rediff.com*, 11 August 2005.
29 'PM apologises for 1984 riots', *Business Standard*,14 June 2013.
30 Bhardwaj, '4 commissions, 9 committees & 2 SITs – the long road to justice for 1984 Sikh killings'.
31 Manjit Singh Sawhney vs Union of India, 13 May 2001, available at: https://supremetoday.ai/doc/judgement/01100000597. Last accessed on 11 May 2023.

Chapter 4: Bihar/Jharkhand, 1983–94: A Few Good Men

1 Founding member of National Forum of Forest People and Forest Workers (NFFPFW). For more information on him, see Ashok Choudhary and D. Thankappan, 'Dr Vinayan', *EPW*, Vol. 41, Issue No. 35, 2 Sept, 2006.
2 Arvind Varma, 'Vinayan had few parallels in the way he lived', *The Telegraph*, 30 August 2006.
3 Farzana Ahmed, 'CM Bindeshwari Dubey's decision to ban MKSS raises doubts about his grip on Bihar', *India Today*, 15 September 1986.
4 Varma, 'Vinayan had few parallels in the way he lived'.
5 Other Backward Castes, the lowest in the Hindu caste hierarchy.
6 Ipsita Chakravarty, 'The forgotten riot: How Bhagalpur 1989 left a memory trace in Bihar politics', *Scroll.in*, 12 August 2015.
7 Varma, 'Vinayan had few parallels in the way he lived'.
8 Ibid.
9 B. Rajeshwari, 'Communal Riots in India: A Chronology (1947–2003)', *IPCS Research Papers*, Institute of Peace and Conflict Studies, March 2004.

Chapter 5: Bombay Riots 1992–93: Months of Madness

1 Ambarish Mishra, 'Remove speakers on mosques, Raj Thackeray tells Maharashtra government', *Times of India*, 3 April 2022.
2 *Srikrishna Commission Report*, Volume 1, *Sabrang*, paragraph 1.27, available at: https://www.sabrang.com/srikrish/vol1.htm. Last accessed on 11 May 2023.

3 PTI, 'Analysis: Srikrishna Commission report', *Hindustan Times*, 19 May 2004; M. Rahman, 'Bombay police standards fall with inadequate training, political interference and corruption' *India Today*, 28 February 1993.

4 Under the Terrorist and Disruptive Activities (Prevention) Act, courts were set up exclusively to hear the cases and deliver judgements pertaining to the persons accused under this Act.

5 M. Rahman, 'Bombay police standards fall with inadequate training, political interference and corruption', *India Today*, 28 February 1993; The local Shiv Sena MLA Madhukar Sarpotdar could not substantiate his own allegation of Behrampada being an enclave of illegal Bangladeshi immigrants in front of the Srikrishna Commission.

6 *Srikrishna Commission Report*, Volume 2, *Sabrang*, paragraph 2.25, available at: https://www.sabrang.com/srikrish/vol2.htm. Last accessed on 11 May 2023.

7 United Press International, 'India Violence Persists as Sikhs Kill 6, Hindus Stage Protests', *Los Angeles Times*, 11 July 1987.

8 'The Bombay-Bhiwandi Riots', Committee for the Protection of Democratic Rights, available at: <http://www.unipune.ac.in/snc/cssh/humanrights/04%20COMMUNAL%20RIOTS/A%20-%20%20ANTI-MUSLIM%20RIOTS/06%20-%20MAHARASHTRA/a.pdf>. Last accessed at 11 May 2023.

9 *Srikrishna Commission Report*, Volume 1, paragraph 1.7 (iii).

10 Khandwani and four others were charged with rioting and voluntarily causing injury to a public servant. They were convicted by a special magistrate's court in 2009. They were acquitted in appeal.

11 Sushobha Barve, *Healing Streams: Bringing Back Hope in the Aftermath of Violence*, New Delhi: Penguin Books, 2003, p. 184.

12 Amit Bhelari, 'An experiment yet to take off', *Sabrang International News Network*, 11 September 2007.

13 'Associates of Mahatma Gandhi: Vinoba Bhave's Thoughts', *MKGandhi.org*, available at: https://www.mkgandhi.org/vinoba/nv.htm.

Chapter 6: Gujarat 2002: A Heritage of Humanity

1 Communalism Combat, 'Who does Gujarat belong to?', *Sabrang*, March-April 2002, available at: <https://sabrang.com/cc/archive/2002/marapril/gbelong.htm>.

2 'An Introduction to KHOJ: CJP's Educational Program for a Plural India', Citizens for Justice and Peace, available at: <https://cjp.org.in/an-introduction-to-khoj/>.
3 Interview conducted by me in 2004.
4 Name changed to protect identities.
5 Ibid.
6 Ibid.
7 Ibid.
8 'A brave officer the Muslims could trust', *Sabrang*, 1 June 2004.
9 Name changed to protect identities.
10 Ibid.
11 Ibid.
12 Ibid.
13 Ibid.
14 Ibid.
15 'We have grown up together; how can we desert them now?', *Sabrang*, 1 June 2004.
16 Aakar Patel, Dileep Padgaonkar, B. G. Verghese, *Rights and Wrongs: Editors Guild Fact Finding Mission Report*, 3 May 2002, available at: <https://cjp.org.in/wp-content/uploads/2017/06/Excerpts-from-Editors-Guild-Report-2002.pdf>.
17 Justice A. P. Ravani, *Concerned Citizens Tribunal: Gujarat 2002*, Citizens for Justice and Peace, May 2002, available at: <https://www.sabrang.com/tribunal/volI/expwitness.html>.
18 Piyush Desai, 'Manavta ka Kaam', *Sabrang*, 1 July 2002.
19 *Crimes Against Humanity: An Inquiry into the Carnage in Gujarat*, Volume 2, Concerned Citizens Tribunal, p. 31, available at: <https://cjp.org.in/wp-content/uploads/2017/06/Crime-agaist-humanity-Vol-2-.pdf>. Last accessed on 11 May 2023.
20 Staff, 'Freedom Song: Dalit Mahasammelan at Una, Gujarat', *Sabrang*, 15 August 2016.
21 Moradabad in 1980, Gujarat in 1985, Meerut, Maliana, and Hashimpura in 1987, and Bhagalpur in 1989 are only among a few of the worst examples of targeted massacres in this period.
22 Teesta Setalvad, Split Wide open, Communalism Combat, February 2001 (https://www.sabrang.com/cc/archive/2001/feb01/costory.htm).
23 Uday Mahurkar, 'Riot victims languish in relief camps as Gujarat govt doles out inadequate compensation', *India Today*, 1 July 2002.

Chapter 7: Violence in Chhattisgarh: Many Peacemakers, No Peace

1 Rahul Noronha, Tribal or not?, 'The court battle over Ajit Jogi's identity continues', *India Today*, 08 July 2017.

2 Supriya Sharma, 'Raman willing to talk peace with Maoists?', *Times of India*, 13 February 2011; Also see, Ramsewak Paikra, 'Chhattisgarh government ready to hold dialogue with Naxals', 23 October 2016, *Indian Express*.

3 Aman Sethi, 'Maoists kill two security guards, kidnap Collector in Chhattisgarh', *The Hindu*, 21 April 2012.

4 Joseph John, 'Maoists to release abducted Sukma collector Alex Paul Menon on May 3', *Times of India*, 1 May 2012.

5 Mail Today Bureau, 'Only justice to people can bring peace', *India Today*, 10 April 2010.

6 P. Chidambaram was retained as home minister in UPA-II government, 2009–14.

7 Astha Savyasachi, 'Interview: When a Quest for Justice Was Treated Like a Crime', *The Wire*, 21 July 2022.

8 Suvojit Bagchi, 'The rise and fall of Mahendra Karma – the Bastar Tiger', *The Hindu*, 26 May 2013.

9 Pravin Sawhney and Ghazala Wahab, 'Camp Fire', *FORCE*, August 2007.

10 Ibid.

11 Ramachandra Guha, 'The Revolution And Its Children', *The Telegraph*, 27 July 2006; Also see, Kanchan Gupta, 'Mao's Horsemen of Apocalypse', *Daily Pioneer*, 4 October 2009.

12 Agarwal spoke to me in the third week of June 2005 in his office.

13 Independent Citizens' Initiative, *War in the Heart of India: An Enquiry into the Ground Situation in Dantewada District, Chhattisgarh*, 20 July 2006.

14 Nandini Sundar & Ors vs State Of Chattisgarh on 5 July 2011, available at: < https://indiankanoon.org/doc/920448/>. Last accessed on 11 May 2023.

15 The Wire Staff, 'Chhattisgarh Police Drop Charges Against Nandini Sundar and Co-Accused', *The Wire*, 12 February 2019.

16 Nandini Sundar, *The Burning Forest: India's War in Bastar*, New Delhi: Juggernaut Books, 2016.

17 Email interview with me, 27 August 2022.

18 Panchayat (Extension to Scheduled Areas) Act, 1996, Ministry of Home

Affairs, available at: <PESAAct1996_0.pdf (mha.gov.in)>. Last accessed on 20 April 2023.

19 Email interview with me, 23 August 2022.

20 Nachiketa Desai, 'Lessons From Chhattisgarh Peace March', *Counter Currents*, 15 May 2010.

21 'Letters from P. Chidambaram and CPI (Maoist) to Swami Agnivesh regarding the possibility of dialogue', *Sanhati*, 25 June 2010.

22 'Condemn The Assassination of Azad', *Counter Currents*. Also see, NDTV Correspondent, 'Andhra Pradesh encounter: Govt orders probe into scribe's death', *NDTV*, 6 July 2010.

23 Ashish Sinha, 'Govt sabotaged talks with Maoists: Swami Agnivesh', *India Today*, 4 August 2010.

24 Aman Sethi, 'Green Hunt: the anatomy of an operation', *The Hindu*, 6 February 2010.

25 Aman Sethi, 'Swami Agnivesh, journalists attacked in Dantewada', *The Hindu*, 26 March 2011.

26 PTI, 'Peace talks with Naxals only if they repose trust in Constitution: Chhattisgarh CM', *Indian Express*, 19 May 2022.

27 Email interview with me, 21 August 2022.

28 'Binayak Sen v. Chhatisgarh', Global Freedom of Expression: Columbia University, available at: < https://globalfreedomofexpression.columbia.edu/cases/binayak-sen-v-chhatisgarh/>. Last accessed on 11 May 2023.

29 Ibid; 'India court grants bail to activist Binayak Sen', *BBC News*, 15 April 2011.

30 'Interview | President, PUCL, Chhattisgarh, Dr Binayak Sen: "The Mitanin Programme has Certainly not been Implemented in the Spirit in Which it Was Formulated"', *FORCE*, August 2012.

31 Divyesh Singh, 'Bhima Koregaon case: Pune Police submits draft charge, claims accused were planning to assassinate PM Modi', *India Today*, 19 December 2019.

32 Scroll Staff, 'Bhima Koregaon draft charges: No mention of plot to assassinate Modi', *Scroll.in*, 23 August 2021.

33 Email interview with me, 21 August 2022.

34 Email interview with me, 18 August 2022.

Chapter 8: Insiders and Outsiders in Assam: The Ant of Rowmari

1 The team insists on writing the name of the organization in lower case i.e., 'the ant' as a reminder to stay humble.
2 For more on the ant, see: <https://.org/ theant en/>. Last accessed on 12 April 2023.
3 Azad Foundation, Women with Wheels: http://azadfoundation.com/our-programmes/women-with-wheels/. Last accessed on 12 April 2023.
4 Avirook Sen, 'Sanjoy Ghose killing: All leads point to a well-thought-out plan by ULFA', *India Today*, 22 September 1997.
5 Children's Development Protection, The Ant, https://theant.org/en/what-we-do/childrens-development-protection/. Last accessed on 12 April 2023.

Chapter 9: Jammu and Kashmir 2004–19: No Peace without Justice

1 A self-professed religious group, Dukhtaran-e-Millat, founded by Asiya Andrabi, claimed to be apolitical because it viewed the Kashmir issue as a religious one instead of political. Until the mid-1990s, it indulged in proselytizing activities despite being a part of the separatist political umbrella organization, All Parties Hurriyat Conference. Married to Qasim Faktoo, one of the founding members of Kashmiri insurgent group Hizbul Mujahideen, Andrabi was arrested for anti-India political activities in 1993 and released in 1994. The organization remained low-key for the next several years, emerging in the middle years of the 2000s as a moral policing outfit. Since then, Andrabi has been arrested and released several times. The organization was banned in 2004.
2 *Islamist Terrorism and 'Feminist' Narratives: The Case of Dukhtaran-e-Millat*, European Foundation for South Asian Studies, 2020, available at: https://www.efsas.org/EFSAS-Dukhtaran-e-Millat-July2020.pdf. Last accessed on 11 May 2023.
3 Satinder Kumar Lambah, *In Pursuit of Peace: India-Pakistan Relations Under Six Prime Ministers*, New Delhi: Penguin Random House India, 2023.
4 'Inshallah, Kashmir Will Become Part Of Pakistan', *Outlook*, 5 February 2022.
5 Surender Sharma, 2006 J&K sex scandal: HC upholds conviction of four,

acquits ex-BSF DIG, *Hindustan Times*, 21 August 2020.

6 Kathwari was also the chairman, president, and chief executive officer of Ethan Allen Interiors Inc.

7 Ghazala Wahab, Season of Challenges, *FORCE*, November 2005.

8 Steve Coll, The Back Channel: India and Pakistan's secret Kashmir talks, *The New Yorker*, 2 March 2009.

9 Jordyn Phelps, Pakistan's Lawyers Movement (2007-2009), International Center on Nonviolent Conflict, August 2009. <https://www.nonviolent-conflict.org/pakistans-lawyers-movement-2007-2009>. Last accessed on 20 April 2023.

10 PTI, '223 people killed in Kashmir unrests in 2008, 2010, 2016: Govt tells House', *Hindustan Times*, 10 February 2017.

11 'Interview: "So Long as Jammu and Kashmir is a part of India, the National Conference Will Always be Relevant": President, National Conference', Omar Abdullah, *FORCE*, September 2008.

12 Ghazala Wahab and Pravin Sawhney, 'Holding Peace to Ransom', *FORCE*, September 2008.

13 'Interview: "So Long as Jammu and Kashmir is a part of India, the National Conference Will Always be Relevant": President, National Conference, Omar Abdullah'.

14 Wahab and Sawhney, 'Holding Peace to Ransom'.

15 Ibid.

16 Ghazala Wahab, 'Halved by Religion', *FORCE*, January 2015.

17 PTI, '223 people killed in Kashmir unrests in 2008, 2010, 2016: Govt tells House'.

18 JKCCS and APDP, *Annual Review of Human Rights Situation in Indian Administered Jammu and Kashmir*, 2019, accessed on 30 March 2023. <Microsoft Word - FINAL_AR 2019.docx (wordpress.com)>. Last accessed on 20 April 2023.

19 Sonali Dhawan, '"An open-air prison": Kashmiri journalists on how travel bans undermine press freedom', *Committee to Protect Journalists*, 19 September 2022.

20 JKCCS and APDP, *Annual Review of Human Rights Situation in Indian Administered Jammu and Kashmir*.

21 'Situation of Human Rights in Kashmir: An Interview with Khurram Parvez', *VideoVolunteers*, 2 November 2020, accessed on 30 March 2023. <((221) Situation of Human Rights in Kashmir, An Interview with Khurram Parvez - YouTube)>. Last accessed on 20 April 2023.

22 OHCHR, 'One year in detention: UN experts demand immediate release of Kashmiri activist Khurram Parvez', 22 November 2022.

23 'Jailed Kashmir rights activist Khurram Parvez in Time's 100 list', *Al Jazeera*, 24 May 2022.

24 Victoria Schofield, *Kashmir in Conflict: India, Pakistan and the Unending War*, London: I. B. Tauris, 2010.

25 Free Khurram Campaign 2021, (@FreeKhurram2021), Twitter post, 22 November 2022, <(4) Free Khurram Campaign 2021 on Twitter: "Who is Khurram Parvez? He is a jailed Kashmiri activist, global human rights defender, scholar, and leader of rights movements. We call upon the government of India to #FreeKhurramParvez https://t.co/kdiE6Mix8w" / Twitter>. Last accessed on 20 April 2023.

26 Parvez's personal details were shared with me by a person close to him who did not wish to be identified.

27 I was the executive editor of *FORCE* magazine.

28 Ghazala Wahab, 'Cost of the Conflict', *FORCE*, August 2009.

29 David Barsamian, '"We are trying to redefine resistance": Khurram Parvez, *International Socialist Review*, 18 February 2011.

Chapter 10: Muzaffarnagar Riots 2013: Sliding Towards Violence

1 A method of animal slaughter in which a single blow to the neck from the side of the backbone kills the animal.

2 Halal refers to food deemed fit for consumption by Muslims. In the halal method of slaughter, major blood vessels, such as the carotid arteries and jugular veins, are cut to ensure the rapid and complete drainage of blood.

3 'Farmers protest against WTO and import of wheat', La Via Campesina: International Peasants' Movement, 21 March 2006; Also see Ravleen Kaur, 'US Not Keen to Trade Freely', *Down to Earth*, 30 September 2009.

4 Rehan Fazal, 'egsUæ flag fVdSr us vpkud fo›kky /kjuk D;ksa [kRe dj fn;k Fkk', *BBC Hindi*, 6 Feb 2021.

5 'Timeline of Muzaffarnagar riots: eve-teasing incident led to murders, then riots', *India TV*, 8 September 2013.

6 Sreenivasan Jain, 'The Mystery of Kawwal: Were Muzaffarnagar riots based on distortion of facts?', *NDTV*, 14 September 2013.

7 Farah Naqvi, 'The chilling familiarity of Muzaffarnagar', *Hindu*, 18 September 2013.
8 Apruva, 'Communal clashes in western UP town, reporter among six killed', *Indian Express*, 8 September 2013.
9 Ashish Tripathi, 'Six including a journalist killed in Muzaffarnagar communal violence', *Times of India*, 7 September 2013.
10 Wahab, *Born A Muslim*, p. 259.
11 Dipankar Ghose, Apurva, '3 bodies of Jat victims fished out of Muzaffarnagar canal, say police', *Indian Express*, 14 September 2013.
12 Bharti Jain, 'Government releases data of riot victims identifying religion', *Times of India*, 24 September 2013.
13 Pragya Singh, 'Kairana Doesn't Just Stand For Riots And Hindu-Muslim Rivalry, We Can Stand For Something Else As Well', *Outlook*, 25 May 2018.
14 PNS, 'RLD plans Bhaichara Zindabad campaign to unite all sections', *Daily Pioneer*, 6 April 2021.

Chapter 11: Delhi Violence, February 2020: The Doctor Who Bore Witness

1 The Wire Staff, 'Delhi Riots Death Toll at 53, Here Are the Names of the Victims', 6 March 2020.
2 Madan B. Lokur, A. P. Shah, R. S. Sodhi, Anjana Prakash, G. K. Pillai, *Uncertain Justice: A Citizens Committee Report on the North East Delhi Violence 2020*, October 2022, available at: <uncertain-justice-citizens-committee-report-on-north-east-delhi-violence-2020.pdf>. Last accessed on 20 April 2023.
3 Arundhati Roy, '#DelhiViolence2020 | It Was A Pre-Planned Massacre', Karwan e Mohabbat, 5 March 2022.
4 Mariyam Alavi, Saurabh Shukla, Sreenivasan Jain, '"No Action", "Case Pending": Delhi Police Call Logs Offer Clue To Why Violence Raged For 4 Days' *NDTV*, 29 February 2020.
5 Lokur, Shah, Sodhi, Prakash, Pillai, *Uncertain Justice*.
6 Apoorvanand, '#DelhiViolence2020 | Communal Violence Breaks All Bonds We Share With Each Other ', Karwan e Mohabbat, 8 March 2022.
7 Amit Shah, (@AmitShah), Twitter post, 1 May 2019, available at: <https://twitter.com/AmitShah/status/1123581776415399937>. Last accessed on 20 April 2023.

8 Ibid.

9 Prabhjit Singh, 'Dead and Buried: Delhi Police ignored complaints against Kapil Mishra, other BJP leaders for leading mobs in Delhi violence', *The Caravan*, 21 June 2020.

10 HT Correspondent, 'Kapil Mishra warns cops: Clear road in 3 days... after that we won't listen to you', *Hindustan Times*, 24 February 2020.

11 Wire Staff, "Delhi Riots Began With Kapil Mishra's Speech, Yet No Case Against Him": Minority Commission Report', *The Wire*, 16 July 2020.

12 Lokur, Shah, Sodhi, Prakash, Pillai, *Uncertain Justice*.

13 LiveLaw News Network, 'Delhi Riots: At Midnight Hearing, Delhi HC Directs Police To Ensure Safe Passage Of Injured Victims To Hospitals [Read Order]', 26 February 2020.

14 Ibid.

15 PTI, 'Charge sheets filed in 361 Delhi riots cases out of 758, charges framed in 67: HC told, seeks update', *Economic Times*, 25 November 2021.

16 Delhi Government's Assistance Scheme for the Help of Riot Victims, available at: < https://cdn.s3waas.gov.in/s3c06d06da9666a219db15cf575aff2824/uploads/2020/02/2020022983.pdf>. Last accessed on 20 April 2023.